FORTITUDE
A PTSD Memoir

APRYL POOLEY

Cover Design by Yosbe Design
Edited by Justin Bogdanovitch

Previously self-published as *Shadow Brain: A Neuroscientist's Journey Through PTSD and Womanhood*

PRINT ISBN 978-0692730027
EPUB ISBN 978-0692731215
Library of Congress Control Number:2015914887

Table of Contents

AUTHOR'S NOTE

Out of respect for anonymity, I changed the names of some of the people who appear in these pages. This book is not intended for anything that could possibly come of using real names.

The purpose of this book is twofold: to give other survivors a sense of hope and to communicate the consequences of interpersonal violence to those who haven't experienced it. We must acknowledge that these atrocities happen to millions of people and affect us all as human beings. Disbelief, ridicule, and blame are absolutely unacceptable first-responses to a victim telling his or her story.

In order to do this, I describe my experiences in much detail. We need to face the details because it's in those details where the trauma and the possibility for healing exist. If you feel triggered or overwhelmed by my story, please stop reading, call a friend or one of the hotlines below. I believe you. I support you. It's not your fault.

Rape, Abuse, and Incest National Network: (800)-656-4673
National Domestic Violence Hotline: (800)-799-7233
National Suicide Prevention Lifeline: (800)-273-8255
National Institute on Drug Abuse Hotline: (800)-662-4357
National Child Abuse Hotline: (800)-792-5200

*To all the survivors who came before me and paved the way to recovery —
the road is still rocky but it led me to a peaceful valley. Thank you.*

DAY 1

THE CRUCIFIXION

IN THE BEGINNING

SOMETIMES I WONDERED if I even belonged to the human race, or *human beans* as my toddler-self called them. I never quite felt at home anywhere. Within the first few years of my tiny life, I became a Chicagoland transplant to an all-American town of 20,000 residents. Charleston, Illinois was large compared to the other surrounding towns within fifty miles that had populations of less than 5,000. I knew Charleston to be of Abraham Lincoln fame—the Lincoln-Douglas debates took place in Charleston, Lincoln's father and stepmother lived in Charleston (in a literal Lincoln log cabin), and Charleston is home to the largest statue of Abraham Lincoln in the world. Originally constructed in 1968, Lincoln held the emancipation proclamation in one hand while his other hand's index finger pointed toward the sky in an eloquent, 72-foot oratory pose. But somewhere along the line, the statue became target practice, and when someone shot Lincoln's index finger clean off, the new shaking-his-fist-at-the-sky pose seemed about right. In the early 2000s, Charleston became widely known as the "meth capital of the country."

Half of Charleston residents were students or employees of Eastern Illinois University, the state school in town. EIU was of Cowboys quarterback, Tony Romo, fame. The liberal college campus occupied half a square mile in the middle of the rural farming community. It was the kind of town where the schools had "bring your tractor to school day," but kids also had opportunities to take kid-friendly summer classes from instructors at the university. Herds of people hung out at Wal-Mart on the weekends out of lack of anything better to do.

I went to school with a hodgepodge of kids, and I could tell whose parents were farmers or factory workers because of their clothes, and whose parents were professors because they didn't go to church. The church families were made up of doctors and lawyers and teachers and real-estate agents, but for some reason, there didn't seem to be a church for college professors. I wondered what they did on Sunday mornings.

For five years, my mom and I tried out different churches in town—Christian, of course, because there weren't any other options. Church mostly bored me, but I liked prayer time before bed. My mom sat on the edge of my bed as I recited the prayer I'd come up with as a toddler, "Dear God, please don't let there be any tornados, earthquakes, fires, floods, burglars..." and my list of potential threats to our safety grew every year.

My mom wanted to belong to a "church family," and when a new pastor came to town from Michigan, the family who used to babysit me suggested we try this church with them. My mom immediately felt at home in the "non-denominational" Charleston Community Church atmosphere (technically it belonged to the Assemblies of God denomination, but nobody outwardly claimed that), and I quickly became friends with the pastor's daughter and only other nine-year-old there, Rebekah. My babysitters, the McCormicks, had a son, Colin, who was two years younger than me, and I was excited to be in church with my best buddy from childhood. My mom and I went to church every Sunday, and I enjoyed the contemporary worship music with drums and guitars, and the programs they offered the kids in the church.

In 1995, within weeks of our joining the congregation, an arsonist demolished the church. After we got the middle-of-the-night call about the fire, my mother and I watched the intricate nineteenth century stone cathedral—elaborate stained-glass windows and all—burn to the ground. I didn't know stone could burn like that.

"You know, this is the building your dad and I got married in ten years ago," my mom said in a zombie-like voice as she stared into the flames.

I wondered if we hadn't gone to this church before the McCormick's suggestion because my mom didn't want a reminder of my dad. Did she miss my dad? Did she wish they hadn't divorced when I was five-years-old? Nobody ever talked to me about why they divorced or that it even happened until I asked why he didn't live with us anymore.

For the next few years, the congregation met in various buildings in Charleston until we raised enough money to build a new church. Despite this fiery history, Charleston Community Church didn't preach fire-and-brimstone teachings—it followed a model of the more contemporary, progressive churches that stayed away from politics and controversy and stuck to the Golden Rule sort of teachings. Most of the services consisted of singing rock-n-roll-style worship songs. Shortly after the fire, I sat on the steps of our temporary church building with one of the adults and accepted Jesus as my personal savior. As a ten-year-old, not entirely sure what this meant, it seemed like a good idea—I liked belonging to a group of nice people who played good music, and I liked that it made my mom happy.

Our church, which grew in population exponentially after the fire, started a new Sunday evening group called Sonlight for all the kids aged twelve-and-under. We memorized Bible verses, sang songs, and did physical competitions in the empty sanctuary with the three hundred chairs pushed to one side. The "coaches" taped off a court in the sanctuary with long strips of Velcro and split the kids into four teams. Different games utilized different lines on the court—sometimes we raced to the middle to grab a bowling pin, and sometimes we ran around the perimeter with metal batons in relay-style matches—I loved it.

In my last year of Sonlight, a church in Rockford, Illinois hosted a Sonlight Olympics competition, and Rebekah and I were two of the few kids from Charleston Community Church who got to compete. Leaving home without my mom for the first time to participate in a big-deal competition excited and frightened me. Our church's head Sonlight coach, Commander John, as we called him, actually competed in the 1972 Olympics as a triple jumper, and I felt privileged attending this competition with a real, live Olympian. I did terribly in my relay event at the Sonlight Olympics, but I didn't mind because the four-hour van-ride to and from the games and the nights in the hotel made everything worth the trip. I loved being amongst my friends, eating gas-station snacks, and telling jokes.

Church quickly became my social life, and Rebekah became my sidekick for the services on Sunday mornings and Wednesday evenings and Sonlight on Sunday nights. Until then, nobody understood me, and I didn't fit in anywhere. I always kept plenty of friends at school, and everybody liked me, but I didn't socialize outside of school.

As a child, I harbored a vivid imagination and preferred to play with Legos or Ninja Turtles by myself rather than join 4-H or go to birthday parties. Science fascinated me, and I wanted to be an astronaut when I grew up. I always tried to figure out how things worked or tried to invent something, which usually resulted in the waste of a lot of Scotch tape. One time, I got the bright idea to cover the plug to my Lite-Brite with aluminum foil to see what would happen when I stuck it in the outlet. I had a feeling this was unsafe, so I asked my mom to plug it in. She agreed, and I got to see a small explosion, hear my mom scream, and learn about the electrical conductivity of aluminum all at the same time.

I played outside, climbed trees, rode my bike, jumped in piles of leaves, built snowmen, and made earthworm retirement communities out of piles of dirt. I made little storybooks about looking both ways before crossing the street and about snakes on skateboards. I went on "bike-walks" with my mom. She liked to go on walks for exercise and I liked to ride my bike next to her or ahead of her or circling around her. Bike-walks were our special activity where I had my mom all to myself. I never felt deprived living in a college neighborhood without any other kids around because I usually had my mom's undivided attention, and that was all I needed.

But like most kids at the time, in fifth-grade, I started to discover my identity apart from my mother—by shaving my legs and becoming a die-hard fan of *The X-Files*. I never watched much TV before, but somehow I caught an episode and remained hooked. The show had already been on the air for a few years, so to catch up with what I'd missed, I asked my mom to buy a case of blank VCR tapes so I could record every re-run that aired on TV. It didn't take long before I had every single episode of The X-Files to-date recorded to watch at my leisure. I drew X-Files logos on my notebooks at school, covered my bedroom wall with X-Files posters, and subscribed to The X-Files magazine.

I daydreamed about being Scully's partner-in-crime, and when I met another girl at school who also liked the show, I blurted out "Isn't Scully beautiful?" at the same time she said "Isn't Mulder hot?" Her statement caught me off guard—I'd never thought about Mulder in that way. I agreed with her and thought, *Yeah but he doesn't have Scully's fiery hair and voluptuous lips…*

I refused to ask anyone what being attracted to other girls meant because I'd just accepted Jesus as my personal savior, and knew I shouldn't think about sex until I got married—I didn't want to be an adulterer! But I had sexually charged dreams involving other girls at school, actresses, and women I'd never seen before. Around this same time, Ellen DeGeneres came out as gay in 1997, four days before my eleventh birthday, and my church collectively reacted with disappointment that Ellen had turned out to be such a bad role model—and then her network cancelled the show. I thought being gay must be a bad thing, but I didn't even know what being gay meant, and I definitely didn't know why people thought of it as a sin.

I decided to ignore my affinity for girls, but in junior high, when everyone cut out magazine pictures of their favorite celebrities to tape on their lockers and bedroom walls, I covered most of my wall space with pictures of Julia Roberts, Gillian Anderson, Drew Barrymore, Kate Winslet, Cameron Diaz, Keri Russell, Lauryn Hill, Alicia Silverstone, Gwen Stefani, and Halle Berry. I realized that my other friends mostly had pictures of heartthrob boys like Leonardo DiCaprio or Justin Timberlake on their walls, and thought that I needed to balance out my fully female-covered wall with some hot guys. I flipped through hundreds of old magazines, angry and frustrated and ashamed that I couldn't find any pictures of a guy I wanted on my wall. I knew this definitely wasn't normal, so I tore down all of my pictures and told myself I needed to grow up.

Beginning in junior high, I "graduated" from Sonlight (we even had a ceremony) and joined the youth group for the junior high and high school kids. I had even more fun in youth group than in Sonlight—we went to Christian rock concerts, church conventions, and community service trips. And after attending my first big three-day-long church youth conference, Ascension Convention in Chicago, something within my twelve-year-old self changed. I decided that I needed to devote my life to following Jesus, which included eradicating my "idol," *The X-Files*, from my life. I took down all my posters and stopped watching the show. Behind the TV in my bedroom, I taped a piece of paper on which I wrote the word NO in huge letters that covered the page. This served as a reminder to not watch "that show" and to not touch myself if I ever thought about women in the way I thought about Scully or any of the other women who used to hang on my wall. With this resolution, my teenage angst and confusion latched onto music.

I grew up with my mom's music in my ears and on my Walkman—the Beatles, Led Zeppelin, Counting Crows, Alanis Morissette, Paul Simon, Pink Floyd, Mariah Carey, Pearl Jam, the Allman Brothers Band—and right around the time I started junior high, I asked my mom if I could take piano lessons. I got in with one of the best piano teachers in town, and took weekly performance and music theory lessons. From the first moment I touched the piano, my connection with music became solidified in my soul with an unbreakable bond. I learned that I could express myself with music in a way that I never could with words, and I craved that outlet, practicing hours and hours a day. I quickly caught up to the skill level of my piano teacher, who often branded me as the most talented student she'd ever taught.

I'd heard this sentiment from teachers in school before, but it never meant as much to me as it did coming from my piano teacher. In school, teachers called me "gifted," and I joined the in-school "Gifted Program" based on my standardized test scores. Apparently I had a "highly superior" IQ, but the testers couldn't give me the exact number. During a parent-teacher conference, my sixth grade teacher asked my mom if she had any other kids, to which my mom replied no.

"Good. You shouldn't have any more children because you'll never get another one like Apryl. She's special," the teacher said.

People always told me I was special, and with that, came special responsibilities. Every year, a teacher paired me with a kid in class who struggled in one way or another—I sat next to this classmate, helped them with their homework, made sure they weren't acting up—I actually enjoyed this responsibility and took it seriously. I considered it an important job, and one that certainly kept me from getting too bored in school.

I also helped clean up the classroom at the end of the day, but that could've been because I usually got picked up from school long after all the other kids were gone. The teacher instructed me to note which kids didn't clean up their areas properly so they could get a punishment, but if somebody left a pencil on their desk, I put it away for them because that was a silly thing to get in trouble for.

But aside from my special jobs, everybody went to school, and while I enjoyed it and soaked up knowledge like a sponge, I needed something to make completely my own—music. Learning music introduced me to a type of knowledge that I knew I needed, and something I could strive to master—something I thought I could use to change the world. Music had no limit, I could always learn something different, create something new and get better, but at school, I didn't have anything to do but get As on my report card.

Since I stopped watching *The X-Files*, I started listening to music whenever I took a break from practicing piano. I replaced my Walkman with a portable CD player that I carried around with me everywhere. I went to the library and bookstore to listen to their music collection, and had my mom buy me a new CD almost every time we went to a store that sold music.

I discovered jazz and classical music, and any time someone at church or school asked what I listened to, my responses of Steve Turre, Herbie Hancock, Thelonious Monk, Beethoven, and Mozart were met with intrigued glances—I wasn't a typical twelve-year-old. I wore neckties as belts around my jeans that had holes in the knees and carried around a box of Grape Nuts to snack on in the school bus or as I sat in the corner of the youth group room to listen to my headphones. Beethoven and Mozart were my favorite composers, as they wrote the only music I'd ever heard that could truly capture the essence of anticipation, disappointment, and anger—feelings I couldn't name at the time and didn't know resonated so deeply within me.

Sometimes I slammed my fuchsia-colored hairbrush against my

bedroom wall so hard that it left dents in the plaster. This satisfied me more than throwing it across the room, as I could feel the deep vibrations from the impact resonate throughout my body and take hold of whatever brewed inside of me that I didn't understand.

"What are you so upset about?" my mom snapped at me.

"I don't know, Mom, I really don't know…" I pondered aloud as my mom walked away.

As it did with *The X-Files*, my involvement in the church often contradicted my love for music—I wasn't supposed to listen to "secular" music, and I scoured Christian teen magazines for articles on Christian musicians and charts with suggestions like if you're a fan of this secular band, then you'll like this Christian band. But Christian music never quite satisfied me; it always seemed too shallow and too calculated and never quite resonated with my soul the way my other music did. When Christian bands would get ridiculed and ostracized from the church community for "crossing over" into mainstream, I knew something had to be wrong with this. And when I read a magazine article exposing the Christian music industry for severe censorship requirements of its artists—I'll never forget reading about the minimum "Jesus-per-minute" rule—I said to hell with it. I couldn't stand by anything that stifled musical and artistic expression. I probably picked up this quality from my abstract artist parents.

In August of 1999, just before my eighth grade year, I went to my first concert—Lauryn Hill and The Roots—with my mom and my cousin, Heather. The experience absolutely blew me away, moved me physically and emotionally, and live performance joined the growing list of things I loved about music. I looked around at the other concertgoers and saw people of all shapes and sizes and ages and colors, and thought that I wanted to belong to this kind of community— it didn't look anything like my all-white church or school.

When I wore my Lauryn Hill concert t-shirt to a youth group sleepover, one of the parents asked who Lauryn Hill was and if she was a Christian. I appreciated my friend who stood up for me and confirmed that Ms. Hill did identify as a Christian and that her music was safe, but I secretly seethed inside for reasons I didn't quite understand. This same friend snuck into the church basement with me on New Year's Eve 1999, while the congregation "prayed in the New Year" upstairs, so we could listen to the conclusion of the top 100 songs of the 90s countdown on the radio.

THE BEGINNING OF THE END

DAWN
2000-2003

I BEGAN TO WONDER if more existed out in the world besides church, and I decided to get involved in something else by taking group tennis lessons through the Charleston recreation department in the summer. When I got to high school, I joined the tennis team, the highlight of my freshman year. We were the Charleston Trojans, with colors described as "maroon and gold," but everything in the school was definitely painted red and yellow. Like McDonald's. I wore my Charleston High School Tennis Team sweatshirt every day, inside-out so the white fuzzy part showed, with a light pink or blue or plaid collared shirt underneath—you could call it a preppy-bum style, and I was the only one doing it.

The only other part about starting high school that I liked was that I could go to the bathroom whenever I wanted, and I often got up in the middle of class to "use the restroom," while I actually wandered the hallways and explored the building for twenty minutes. Nobody ever questioned my long bathroom break absences, which was fine with me. I loved school, but not the sitting in class part—I looked forward to study hall and going home where I could read the textbook myself and do my homework alone.

I never struggled with my schoolwork, and I quickly acclimated to being in a building with a thousand other students—I liked the anonymity of it. Freshman English class became my favorite subject, probably because Mrs. Whitmer became my favorite teacher. I respected her intelligence and creativity, and I'll never forget when she taught us about how different people learn differently. She taught us to "think about how you think," and that's exactly what I did. I tried to analyze everything I did and said and why I was the way I was, but in doing this, I neglected to turn in a lot of my homework.

Most of the assignments seemed silly to me, so I didn't bother doing them, but I loved these more complex "think about how you think" type things. I loved when she asked the class to find a modern-day reference to Greek or Roman mythology and explain the relevance of it. When I noticed the bottle of Ajax in another classroom, I excitedly grabbed it and ran it upstairs to Mrs. Whitmer to explain to her that Ajax was the strongest warrior, which would make for a good tough-on-stains detergent. I felt so proud of myself. One day after class, Mrs. Whitmer called me over to her desk to encourage me to turn in my assignments.

"Listen, Apryl. I know you're brilliant, and you can do this work. It might be boring for you, but I can't give you any credit if you don't turn in any assignments." She guided me in a nurturing tone. I didn't feel like I was getting in trouble.

I realized if I didn't do my assignments now, I'd never get out of high school and onto more interesting things later. She explained to me how much each assignment impacted my grade, something nobody had ever done before. My grades always appeared out of nowhere at the end of the term, but now that I knew how many points the assignments were worth out of the total points in the class, I turned it into a math game that I enjoyed. For the most part, I enjoyed school more than it frustrated me, but unexpectedly, anxiety crept into my mind and body.

I experienced my first anxiety attack during the summer between my freshman and sophomore years of high school. I went to a Bob Dylan concert with my mom and one of the more musically-liberated couples from church. Seeing a legend like Dylan for the first time excited me so much, but I couldn't stop thinking about tryouts for the tennis team, which were scheduled for the next morning. I did well in tennis freshman year, and knew I'd make the team again, but I couldn't relax.

As the concert went on, I questioned whether I wanted to stay on the tennis team, whether I wanted to commit the time to it, and what people would think if I decided not join the team again. Would I be a quitter? A failure? I knew this issue wasn't significant enough to freak out about, but the concerns in my head grew louder and more repetitive, and the people around me in the crowd piled on top of me like a violent avalanche. Even the decrepit Dylan, whose barely-audible voice screamed directly at me, "DON'T THINK TWICE, IT'S ALRIGHT!" over ten thousand other people in the grandstand

My heart raced. I couldn't breathe. I became nauseated, and collapsed into my seat with my head in my hands. After what felt like hours, I finally regained control of my thoughts, and made the decision to not tryout for the tennis team again. I felt relieved, but what I just experienced concerned and confused me. I knew whatever had happened related to more than high school sports.

Since I didn't belong to the tennis team anymore, I decided to start playing guitar. My dad bought me an acoustic guitar for my fifteenth birthday, and I picked up the craft almost as quickly as I had with piano. I continued discovering music and fell in love with Dave Matthews Band after I started playing guitar. I had my mom take me to all the Dave Matthews concerts in the area—I saw them in Indianapolis, Chicago, and St. Louis all in one year. I decided that I needed to get a job as soon as I turned sixteen so I could buy all the CDs I wanted.

For my sixteenth birthday, I had my mom take me to see a performance of Beethoven's first and ninth symphonies by the Saint Louis Symphony, and then I got a job at Little Caesars where Rebekah started working when she turned sixteen a few months earlier. Little Caesars introduced me to the "real world," as we worked alongside college students and full-time food service employees who were in their mid-20s or 30s. Unlike at home, church, or school, I could do and say just about whatever I wanted at work—I swore, asked questions about sex, and smoked cigarettes. I bummed cigarettes from my co-workers as I found it relaxing to take a break from the hot kitchen to step outside to smoke. I drank all the pop I wanted, ate pizza every day, and worked with Rebekah, all while making money to buy CDs.

Aaron, who was a year older than us, also worked at Little Caesars, and he and Rebekah started dating during our junior year of high school when he asked her to the homecoming dance. At first, I vehemently disliked Aaron. He'd belittle and harass everyone at work with his loud and obnoxious voice, and he looked like Eddie Munster but twice as animalistic and four times as large. But Aaron started coming to church with us, since Rebekah could only date other Christians, and I began to tolerate his company more. It was a typical pastor's-daughter-with-the-bad-boy love story.

On the Fourth of July 2003, the summer before our senior year, Rebekah called to tell me that Aaron had some whiskey, and they were going to drink and watch the fireworks at the airport. Aaron had graduated high school and had connections to things that we didn't have. I'd never drank before, and the thought of it honestly made me nervous. I sat on a stump next to my mom at an Independence Day whiffle ball tournament and asked her advice on going with Aaron and Rebekah, but she didn't have much input. She'd warned me previously that a lot of people in our family had problems with alcohol, and that I needed to be aware of the risk of alcoholic tendencies I may have. I weighed the pros and cons of going with Aaron and Rebekah for a long time before I decided to go meet them. I asked my mom if I could try some of her drink—champagne—and decided it wouldn't hurt too badly to have a drink or two.

We went to the fireworks and had a great time drinking warm whiskey out of Little Caesars cups that eventually disintegrated when the alcohol ate through the wax. We were like rebels drinking on the side of the country road and peeing in the cornfield. After the fireworks, Rebekah went home, but Aaron and I went to hang out with a couple guys who worked at Little Caesars. I'd never been to anyone's apartment before, and for the first time, I didn't feel like a child.

That summer, Aaron and Rebekah's relationship became more serious, and the three of us hung out a lot. We scheduled ourselves to work at Little Caesars together often, and occasionally, Aaron scored some cheap beer. The three of us went to the park on the edge of town to drink, and I have no idea how we never got caught. The park sat right next to one of the main highways in town, and we drank beer completely out in the open. I reached my limit after two or three beers, and we always had fun at the park laughing and swinging and going down the slides.

One time at the park, Aaron brought some marijuana that he got from someone at school. I'd never smoked before, but it intrigued me. I told Aaron and Rebekah that I didn't think the pot did anything to me. As I sat cross-legged on a picnic table with my back perfectly straight and my hands folded in front of my chest, I declared in my best British accent, "There's no way I'm high. I am prim and proper like a perfect English lady." We all cracked up laughing and then went to Taco Bell and ordered enough food to feed twenty people. Life was good. We had fun exploring our independence, but I disliked always being the third wheel, so I attempted to find a guy to date during the summer before my senior year of high school.

* * *

BOYS: FIRST ATTEMPT—
I'd worked at Little Caesars with Scott for almost a year, and everybody knew he liked me but my age deterred him from asking me out—he was twenty-three-years-old, and I was seventeen. Aaron encouraged me to ask Scott out, but nothing about that prospect sounded appealing to me. But Aaron said it would be fun to go on double dates together, and I did enjoy the idea that somebody liked me, so I asked Scott if he wanted to hang out sometime.

We went to dinner and a movie (pizza and *Terminator 3*), and the whole time my nerves burned at the thought of Scott putting his arm around me or holding my hand. I couldn't tell if that feeling stemmed from anticipation or dread, but when Scott did hold my hand, it tingled and sparked a curiosity in me. I didn't recognize this feeling, and didn't know if I even liked it. The perplexing touch continued as he held my hand on the drive home from the movie theatre. Before I got out of his truck, Scott leaned in for a kiss that lasted only a few seconds. The awkwardness and sliminess surprised me, as did the taste of stale cigarettes and spearmint gum. I didn't like it one bit, so I dove back in for another to make sure that's really what a kiss was supposed to be like.

The next night, Scott called me in one of his drunken stupors to tell me that I was a bad kisser. I agreed with him and apologized. It must've been something I did wrong. For our second date, he drove me out to a graveyard in the country, a strange place to take a date, but we both lived with our mothers so we had nowhere else to go. We sat in the back of his green Ford pickup truck and kissed for a while under the starry summer night sky, amongst the crumbling nineteenth century gravestones. I'd resolved to get this kissing thing right, but I was still so relieved when my mom happened to call to summon me home right when Scott reached up my shirt to unhook my bra. I faced away from him to re-hook my bra, and while my legs dangled off the tailgate of his truck, I wondered what the hell I was doing in a graveyard with this guy. A couple weeks later, when Scott and I bought saltwater taffy from a toothless man at the county fair who directed the phrase "Father knows best" at us, I knew this relationship wouldn't work out.

*   *   *

BOYS: SECOND ATTEMPT—
Brian was twenty-six-years-old and had gone to Charleston Community Church since he was a kid, even before Rebekah's family took charge. He helped out with the youth group, and all the girls adored him—Mr. Perfect. He did kind of look like a GI Joe action figure or Kenneth from *30 Rock*. But I hadn't paid any attention to Brian until I found out he'd consulted with the pastor and the elders at church about whether it would be appropriate to date me. Appalled that these old men discussed my dating life—and at Brian's assumption that I'd even want to date him—I thought of course it wasn't appropriate for us to date. But everybody at church liked the idea. I guess I should've felt lucky that such an attractive, nice, Christian man wanted me. So we went to a movie, and right before it started, he told me that his parents sat a few rows behind to keep an eye on us. I had a hard time not laughing in the face of this twenty-six-year-old man whose parents chaperoned his movie dates.

He came over to my house and watched a movie in my room (with the door open, of course), and I went over to his house and watched a door-open movie, *Office Space*, one time (he also still lived with his parents). Brian told me that I looked like Jennifer Aniston, but I wished *he* looked a little more like Jennifer Aniston. He enrolled in a couple classes at EIU, and I often met him at the library on campus in the evenings to do my homework and help him with his French. When he suggested we take a study break to go for a walk around the cross-country path, I led him out of the library and enjoyed his observation that I walk down a flight of stairs with such smooth control that my head and shoulders don't bounce up and down at all.

Brian brought a blanket with him, and once we got far enough away from campus, he spread the blanket out in the grass and we lay down. After looking at the stars for about ten seconds, he rolled over and propped himself above me. He moved in for a kiss, but then stood abruptly.

"No. I can't. It's too soon," he said. His dramatic and breathy delivery made the moment comical.

Again, I found it hard to contain my laughter, but I didn't care if Brian kissed me or not, so going back to the library sounded just fine to me. After that night, he sent me a text message telling me he didn't think it would be appropriate for us to be alone together anymore, which also sounded fine to me.

*   *   *

BOYS: THIRD ATTEMPT—

Matt was in my grade and lived down the street from me. We took a lot of classes together at school, and hung out occasionally the summer before our senior year. We both played guitar and had a lot of common interests in music and movies and school. After driving around listening to Led Zeppelin in my car one night, Matt asked if I wanted to go out with him. After the relief of getting my last two dating attempts over with, I'd begun to actively avoid any interaction with boys that might lead to them asking me out, so this coming from Matt disappointed me. I told him I didn't want to risk ruining our friendship if dating didn't work out (a legitimate concern because I already knew it wouldn't work out). He insisted that it didn't make any sense for us not to date since we shared so many interests and got along so well. I couldn't argue with his reasoning, other than the fact that I felt no attraction or excitement about this whatsoever. I told him I'd think about it, and hoped he wouldn't bring it up again.

But shortly after that, Matt asked if I wanted to watch a movie at his house for our date. I reluctantly agreed and planned to give him one date before I told him it wasn't working out. We watched *Memento*, which I actually wanted to see, but I pretended to fall asleep when I became nervous that he'd move in closer to put his arm around me or kiss me or whatever he planned to do. We still remained good friends, but he got the message that I wasn't interested.

I began to think that something was wrong with me. I felt left out when my classmates went on dates, went to parties and movies, shopped, and had sleepovers, but those things didn't interest me that much. I still took weekly piano lessons, and I embarked on a quest to discover as many bands that I hadn't heard yet as I possibly could. I composed music and wrote poetry and taught myself how to play the guitar and went to art museums.

"Mom, I'm lonely."

"You're just too mature for high school. You'll find people to relate to in college," was one of the more heartfelt things my mom ever said to me.

I considered my mom the only person I could truly relate to, but right before my senior year started, she got engaged to Jim, whom she'd dated for the past year. My mom spent some nights at Jim's house, which gave me more freedom to separate myself from her, and I decided to be more proactive about my social life.

Adrianne, who quickly became my other best friend, bonded with me our senior year. Our friendship flourished the year before when we happened to have most of our classes together, and we decided to sign up for identical schedules for our last year of high school. From day one of our senior year, we were inseparable. It was Adrianne and Apryl against the world. She held the Queen Bee title of our group of friends—the honors kids, as the teachers called us—and I felt special to be her sidekick. Adrianne and I sat together in class, ate lunch together, and studied in the library before school. We joined the National Honors Society, the French National Honors society, and the French club, and for the first time in my life, I felt like I belonged in a group of my peers.

Adrianne and I applied to the same colleges together, and I got accepted into one of the top-ten physics programs in the country at the University of Illinois. I couldn't believe that two months before, I'd started my senior year of high school, and in less than a year, I'd be embarking on my voyage into adulthood. I hadn't ever shared a living space with anyone other than my mom, but I looked forward to hopefully rooming with Adrianne in college.

Unlike me, Adrianne always had school spirit and liked getting involved in a lot of activities. She convinced Rebekah and me to walk with the senior class float in the homecoming parade that October. Each class had a theme from a different decade, and the senior class got the coveted 1920s theme. Adrianne, Rebekah, and I dressed up like flappers, and a few boys dressed like gangsters. We had a blast dancing around in our ridiculous outfits throughout the parade route around town, and I decided that being more involved in school would be fun.

Adrianne and I joined the girls' Powderpuff football team that year, and I started to bond with the girls in my class. I even chanted our school cheers in the hallway.

C-H. A-R. L-E-S-T-O-N! Charleston TROJANS, GO. FIGHT. WIN!

I wanted to go to football games and dances and hang out with my friends and enjoy my senior year.

That Friday, Adrianne asked if I wanted to go to a movie with her and a couple other girls from school. We planned to see *Radio* on opening night—October 24, 2003—and going out to do something with my friends excited me so much. My mom had already gone to Jim's house by the time I got home from school, so I danced around the kitchen and bounced from room to room as I waited for my friends to pick me up. I decided to take a couple swigs from my mom's baking Amaretto. It tasted like cough syrup.

"Let's go, Apryl! Wait, are you drinking?" Kelly said, surprised, as she walked through the front door.

"Not really, just a couple pre-game shots." I giggled. I'd heard that term from the college kids at work.

The previous week, Kelly came over to my house with Aaron and Rebekah to have a couple Bud Lights because we got out of school early for Columbus Day, so I didn't think I needed to hide my Amaretto from her. It tasted gross anyway, and I didn't want it ever again. I put the bottle back in the cabinet and hopped in the car with my friends.

That was the first time I'd ever been to a movie with friends from school, and I finally felt like a normal high school student. That was also the last time I ever went to a movie, or did anything, with friends from school, as the decision to go to Adrianne's ex-boyfriend's fraternity house after that movie changed my life.

NOT IN GOD'S EYES

ADRIENNE AND JARED started dating when he still went to high school with us, but he'd graduated the previous year and now went to EIU, as most Charleston High School graduates did. They had a tumultuous, on-again/off-again relationship, and none of Adrianne's friends liked him. Adrianne still totally loved Jared, and while nobody could ever figure out their official relationship status, everybody knew they were still sleeping together.

Jared lived in a fraternity house on campus, and we went over there along with Jessica, who came to visit Adrianne from out of town. Jared had a fake ID and asked us if we wanted to go get some beer. Adrianne and Jessica didn't want to drink, but the fake ID impressed me, and I thought I could go for a couple beers. We all got in his car and pulled up to the drive-thru window at the liquor store, which sported what sounded like a fire truck bell to alert the employees of a car at the window. Jared asked what kind of beer I liked, but I didn't know what to say because the only beer I'd ever tried was Keystone Light and Bud Light, and I knew that probably wasn't good beer. He got a six-pack of Michelob Ultra and called it "quality stuff."

We all went back to his room, which spanned about ten square feet and boasted only a bunk bed, dresser, mini-fridge, and TV. Jessica planned to stay the night at Adrianne's house, so I called my mom to tell her I wanted to stay at Adrianne's that night, too. The night felt relaxed—we sat around and watched a kung fu movie, but

I enjoyed this so much. I'd never hung out on campus before, and I felt like a badass drinking beer at a frat house.

After my second beer, I announced that I didn't want any more to drink because I didn't want a hangover for the football game the next day. I wanted to get up early to hang out with Adrianne and Jessica, but Jared perked up when I said I was done drinking.

"Wait, have you ever tried Bacardi Razz?" I didn't pick up on his eagerness.

I'd never heard of Bacardi Razz, but Jared described it as awesome rum that tastes just like raspberries and insisted I try it. He didn't have to twist my arm too much, but still, he pitched the stuff as though he were a used-car salesman. When I agreed to try some, he said it needed to be mixed with Sprite, so he went downstairs to get cups and soda, and handed me my drink when he returned to his room. He watched attentively as I tasted his concoction and asked what I thought of the drink. I told him I loved it, and it actually did taste like raspberries.

Up until that point, I'd only drunk cheap beer, warm whiskey, and that syrupy amaretto that my mom bought to bake in her cookies. I decided that Bacardi Razz was my favorite alcohol. Who knew liquor could taste so good!

I don't remember the kung fu movie ending or much at all over the next sixteen hours. Within minutes of drinking that raspberry elixir, everything around me moved so quickly, but I remained stationary, like looking out the window of a moving train. One minute I found myself downstairs in the common room, vomiting in a water fountain, and the next second I found myself on the third floor vomiting out of a window from which somebody (probably me) had pushed the screen out.

I tried to tell myself this was fun, but being so confused about why I was sick and unable to walk straight or even stand scared me. With my back pressed hard against the hallway wall, I slid down to the carpet adorned with stains to match the yellow paint, and watched the outlines of the bodies towering over me quickly fade away to black. I hadn't had a lot of experience with alcohol, so I assumed this was supposed to happen. I don't remember Adrianne and Jessica leaving, abandoning me to my fate.

I woke, fully clothed, flat on my back, arms to my sides in the bottom level of a bunk bed. Glowing red numbers of an alarm clock glared at me from across the room that read 1:00. One o'clock—was it one o'clock in the morning? I tried to think of the last thing I remembered, which was watching a kung fu movie around nine o'clock the night before. Then I noticed the blinding sunlight that peeked in from behind the dark fabric curtains.

Oh my God, it must be one o'clock in the afternoon.

I counted the hours backwards and realized that the last thing I remembered was sixteen hours ago. Unless it was one o'clock in the afternoon on Sunday. Or Monday. I had no idea what day it was; for all I knew, a week could've gone by. I knew something wasn't right. I felt unsafe and terrified. I had to get home, but when I tried to get up, my body was completely paralyzed.

The feeling reminded me of waking up in the middle of the night with my arm asleep, not being able to move it for a few seconds until it started tingling again. Except this overtook my entire body, and it didn't start tingling after a few seconds. I tried to scream *get up!* in my head, but I didn't even have the strength to do that.

Not being able to move my body when I willed it to move was one of the most horrifying feelings I'd ever experienced. Did I have a stroke? I imagined that this was what it would feel like to wake up strapped to a cold gurney in a strait jacket, peppered with electrodes and needles, having no idea why or how I ended up in the hospital. I could only move my eyes and twist my neck a little bit, and I saw that Jared lay next to me. I felt a little relieved to at least know where I was, so I fell back asleep.

When I woke the second time, a couple hours later, I mustered the strength to lift my body out of the bed. I kept my balance by holding on to the posts of the bunk bed and leaning against the walls, and I stumbled into the tiny tiled bathroom that adjoined Jared's room to his neighbors' room. I vomited in the toilet. Moving my body was extremely difficult. My balance was off, even with trying to look at the horizon—a seasickness remedy my aunt had taught me on a boat tour of the Chicago River. I had to think about moving each of my legs, which weighed a thousand pounds, step by step. I plopped myself back down on the bed and wondered why I wasn't at Adrianne's house and where Adrianne was anyway, and I wondered whether my mom was worried about me. I needed to get home immediately. Jared awoke and rolled over to me.

"We need to get this shirt off of you," he stated.

"No. Home," were the only words I managed to squeak out. Talking was difficult.

"You have vomit on your shirt. We need to take it off."

"No, I need to go home," I said, my eyes barely open, drifting back to sleep.

"You're still too fucked up. I'll take you home later." It was neither an offer nor an option.

When he tried to take off my shirt again, and I told him to stop, Jared said, "It's my bed, and I don't want vomit to get all over it." I guess I could understand why he wouldn't want vomit in his bed.

He took my shirt and bra off, propped himself over me and kissed me. I drifted in and out of consciousness, and didn't understand what was happening. I felt like I was in a dream, except this large, hairy man would've never appeared in one of my dreams. I couldn't tell if I kissed him back or not. I didn't know what actually happened and what I may or may not have dreamed as I continued to doze off. I didn't want this to happen. I just wanted to be home, safe in my own bed. At some point when I awoke from dozing off again, I saw that I was completely naked, and Jared lay at the end of the bed, inserting his fingers into me. I couldn't feel anything, but I saw his hand moving in and out of view so fast, and it was covered in my blood. Mine! He'd scolded me about vomit in his bed, but this much blood was okay?

Nothing had ever been inside me before—not a finger, not a tampon, not a penis. A few years earlier, I was at Disney World with my mom, and I was on my period. I wanted to go swimming, and she told me to try one of her tampons. I couldn't figure out how to get the tampon in, and my mom tried to help to no avail. I tried to at least get my finger in there, but my vagina was like an iron vault. In high school, I got sick of wearing pads, and tried to break into that vault a couple more times, but it was sealed off to the world. I'd heard stories of girls' hymens breaking while horseback riding or strenuously running, so I decided to wait for my hymen to break on its own. I never envisioned Jared's dirty, chubby fingers doing the job.

Jared stayed down at the end of the bed for what could've been hours, and when he came back up to my face, his pants were off. He tried to put his penis in me, but he couldn't get an erection. I'd never seen a penis before, and didn't know the difference between an erect one and a flaccid one or that it needed to be hard in order to go into a vagina.

"You're gonna have to help me out here," Jared said. His tone remained flat as if he didn't care what was going on. But if he wasn't enthused about this and I certainly didn't want to be doing this, then why was it happening?

I didn't know what he meant or how I could possibly help him in my helpless state. I could barely stay awake, let alone move my weak limbs. He placed my hand on his penis and told me to rub it. It reminded me of a miniature roll of Pillsbury cookie dough that'd been left out on the counter too long. I didn't have the strength or physical dexterity to grasp anything, and I definitely didn't want to touch Jared's penis. I tried moving my hand around his crotch, but I didn't know what I should do or what was supposed to happen with his penis.

Then he grabbed my torso and lifted me up so my body straddled his. I couldn't maintain my posture, so Jared had to hold me up to keep me from just slumping over on him. I felt his hands burn into the sides of my ribcage. I don't know if he got an erection or went inside me at that point, since I still couldn't feel anything, but he sure moved my body around a lot. My forehead bashed into the wooden frame of the bunk bed as he maneuvered me. After my head hit the bed frame a couple more times, I shifted my weight so I could keep my forehead firmly pressed against the splintered wood, and realized that something wasn't right. I didn't know how long this had been going on, but with all the bleeding and head bashing, I became more aware of what had happened.

Jared laid me back down and grabbed a condom from the end of the bed. Something about seeing that condom in his hand made me realize, for the first time, that I was having sex.

Oh, my God.

I'm having sex.

This is my first time having sex.

I'd always heard that your first time having sex would be awkward, but being the good Christian girl I learned to be, I planned to save myself for marriage. I felt that I'd done something incredibly wrong because I'd never be a virgin again, not in God's eyes nor my own.

I felt how much pain my body was in—my muscles ached, my forehead pounded, I was nauseated, and my vagina felt like it had been repeatedly stabbed with a machete. I had no way to reverse what Jared had already done to me or to stop what was about to happen with the condom he put on his half-erect penis. I knew I'd already been permanently damaged, and I would never be the same person again.

I can't recall exact details of what happened next because I retreated so far into my own head. Once I realized I had no control over the situation, over Jared, over my own body, and that I'd slowly and painfully lose my virginity whether I liked it or not, I decided I should at least try to enjoy it. Try to make it good. Sex was supposed to be good, right? I felt a responsibility to make this experience enjoyable for Jared, and I didn't want him to know how horrible it was for me. I thought if I could give him what he wanted it would be less painful for me and end more quickly.

But I didn't know how sex worked other than what I'd seen on TV or movies—in the time of dial-up internet, the abundance of all the high-speed free porn to satisfy any teenager's curiosity was just a far-fetched dream. I remembered that fake orgasm scene in *When Harry Met Sally*. And I thought of those orgasmic Herbal Essences commercials. I pretended I was that girl in the shower washing her hair with Fruit Fusion shampoo or Meg Ryan with Billy Crystal in that deli.

Yes.

Yes!

YES!

"I'll have what she's having," said the old woman at the table next to me.

I don't know how it finally came to end, but I must've performed well enough that Jared decided we were done. He never even took off his dirty white t-shirt. I went to the bathroom to try to clean up the blood that stained my legs, and when I realized I wouldn't stop bleeding anytime soon, I put my clothes on and told Jared to take me home. He refused to drive me home, but offered to take me to Adrianne's house. Adrianne was the one person I wanted to talk to about what'd just happened to me, and Jared must've read my mind.

"How about we don't tell Adrianne about what just happened?" Jared said as he stared at his shoes. "You know, because she's still in love with me. It would just upset her."

Jared assured me that he has sex with other girls all the time, and that he and Adrianne weren't dating anymore, so what happened between us was okay. But he said I still shouldn't tell her because she might get mad at one or both of us. Now I felt conflicted—I hadn't taken into consideration that it was Adrianne's ex-boyfriend and current lover who raped me, if I could even call it that. I wanted some comfort and advice from the person I considered my best friend.

He drove me to Adrianne's, and I sat down in her living room. I felt like death as I sunk into a plush loveseat, and I felt my vagina still bleeding. I decided that I needed to go to bed and figure out what to do about talking to Adrianne when I felt better. When Adrianne came into the room, "Why did you leave me there last night?" spurted out of my mouth. It was the only thing I could say when I saw her. I wanted some answers. I wanted to know how I got so fucked up.

Was it really just from a few drinks? Did I smoke pot? Did I drink a lot more than I realized? What time did Adrianne leave? What happened before she left? Why didn't Adrianne take me home with her? What happened in the sixteen hours I don't remember? What about Jessica? Maybe she knows what happened. Should I ask her? Was anybody else in the frat house? Why do I have incoherent voicemails on my phone from myself? Did I call myself? Was I trying to call someone else? Did we order pizza? Why was I paralyzed when I woke up? Is that what happens when you drink too much? What am I supposed to do now? Should I call the police? Should I go to the doctor? Was I raped? Or did I just have sex? Is this just what happens when you drink a lot?

But I never got the chance to ask any of those questions.

"You were really fucked up," Adrianne answered. "Jared said you could stay there, and he would take you home when you sobered up, so we left," was the only answer I got to the million questions that circled through my head.

Adrianne drove me home in silence. I don't remember the encounter with my mom when I walked into the house, or if she wondered where I'd been. Normally, my mom would've been worried sick over my whereabouts, but she and Jim were getting married in six weeks, so she was preoccupied with the wedding. I made a beeline for my bed, but it didn't take too long for my mom to come in to ask me what was wrong.

"I drank too much. I'm never drinking again. I feel so sick," I said. I moaned with discomfort, like a bloated cow.

I didn't even know what'd happened to me, so I certainly couldn't form the words to tell my mom. But I knew I drank too much and whatever happened was probably my fault. My mom said she hoped I'd learned my lesson and stayed away from alcohol, and that she was glad I was okay. But I didn't feel like I was okay. Nothing was okay. I stayed in bed the rest of that Saturday and all of Sunday, and I vomited and bled for two days. I thought I was going to die. All the questions I had about what had happened to me were constantly going through my head like a broken record that got louder and louder every second. I still wondered if part of it could've been a dream, or at least that's what I hoped.

I listened and re-listened to the incoherent voicemails I'd left myself on my phone from that night. I heard people laughing in the background. I heard Adrianne say she loved me and me tell her I loved her back. I listened to Adrianne's giggly "I love you" over and over, and each time I heard her voice, I wanted to cry. But I couldn't cry—I couldn't feel anything.

MORNING AFTERMATH

I STILL FELT NAUSEOUS when I got up for school on Monday morning, but I wasn't vomiting anymore and the bleeding had finally stopped. I felt my sore underside sink into the bucket seat of my car on the short drive to school. I'd never been more aware of my reproductive system than when my aching vagina was the only part of my body that I could feel. As soon as I walked through the doors of my high school, I realized that I wasn't the same person I was when I'd walked through those doors just a few days prior.

The hallways darkened and became convoluted, and a powerful sense of dread weighed me down. This building that used to be so familiar now scared me in a way I couldn't understand. At the end of the thousand-mile-long hallway, Adrianne stood by her locker with a few of our other friends. They were so close, but walking over to my friends seemed like a huge endeavor. I stopped at my locker to drop off my bag and get my books, where I lingered with my fingers on the dusty red metal. I didn't understand why I hesitated to see the people I always loved catching up with after the weekend. I walked up to the group, and Kelly asked me if everything was okay. I knew I looked sick, and I'd planned to tell everyone that I was coming down with a cold or something, but Kelly's tone unsettled me. I wondered if she already knew what'd happened—or could see it on me like it was written across my forehead. Without a word, I just shrugged and stood there. I still don't know what virginity looks like, but its absence in a person must be pretty obvious.

"Oh my God, did you lose your V-card this weekend?" Kelly said without delay.

I wondered if that was the typical assumption everyone made about a girl who walked into school Monday morning looking like shit. Are people supposed to look like shit after losing their virginity? And was that the only excuse a girl could have for looking like shit? It shocked me that any of my friends would assume that about me. I'd never even had a boyfriend, and openly claimed my Christian beliefs of wanting to wait to have sex until I got married. Maybe since I experimented with alcohol and pot a little bit over the summer, everyone thought my entire moral compass had been destroyed.

I wished I'd never drank alcohol, not only because I thought that might've prevented me from losing my virginity, but because if I was still that innocent girl everybody thought I was, maybe people would believe that I actually didn't want that to happen. But now I was just the girl who drank too much and had sex with my best friend's sleazy ex-boyfriend.

When I couldn't vocalize a response to Kelly's inquiry about my virginity, Adrianne immediately took off down the hallway to call Jared. The rest of that school day lasted an eternity, and Kelly mediated conversations between Adrianne and me via text messages because Adrianne refused to look at me or even text me directly. I told Kelly that Jared and I did have sex, but I was fucked up and didn't want it to happen at all. Kelly said Jared told Adrianne that he didn't remember having sex, so if I said that it happened, it must've been after he passed out. Great, now people could call me a rapist.

This back and forth texting got tedious, and I wanted to talk to someone face to face. I hesitated to tell Rebekah about what had happened, with her being the pastor's daughter and all. I didn't want her to know that I wasn't a virgin anymore. But I figured she'd hear it from someone eventually, so I gave her a brief synopsis of the story.

"Well, you probably shouldn't have been drinking over there" wasn't the support I hoped for from my other best friend.

I knew it. This is what happens when you drink too much. I shouldn't have been drinking. It was all my fault. I realized I was the one to blame for what had happened to me, but I still didn't want people thinking I somehow had sex with Jared after he'd passed out drunk. That was untrue and ridiculous, so I asked Kelly for Jared's phone number and went out to my car to call him. Hearing his voice on the other end of my long-antenna'd flip phone sent painful chills down my spine.

"How could you tell Adrianne that I took advantage of you while you were passed out? You know we had sex. You put the condom on yourself!" My chest and face reddened, my heart pounded. I didn't know if I'd survive this conversation.

"I don't remember anything about a condom. I didn't find a used one in my room, and I cleaned today," Jared said. I wondered if he wanted me to praise him for cleaning his room.

"Well, I saw you throw the condom wrapper away when you told me not to tell Adrianne what happened. Plus, I pulled part of it out of me later that day."

"What? It broke?!" Now he suddenly believed me. "You need to get the morning-after pill right away."

I had no idea how to go about doing that, so he offered to meet me at the county health clinic as soon as I got out of school that afternoon. I dreaded having to see him again, but I willingly went— it relieved me that somebody finally told me what to do. I didn't know what to do while I lay trapped in Jared's bed. I didn't know what to do afterwards about telling Adrianne or my mom about what'd happened. I didn't know what to do about calling the police, going to the doctor, or what to do to prevent this from happening again. I felt this immense pressure to do something about what'd happened to me, just do *something*, but I didn't know what'd happened and I certainly didn't know what to do about it. I just needed somebody to tell me what to do because I felt completely helpless, and I welcomed Jared's offer to take me to the health clinic.

I met Jared at the health clinic right after school, and wanted to vomit as soon as I saw him, but I thought if I could survive this short encounter, I'd never have to see him again. I don't remember what I told my mom when she called to ask why I wasn't home from school yet, but I felt guilty about lying to her. Jared told me exactly what to say to the receptionist, including the time and day that we had sex, which he told me to lie about because it would ensure a better chance they'd give me the pill. My life suddenly became a web of lies. In the waiting room, I saw my stepmom's niece, Laura. We were the same age and used to see each other occasionally when I visited my dad. Apparently there was only one reason anybody went to this part of the clinic.

"Morning-after pill?" Laura asked.

I nodded.

She smiled and said, "I won't tell if you won't."

We both laughed, but there was nothing funny to me about this. Then, a girl from my church walked in. Shit. I definitely didn't want anybody from church to see me there. I told her I was getting the morning-after pill.

"Eh, it happens," she said with an offhand tone as she continued to read her magazine.

"Yeah I guess, just don't tell anyone," I said. I told myself to stay as calm as possible.

Then a concerned look came over her face, and she asked if everything was okay or if I needed to talk. I didn't know she would be the only person to offer me help when I desperately needed it most. I wish I would've told her everything right there in that harshly lit waiting room, in front of Laura, in front of the nurses, and in front of Jared, who sat on the other side of the room with his hands folded behind his head looking like Jack Nicholson in *The Shining*. I wish I could've told her that my virginity, my innocence, and my free will were stolen from me, and the man who took them sat right across the room from us. Instead, I assured her that everything was fine. I needed to wait until I felt safer to tell anybody about what had happened to me.

I hoped the nurse would notice my distress or at least inquire about why I needed the morning-after pill, but she just gave me the pills and charged me twenty dollars. I went back out to the waiting room to find Jared being loud and obnoxious talking to everyone. I realized that I hated Jared, but immediately felt guilty for feeling that way about another person. The receptionist offered him some condoms, and when he saw what kind they were, he raucously proclaimed that the condoms he uses with spermicide are far superior to whatever they offered. I gave him my shut-the-fuck-up face.

"What? I just like to leave my mark wherever I go." And with Jared's declaration, it became my mission to erase whatever mark he'd left on me.

The nurse instructed me to take one pill with dinner that evening and the next pill twelve hours later. I brought the packet of pills home, put them in a box that I kept on my dresser, and hoped my mom wouldn't see them. My mom had given me the small box that was covered in faux cow fur several years earlier, and I always took the cow box with me when I traveled away from home to conventions or concerts with my youth group. Along with my lip gloss and nail polish and makeup, I kept an Oscar Mayer wiener whistle and two rubber smiley-faced hot dogs that reminded me of my childhood inside the box.

As I placed the box of morning-after pills in my cow box, I remembered all the trips I'd taken with my youth group and all the hotel nightstands on which I'd kept the box, all the sparkly fruity flavors of lip gloss, all the times my friends petted the cow fur, all the times I accidentally spilled the contents of the box in the church van, all the times I played the Oscar Mayer jingle on the wiener whistle—I remembered all of my innocence and realized how quickly it had been taken from me as I now put emergency contraception into a box that I always associated with laughter and fun and friends.

I never imagined myself as someone who would ever need to worry about unwanted pregnancy, and I felt like I'd become a completely different person overnight. I never took any more trips with my youth group, and I threw away the cow box shortly after I took the morning-after pills. I replaced the cheery cow box on my dresser with the dark wooden box inside which my mom used to keep her marijuana.

By the end of that first day back at school, Adrianne became irritated by the conflicting stories that Jared and I told her, so she sent me a text that read, "I don't know who to believe. I want to know everything, and I mean EVERYTHING, that happened according to you. Send me an email." So after the morning-after-pill fiasco, I went to the EIU library to use a computer to email Adrianne, and composed a detailed account of everything I remembered from that night. I knew my words were a little graphic, but she said she wanted to know everything that happened, and I didn't want to leave Jared any room to twist my words around, so I provided a thorough explanation.

Walking into school the next day was as gut-wrenching as the day before, but I felt a little bit of hope. I'd taken my second morning-after pill with breakfast, so I didn't have to worry about getting pregnant, and I expected that after Adrianne read my email, she'd understand what a horrible experience I'd had and would comfort me like I needed. Instead, she saw me in the hallway before school and walked in the opposite direction. The image of Adrianne's silhouette disappearing into the blinding sunlight coming in through the glass doors was permanently branded into my mind. I should've run after her. Adrianne never showed up to our first class. Kelly told me that Adrianne went home sick because the email I sent her made her sick, and seeing me that morning made her even sicker. I didn't understand.

LOSS

AFTER JARED VIOLATED ME, Adrianne never spoke to me again. I don't know who told what to whom, but everybody at school knew what'd happened to me. Not my story, but whatever distorted fabrication high school students found the most scandalous. Adrianne remained the Queen Bee of our group of friends and ostracized me. I couldn't sit at our lunch table, so I usually went out to my car to sleep in the backseat during lunch. Instead of smiling and chatting in the hallway, everyone looked away from me. A few of our friends still talked to me, but I couldn't join the group if Adrianne was around.

I felt all the awkward glances and heard the whispers penetrate into my soul as painfully as when Jared had done the same to me. Going to school was like reliving every day what'd happened with Jared—it was worse than that. Jared was a single event that had ended. But going to school and feeling everyone looking at me, knowing that whatever they were thinking about me was probably disgusting and untrue, ensured that I'd never forget what'd happened.

When we stopped for lunch on a French Club field trip, I sat at a table by myself in McDonald's and watched my friends all sitting together and laughing. I wondered if they talked about me, but mostly I wondered why no teachers or other kids came over to ask me why I sat by myself.

I tried desperately to make amends with Adrianne, but she wouldn't even make eye contact with me. I left Christmas cards and

Valentines on her desk at school, only to watch her throw them in the trash in a dramatic scene in front of the class. I couldn't believe these people with whom I'd grown up—these people who knew that I was a good person—would turn their backs on me in one day and never look back. We read *The Scarlet Letter* that year, and I related to Hester Prynne in a way I wished I couldn't.

It's quite possible that the ostracization I felt wasn't an accurate interpretation of what actually happened at the time—maybe it wasn't true that I repulsed everybody and rumors spread about me—but I knew that my best friend couldn't stand to look me in the eye, so I didn't see how anybody else could either. I knew I was a vile, disgusting person, and I didn't even want to be around myself, so I completely withdrew. I had nobody to talk to. Nobody would believe that what'd happened to me was out of my control, and I wasn't even sure of that myself.

"I had sex one time when I was drunk, but I really didn't want it to happen at all," I admitted to a coworker at Little Caesars during a typical conversation about sex.

"Well, you know, you never really do anything drunk you don't secretly want to do sober," she said before walking away as if she'd just explained my whole situation and no further discussion was warranted.

I knew I'd done something wrong and just needed to live with it. I'd be out of high school in seven months, and thought I'd never have to see those people again. I wouldn't admit to myself or anyone else that what'd happened with Jared had any negative effect on me. So much had already been taken from me, and I couldn't bear to lose any more.

I told Rebekah that I was glad I had sex with Jared. I told myself it was good that I got the initial clumsiness of losing my virginity over with, so when I actually wanted to have sex, it wouldn't be so awkward. I told myself I was happy I could use tampons now. I told myself this was a minor setback that happens to a lot of people. I knew of the rape statistics, and I didn't see one out of every five women wandering around town disheveled and broken. Other people moved on with their lives, and so would I. I'd plaster on a fake smile, and press onward.

But I remained in a constant state of panic. I knew it would only be a matter of time before what'd happened with Jared would happen again, either with him or somebody else. I didn't ever want to have to get the morning-after pill again, so I started taking birth control. But getting my first gynecological exam by myself scared me even more than getting the morning-after pill with Jared. They made me take my clothes off. They put sticky jelly on me. They put cold, plastic duck lips inside me. I involuntarily clenched my muscles so tightly and squeezed my legs so hard against the nurse's temples that she couldn't get the duck lips inside me. She told me to relax, to loosen up, that this wouldn't feel any different than just having sex, which was exactly what I feared, and I felt violated all over again.

Just like at the morning-after pill clinic, when I hoped that maybe a nurse would notice my distress or that I could form the words to tell her what had happened to me, I had an in-and-out visit, only leaving with some pills and the feeling of Jared's fingers inside me. And the feeling of warm blood dripping down my legs. And all the confusion and fear that burned a permanent brand into my soul.

I no longer walked around barefoot everywhere because I wanted to "feel the earth beneath my feet." I stopped eating my favorite snack, Grape Nuts, out of the box. I didn't buy any more old men's neckties at the Salvation Army to wear as belts around my baggy jeans with holes in the knees. I didn't care to rake leaves in the fall or collect live Dave Matthews Band recordings to send to other fans across the country in glitter-decorated bubble mailers. I stopped writing poetry and making drawings for every holiday to give to my friends at school. I threw away the symphony that I'd been composing. I stopped passing intricately-folded notes to my friends at school, which usually included a funny stick-figure drawing. I no longer ate Hostess HoHos at lunch, not even at Christmastime when they were called HoHoHos.

Now, I lived simply to minimize the pain as I waited for my time to die. I didn't have senior pictures taken. I didn't go to prom. I didn't have a graduation party. I didn't even take my AP exams that would've earned me college credit for the advanced courses I took in high school.

Some days when I pulled into the driveway after school, I felt so exhausted from having endured a whole day in hell that I immediately fell asleep in the driver's seat of my car until I had to go to work at Little Caesars an hour later. I put pillows and blankets in the backseat of my beat-up red 1991 Geo Storm hatchback so I could nap during lunch at school.

I never admitted it at the time, and I didn't even begin to realize it until I lost her, but I was in love with Adrianne, and I'd hoped that maybe she loved me too. I daydreamed about us living together in college, cooking dinner together, watching movies on the couch together, and maybe cuddling. But now that I'd lost my virginity, I knew nobody would ever love me again.

Earlier that year, around Valentine's Day, all the girls at my church went to a True Love Waits conference, a Southern Baptist creation to promote sexual abstinence outside of marriage. I don't know why I didn't go to the conference, but when the girls returned home, they were honored in front of the congregation at church; they each received a plaque, and recited the True Love Waits pledge:

"Believing that true love waits, I make a commitment to God, myself, my family, my friends, my future mate, and my future children to be sexually abstinent from this day until the day I enter a biblical marriage relationship."

When I saw my friends getting their plaques and how everyone at church congratulated them, I felt left out and wished I'd gone to the conference. I'd never received a plaque for anything before. But even though I hadn't taken the True Love Waits pledge, I knew I had broken an important rule—maybe what'd happened with Jared happened because I hadn't taken that damn pledge.

I felt something new and shadowy within me that I now know to be hatred. I didn't hate Adrianne for leaving me—I just wanted her back in my life. I didn't hate Jared for whatever he did—I thought he was just drunk and thinking with his dick. I did, however, hate myself, and I felt ashamed of this darkness within me. I thought it would only be a short matter of time before I'd die, and my life became a temporary hospice regimen.

UNDER CONTROL

ON THE DAYS I ACTUALLY WENT to school, I made it through the day by sleeping through most of my classes. I liked working at Little Caesars—it distracted me from myself, and I could drink at work if I wanted to. Almost all of the people who worked at Little Caesars were heavy drinkers and occasional drug users; as long as we could still make pizzas, the owners didn't care what we did at work. We often called up the liquor store down the street to make a deal with them to trade a couple pizzas for a bottle of booze. There was always someone at work without a driver's license or a car at any given time, so I'd give them a ride home after work and hope that they wanted to stop at the liquor store to prepare for their own evening. This usually panned out, and I'd casually ask if they'd pick me up a fifth of whiskey as I handed them a twenty dollar bill. Now instead of spending my paycheck on CDs, more and more of it went toward alcohol.

When I wasn't at work or school, I sat in my room and drank whiskey from my grandma's old stainless steel double-sided shot glass. I carefully poured my whiskey into the regular-sized side of the shot glass a few times until my throat became numb enough that I could swallow a jigger-sized shot from the other side of the glass. If I didn't have any alcohol, my heart pounded, my mind raced, and I couldn't focus on anything except the feeling of imminent danger. When I slept, I had nightmares about Jared, and when I was awake, I constantly replayed the events of that night and next afternoon in my mind.

The nightmares weren't like having a bad dream where you wake and realize it was a dream and everything's okay. The nightmares were like physically re-living every moment of being physically invaded and violated and the shame and torture of being ostracized at school thereafter. Even upon waking, my body still felt exactly as it had when those events actually occurred.

When my alarm clock went off in the morning, I bolted out of bed, my heart pounding so hard that I knew everyone in the neighborhood could hear it, every muscle in my body rigidly frozen. I surveyed my surroundings, wondered what'd happened, what day it was, terrified of waking up next to Jared or some other man, as unexpectedly as I had in October. Sometimes I curled into a ball on my bedroom floor and tightly closed my eyes, trying to escape my thoughts. I thought my mind was the one thing nobody could steal from me, the one place I could be safe. But I didn't even feel safe there anymore.

I wanted to drink as often as I could, and it frustrated me so much that I couldn't buy my own alcohol. So whenever I had the opportunity to get some liquor from someone at work, I added it to the stockpile it in my bottom dresser drawer, and rationed it out so I always had some alcohol in case I needed it. I didn't drink every day, only when I thought I'd die if I had to endure one more second of the pain I felt, but I knew I probably drank more than most of the other kids at school. My classmates told stories of the parties they went to over the weekend with their older siblings and what alcohol they tried, and I knew my stories of sitting alone in my bedroom listening to Pearl Jam and drinking whiskey straight out of the bottle wouldn't be well-received.

I didn't let myself drink before or during school though because that was too risky. I wanted to get the fuck out of high school, but not via expulsion. One day, as I sat in my senior-level Consumer Education class, my mom walked into the classroom and asked to see me.

"I'm sorry to interrupt. I need to see my daughter."

The teacher gave me permission to leave, and I got up from my desk to go out to the hallway with my mom. I thought my grandma must've died. Or my dad. Something horrible.

"I know what you've been doing and this has to stop. Give me your car keys. Give me your keys now!"

I had no idea what my mom ranted and raved about, but she was clearly agitated. Something infuriated her, and she talked so fast I couldn't keep up with the conversation. I didn't know why she wanted my car keys, but they were in my locker on the other side of the building.

"I know you've been drinking, and I'm not letting you drive home from school drunk!"

I was so confused—I never drank before or during school. My mom had known for weeks that I drank at home, so I didn't know why she was suddenly hysterical about it. She said she found empty liquor bottles in my dresser drawer that morning, which made her think I'd been drinking that day at school. I assured her that those bottles were from the past several weeks, but I didn't know how to discreetly dispose of them (which was the truth). She finally calmed down, said we'd talk after school, and left without taking my car keys. I needed to find somewhere else to drink besides home.

I was relieved once the guys at Little Caesars invited me to hang out with them, and sometimes Aaron and Rebekah even came to hang out too. I still made a point to drink Bacardi Razz occasionally because I didn't want to intentionally avoid it just because that's what Jared had given me to drink. I wouldn't allow Jared to take my freedom of drink along with everything else. But when I drank Bacardi Razz, the memories from my time with Jared were so much more difficult to wash out. One evening, my glass of Bacardi Razz slipped through my fingers and shattered all over the tiled kitchen floor of my coworker's apartment. I crawled around on the floor trying to pick up all the broken glass, and saw blood all over my hands.

Then, Josh, who used to work at Little Caesars, asked me if I wanted to go for a ride with him in his van. Rebekah told me it was a bad idea to do anything with him, and she made a point to let Josh know I was still seventeen-years-old. Jailbait. I wasn't attracted to Josh in any way, but my goal was to have sex normally—to enjoy sex without fear or pain. If I could manage that, then I could gain back one of the things that Jared had taken from me.

The problem was that I didn't want to have sex, especially not with a man. I had an inkling that I might be gay or bisexual or something other than what I thought everybody else was, but I didn't know how to figure it out. It seemed so complicated and confusing. And now that I'd been with Jared, I didn't think I could tell people I wasn't interested in men. If anyone actually believed that I hadn't wanted that to happen, they'd think I hated men or feared them because boys had been mean to me in the past. And the people who thought I did choose to have sex with my best friend's lover wouldn't believe I was a lesbian because lesbians don't have sex with men. Not being believed when I told somebody the truth of my reality was one of the most disempowering feelings, one that was difficult to survive. So I decided to keep trying to be straight.

I got in Josh's van, and when he drove out to the country, I got anxious—every muscle in my body contracted, my heart pounded, and I couldn't breathe. We kissed for a little bit, but the fear of not knowing what would to happen to me in the next few minutes consumed my body like flames, so I abruptly told him I needed to go home. He looked confused, but agreed to take me back to town. I didn't know why I thought it was a good idea to go to the middle of nowhere in some guy's minivan.

These are the stupid kinds of things girls do to get raped, I thought.

Josh dropped me off at my car, we kissed for a few minutes, and then he reached down my pants and shoved his fingers into my vagina in one swift motion. I didn't expect that. I didn't stop him right away as I wanted to see if I could enjoy this, but Jared's dirty, chubby fingers and the cold, plastic duck lips at the gynecologist filled my mind. It'd only been a month since I lost my virginity, but that month felt like a year to me, and I didn't know why my vagina was still torn and sore. I grabbed Josh's arm, pulled it away from me, and got out of his van.

When I got home I realized I'd been bleeding a lot. I felt so embarrassed and terrified that Josh's hand was all covered in blood. Would he think I was a virgin? Would he think I was on my period? I hoped he thought it was blood from when I cut my hands earlier. I never found out if he noticed any blood or not, but I didn't want anybody going near my vagina until I got it under control.

LUSTER LOST AND FOUND

Sunset
November 2003

THANKSGIVING BREAK CAME, and I was so glad to finally get some time off school, away from that prison. Rebekah went out of town with her family for a couple days, so Aaron invited me to this "Black Wednesday" party that people from town threw every year the night before Thanksgiving. Aaron told me they'd have kegs and it was always a wild party. I'd never been to a real party before, and I was so excited. I brought a bottle of whiskey just in case the beer at the party didn't settle well with me. Sometimes even a couple sips of beer made me vomit.

I recognized some people from school there, but they were mostly college kids, who were impressed when I took swigs of my fifth of Jim Beam. I liked the attention, and my whiskey, so I kept drinking straight out of the Beam bottle. I had a great time drinking and talking to people, but somebody realized that I drank almost an entire fifth of whiskey in a short period of time and warned me that I'd probably get really drunk. I felt fine, but they told me it would catch up with me in a little bit. I definitely felt drunk, but I didn't feel out of control—I walked around and spoke just fine.

I went to use the bathroom and woke up on the toilet when someone banged on the door and told me to hurry up. I figured I'd just dozed off for a few minutes, but when I tried to stand, I fell face first into the porcelain bathtub. I guess the whiskey caught up with me. I walked out of the bathroom and saw a long line of people waiting, and the ominous oh-my-Gods and are-you-okays filled the small, dark hallway like smoke. I didn't know what they were talking about. I didn't think I'd been in the bathroom that long. I apologized for holding up the line and tried to walk back into the party, but a couple of fire-eyed girls pushed me back into the bathroom and asked if somebody had punched me.

They were concerned, and I didn't know why they thought somebody had punched me. They had me look in the mirror, and I saw my nose completely busted open, my face covered in blood. The girls cleaned me up and took me outside for some fresh air. I felt slightly embarrassed, but I mostly laughed it off with everyone as I sat in a vinyl folding chair while blood pooled on my face again.

"Come on Apryl, we need to leave," Aaron said with a hint of sympathy.

"No, no. My curfew isn't for another hour. I'm fine," I said as if I was actually aware of the time.

But Aaron insisted that we leave, and he drove me home. In the car he told me that the owners of the house were afraid of getting in trouble for underage drinking. I was a liability that nobody wanted around. I stumbled into my house, and woke my mom when I knocked over pretty much every piece of furniture and picture frame in the living room. I fell face first into my bed.

I heard my mom's voice resound, "I'm going to leave this mess so you can see what you did when you wake up," as I passed out.

When I got up in the morning—Thanksgiving morning—I saw that the living room looked like a tornado had gone through it; I had no idea how I managed that much destruction. When I saw the blood and vomit caked on my face and all over my shirt, Jared's voice echoed in my head. *It's my bed and I don't want vomit to get all over it.* My mom asked me what'd happened, so I told her the story, and she said that I needed to come up with some other explanation to tell the family.

For Thanksgiving dinner with the family that day, I felt so hungover and had to recite some lame story about slipping in the shower to explain my busted-up face. I told myself I'd never drink again. Drinking wasn't fun anymore like it had been earlier that summer when I drank for the first time with Rebekah and Aaron at the fireworks show.

The Saturday evening after my Black Wednesday fiasco, I sat in my room drinking whiskey—I'd since retracted my resolution to never drink again—when Colin McCormick called me. I usually ignored calls from Colin, but I was extremely lonely and pretty drunk, so I answered my phone. I referred to Colin as "my oldest friend." He was almost two years younger than me, but we grew up together. His mom started babysitting me before either of us remembers. We were best buddies as children, and the McCormicks were the reason my mom and I started going to Charleston Community Church. As we got older, Colin and I didn't spend much time together outside of church, but we were both active in the youth group and still friends. For the first time in probably ten years, hanging out with Colin actually sounded exciting. He went to the Christian school in town, so he had no idea about anything that'd happened to me. Plus, I knew he wouldn't try to stick his fingers in my vagina.

Colin had recently earned his driver's license, so he picked me up at home. We drove around and talked for hours, and I felt so relieved to be with someone who didn't have any idea how broken I was. We stopped at Little Caesars, and I went back to the kitchen to make us some food. We ate freshly-baked pizza and breadsticks in the car, laughed and reminisced about our childhoods. I almost felt normal again.

Colin told me about some guys who got together every Sunday night to play video games, and he invited me to go the following week. I would've normally never been interested in this, but I would've done anything for some friends at that point.

I went over to the house that Sunday and at least twenty nerdy boys playing video games, drinking soda, and eating junk food greeted me. All of the furniture in the house had been acquired from dumpster diving excursions, the metallic blue velvet-flocked wallpaper hailed from another era altogether, and there were more TVs and computers in the house than people. The wall decorations ranged from an old picture of anonymous sorority girls to a Texas-shaped plaque displaying all the different types of barbed wire. They had weekly Halo parties where they connected four Xboxes and four TVs together so sixteen people could all play each other in the game at the same time. They screamed friendly "your mom" insults at each other and used words like "noob" and "pwned" and talked about computers. I didn't know parties like this actually existed—it was a whole new culture to me.

We all grew up in the same town, but these guys were a few years older, so we were never in school together. Colin and I stayed and played video games for hours, and I'd never had so much fun in my life. Nobody there knew anything about what had happened to me, nobody judged me for drinking, and nobody tried to stick their fingers in my vagina. I was safe there.

In the days and weeks—and as it turned out, years—to come, I became a regular at the Halo House, as somebody aptly named it. I went every Sunday to play Halo with the guys, and then I started going to their weekly movie nights on Thursdays. They pretty much had an open-door policy at the house, so sometimes I dropped by to use the Internet or see who was home. I often felt like something horrible could happen to me any second, and going to the Halo House made me feel safe. There was always somebody at the house hanging out, and they welcomed me to join anytime.

They had more traditional parties occasionally, but these guys weren't big drinkers like the guys at Little Caesars. I still drank there, even if nobody else joined me, but nobody said anything about it, and I liked it that way. At first, my mom wasn't too thrilled about me hanging out in a house with a bunch of twenty-something boys, but I assured her that these guys were completely harmless. Really nice kids. A lot of them were even involved in the Christian Campus House at EIU. I was safe.

NEW BEGINNING

LANCE HAD JUST TURNED twenty-one and also regularly hung out at the Halo House. We both lived in Charleston for most of our lives, but I didn't know him until I worked at Little Caesars where he'd started working just a few months before I did. One day at work, the delivery driver asked me if I liked Lance. I'd never thought about it. I looked over at Lance across the store—he was covered in flour, leaning against the pizza dough machine, and he was kind of cute I guess. He looked exactly like Elijah Wood, only slightly less Hobbit-like. I shrugged it off, but once we interacted outside of work at the Halo House, I began to like him. Lance was goofy and fun and an excellent musician.

I hung out at the Halo House even more now, especially when I saw Lance's car there. Sometimes, I changed my work schedule around so I could work with him at Little Caesars. Out of all the guys at the Halo House, Lance had a drinking habit most on par with mine. He became my main supplier of alcohol, I enjoyed drinking and spending time with him, and we became good friends. Lance was a devout Christian, and he openly shared the fact that he was a virgin saving himself for marriage. I felt safe with him, especially for that reason.

But somehow, our friendship progressed into making out in our cars for hours and hours. We often went to the Halo House together after work, so one of us would drive the other home later that night, and we'd sit in the driveway until two or three o'clock in the morning where we kissed, talked, laughed, and listened to music.

We talked about our childhood experiences, our religious beliefs, our taste in music and movies. I'd never been so open with anyone in my entire life. I could truly be myself around Lance. I felt comfortable with him in a way that I'd never been comfortable with anyone else. Inevitably, the topic of sex came up. I already knew that Lance was a virgin, and when he asked if I shared the same status, I told him that I'd had sex a few months ago but that it was "not consensual" because I was fucked up and hadn't wanted it to happen.

This was the first time I talked about what'd happened with Jared since that first day back at school afterward. I referred to Jared by name because I knew he and Lance had gone to school together, and hoped that maybe Lance had heard something about him — about my experience with him, or about someone else who had something similar happen. I still desperately searched for answers.

Lance said Jared had always been a scumbag and he hoped they'd never run into each other anywhere. I still couldn't talk about the details of what'd happened or how it made me feel, and casually telling Lance that I'd had "non-consensual sex" made me feel like it wasn't that big of a deal, especially with his rather blasé reaction.

I thought that maybe I could re-claim my virginity and told Lance that I also wanted to save sex for marriage. But in the short time between when he told me he wanted to remain a virgin until marriage and when I told him I'd already had "non-consensual sex," Lance changed his mind.

"I think we should have sex. I don't see the point in waiting until marriage. We should live for the moment!" Lance boldly said during one of our drunken make-out sessions in the car.

This took me by surprise. I felt comfortable with the idea that we weren't ready for sex. With all of the kissing and touching we did in the car almost every night, we were comfortable with each other's bodies, but I didn't think it would head in the direction of sex, at least not so quickly. Where were we even supposed to have sex? We both lived with our parents. We weren't even officially dating — Lance kept telling me he didn't want to be "tied down." I told Lance that we shouldn't make a decision about sex while we're both drunk.

"Hey. I'm the virgin here. I should get to decide if we have sex," he snapped back.

That comment penetrated so deeply into my soul, all of the air left my lungs and the blood rushed from my face. Lance had just inflicted the exact same pain that Jared had. He told me that by not being a virgin, I had no power to decide the fate of my body anymore. It didn't matter whether or not I lost my virginity by choice; I wasn't a virgin—not in God's eyes, not in my own eyes, not in anyone else's eyes.

Lance and I didn't have sex that night in the car, but a few weeks later, we officially started dating. We saw each other every day, and this made me think that my life could return to normal. I had friends, a job, a boyfriend, a car. I was normal by most high school standards.

Unfortunately, my life at school was still hell, and it became even more unbearable once I had a good life outside of school. Sometimes Lance and I stayed up so late playing video games and watching movies in my bedroom that I'd sneak him out of the house when my mom got in the shower in the morning. Staying up with Lance until three or four or even five o'clock in the morning made it almost impossible to stay awake at school, but I didn't want to miss one minute of the only time I felt happy. I'd rather sleep at school anyway, and I still had good grades. But I missed a day of school almost every week and got detentions for truancy for the first time in my life.

Only one teacher ever asked me if I was okay when he noticed this sudden change in my behavior, but it caught me totally off guard and I didn't feel safe talking about it in the three minutes we had in between classes, so I just assured him I was fine. Again, I didn't know he'd be one of the only people to offer me help when I needed it most.

I just wanted to finish high school so I could move on with my life. I still drank quite a bit, and my anxiety worsened, especially about having to go to school. If anyone at school or work brought up the rumors about me and Jared, I brushed it off as an awkward first-sex experience toward which I felt completely indifferent. I desperately tried to convince myself that what'd happened wasn't that big of deal, that I'd get over it soon enough, but all that mindset did was leave me with an unbearable amount of anxiety to which I couldn't attribute a cause. Really, it never crossed my conscious seventeen-year-old mind that the reason I was anxious, afraid, not sleeping, not eating, and suicidal had anything to do with Jared—despite the fact that I awoke from nightmares every night and couldn't ever stop thinking about being penetrated and ostracized.

My mom noticed my increased anxiety and thought medication might help, so we made a doctor's appointment. First, we saw a nurse practitioner who asked if anything significant had happened that might've caused my anxiety. I quickly replied that no, nothing had happened. She asked if I slept okay and if I felt sad or lonely or unmotivated, and I explained that school stressed me out and that I couldn't ever relax. When I answered the final ominous question, have you ever thought about hurting or killing yourself? with, "Well, yeah, I've thought about it, but I'm not going to," I immediately put my hand over my mouth. I didn't mean to say that, and by the look of shock on my mother's face, she didn't expect it either.

I explained to the nurse and my mom that sometimes I felt like it'd be easier if I could do something to make the anxiety go away. I wondered what would've happened if I said that I'd rather be dead than have to live one more second in my nightmares and thoughts—that I'd rather be dead than have a constant reminder of my transgression by being ostracized at school. But I couldn't even understand, let alone vocalize, my pain, and with everyone at school knowing what'd happened to me, the fewer people in the world who knew what a dead, broken girl I was, the better. I didn't think anyone could do to anything help me anyway—nobody could undo what'd already happened, so I just had to live with it.

The nurse sent us to see a psychiatrist, Dr. Byrd, who actually looked like a bird—like a weird, old emu. He spoke with my mother and me for about five minutes before he diagnosed me with bipolar disorder. My mom and I both knew he had no basis for this diagnosis, but he prescribed an antidepressant, Paxil, that I agreed to try.

I now know that prescribing an antidepressant, like Paxil, alone isn't an appropriate treatment for bipolar disorder, which wasn't even a correct diagnosis for me. My mother shouldn't have been in the room as I spoke with the nurse or the psychiatrist, and these health professionals should've known that. Maybe I would've been able to talk to them if I wasn't so afraid of what my mom would think of me if she knew what'd happened. But then again, acknowledging to myself, alone, what had happened scared me just as much.

I didn't tell my mom about what happened with Jared right away because I didn't even know *what* had happened to me; I thought I'd done something terrible. I wanted to be her innocent little girl, and it made me feel a little better knowing somebody could still think of me that way. My mom was so happy about getting married, and I didn't want to ruin her wedding. Plus, I'd already been shut down by my best friends, and knew I couldn't handle any kind of similar response from my mother or anyone else.

A few weeks after starting Paxil, I noticed that my anxiety had diminished. I relaxed and slept better. Being in school became a slightly more manageable hell. The nurse warned against drinking while taking an antidepressant, but I went to a party at the Halo House and drank some beer. After two beers, I became woozy and tired, sat on the couch, and fell asleep for a while. When I woke up, I panicked. I felt exactly how I had when I woke up in Jared's bed, and thought I would die, but then I saw my friends, who laughed and welcomed me back into the world. Nothing bad happened. I was safe there.

My new friends didn't drink much, and I felt better anyway, so I decided I shouldn't drink anymore. I took Paxil for about nine months and didn't drink the entire time. But after about three months of taking Paxil, my anxiety came back. I was in Wal-Mart with my mom, and I was shaking and scared and thought I'd never get out of there alive. We went back to the doctor, who increased my dosage, which worked for a while. But the same thing happened a couple months later, and again, my mom and I returned to the doctor for a Paxil dosage increase.

My youth group leader, who I adored, moved away and my already dwindling attendance at youth group became even scarcer when the new leaders came in. One of them pulled me aside, and told me that she noticed I struggled with things and that she knew it was because I had a hard time with my parents' divorce and not growing up with a father in the house. I gave her a look that said, *You have no fucking idea what you're talking about, lady; this has nothing to do with my goddamn parents' divorce thirteen years ago.* I walked away and never went back. I started going to the Christian Campus House with Lance. This was another "non-denominational" contemporary church that mostly EIU students attended, and I liked the idea of belonging to a group of people who didn't know anything about me.

I decided not to move away to start the physics program at the University of Illinois. Even though it was less than an hour away from Charleston, I didn't want to leave the safety of my new friends or Lance for the unknown. I didn't even see the point of going to college anymore, so I decided to just work at Little Caesars and spend time with my new friends.

Two months before I graduated high school, I got an apartment in town and moved out of my mom's house. Jim had lived with us for a few months since he and my mom got married, and I couldn't stand living with a new person in the house for the first time in my life, having no private space to be alone. I don't know how I rented an apartment as a seventeen-year-old—the landlord never asked for any information from me and I'd saved enough money for the security deposit and first month's rent.

Having my own space was so liberating and I knew I was one step closer to getting out of high school and adolescence. When I finally graduated high school, the teachers who sat near the stage all cheered for me as my name was announced as graduating with high honors.

"Way to go, Detention!" my English teacher said. Students who got detentions rarely graduated with honors, which made me feel a shred of pride that I wouldn't have otherwise felt.

I would've been at the top of my class of two hundred graduating seniors, but in my last semester of high school, I got the first C on a report card in my life. It was in physics class, which I thought ironic considering I'd been accepted into a top physics program. It wasn't that I struggled to understand the material, it was that I struggled to survive and my education lost its value. Trying to figure out how I got a C, I looked back at my homework assignments and saw liquor stains on the pages of my physics lab notebook.

But now, I'd survived high school, and aside from Rebekah and Matt and a couple other people who I remained friends with, I thought I'd never have to see anyone from high school again. I finally escaped that prison, and grasped a sense of calm. I was happy, and didn't feel any need to drink. I decided that maybe I should go to college after all, so I accepted my old admissions letter from EIU, as I'd applied there at the same time I applied to the University of Illinois.

Being in the top ten-percent of my graduating high school class and scoring in the 98th percentile on the ACT, I probably could've found scholarships, but I didn't apply for any since I didn't think I'd be going to college. Fortunately, when I turned eighteen, I gained access to a savings bond that my grandparents had opened for me ten years earlier. The bond, worth $30,000, paid for my college, and the money I made at Little Caesars paid my bills and bought my cigarettes, the first thing I bought on my eighteenth birthday.

I applied to the EIU Music Program, and my piano teacher helped me prepare pieces from the required musical eras for the audition. The music director told me that he was "blown away" by my performance, and he admitted me to the program on the spot. But for some reason, this didn't excite me at all—I just dreaded it. After having a panic attack during my senior piano recital, I found that my passion and ability for piano had vanished. I could no longer play or write music—something within my brain had broken.

SILENCE BEGINS

Evening Twilight
June 2004- August 2005

AS SOON AS we graduated high school, Aaron and Rebekah got married. I think they were so desperate to have sex, which they obviously couldn't do outside of a "biblical marriage," that they didn't see any other option. Rebekah asked me to be her maid of honor, and I went dress shopping with her and hosted a bachelorette party, but my heart wasn't in the role of maid of honor—I didn't think I'd even survive long enough to make it to her wedding. Still, I did the best I could, and being in a wedding party for the first time excited me.

During the rehearsal dinner the night before the wedding, all of the bridesmaids lined up outside the church sanctuary to run through the order of the ceremony, I in the front of the line. Just as we were about to walk down the aisle, Rebekah's mother told me to stand behind Rebekah's sister, and just like that, she stripped me of my maid of honor title. The way in which she replaced me as maid of honor, with no explanation or advanced warning, shocked and hurt me. I don't know who decided that I shouldn't be maid of honor or their reasoning, but I thought that such an impure person as me shouldn't represent the pastor's daughter. I was no longer a virgin. I drank. I smoked cigarettes. Of course Rebekah's family wouldn't want me standing up there in front of the whole congregation next to their daughter on her wedding day. I wasn't "honorable" in any way, and I was no longer worthy of respect—not in God's eyes, nor anyone else's.

I could never escape the high school nightmare I tried so desperately to forget. I had dreams that I had to return to high school to finish some classes I neglected to take, and heard everyone talking about my repulsiveness. I felt exactly as I had in high school; like it would never end. And seeing Adrianne certainly didn't help me move on either. I saw her around town occasionally—she also decided to stay in Charleston to attend EIU, and she worked at the only grocery store in town. If my company included someone she knew, we stopped and chatted, but Adrianne never made eye contact with me or acknowledged my presence. I even saw Jared a couple times—actually, I saw him everywhere. Every man with that particular short, round build, every man with that dark receding hairline, every man with that gummy smile. He looked like Butt-Head without the Bevis counterpart.

My new apartment shared a parking lot with Little Caesars; it was only one block from the Halo House and only half a mile to campus. I never had to travel far, and I felt safe in my own space. But I still had trouble coping with my ever-increasing anxiety. I remembered going for regular jogs while playing on the tennis team in high school. I'd always enjoyed those jogs, so I decided to go out for a run to see if it would make me feel better.

About two minutes into my run, I saw Jared walking down the sidewalk in my direction, and I absolutely panicked. I bolted in the opposite direction, sprinted across a four-lane highway without looking, ran in between houses and ducked behind trees, the whole time wondering if he recognized me and if he followed me. I hyperventilated and could hardly breathe, but I didn't want to stop running for fear that Jared would catch up with me. And I didn't want to go back home in case he watched to see where I lived. I ended up running straight into the living room of Lance's parents' house. I sat on their couch. I didn't think anybody was home, but I didn't bother to check. I stared at the blank TV and tried to catch my breath. Lance's mom eventually came home, surprised to see me sitting on her couch—she'd seen me before, but I don't think she knew Lance and I were dating.

"Oh, hello there," she said as her eyes shifted and face scrunched as if trying to figure out what I wanted.

"Hi. I'm just waiting for Lance to get off work."

"I think he'll be home in about three hours."

"Okay."

It was definitely odd for me to hang out in their house with nobody else home, but she left me alone and I felt safe there. I needed to hang on to any shred of safety I could find, which meant hanging on to Lance.

I thought myself crazy for getting so scared, but as it turned out, Jared did find out where I lived and he still had my phone number from when we spoke about getting the morning-after pill.

I was in bed asleep when my phone rang and Jared's name showed up on my caller ID. I hadn't spoken to him since that afternoon at the health clinic nine months earlier. I didn't want to talk to him, but I was curious why he called me in the middle of the night. Did he call to apologize? Did he call to see if I was okay? I had to know. I wanted to ask him all those questions nobody else could answer—he was the only person who knew what happened that night.

"Hello?"

"Apryl? Hey, it's Jared. What are you doing?"

"Umm, sleeping."

"I'm hanging out in my buddy's garage just down the street from your apartment. Wanna come over and have a beer?"

His voice and invitation absolutely shocked me. How did he even know where I lived? I couldn't believe Jared had the audacity to casually call me at two o'clock in the morning to see if I wanted to hang out in his friend's garage when the one and only time we ever interacted was a nightmare from hell. Did he not realize what he'd done to me? Still, I felt torn between leaving the safety of my apartment and going to meet him in that garage—it could be my only chance to find out what'd happened. The mystery surrounding that night still haunted me.

I always thought that if I'd gone to the hospital to get one of those rape kits I'd heard about, I'd know for sure what had happened—I'd know for sure that I really did tell him no (or couldn't tell him no), that I really didn't want it to happen. But that window had closed months ago, so I told him I might come.

I hung up the phone, fell back to sleep, and awoke to forceful bangs on my apartment door. Within seconds, I went from sleeping to looking at Jared's terrifying magnified face in my tiny peephole. I ran into my bedroom to hide under the covers. I put my phone on silent so he wouldn't hear it ringing should he call me again, and I prepared to call 911 in case he broke down my door. I guess all that practice of bolting out of bed every morning finally served its purpose.

I heard him pleading, "Apryl!" as he pounded aggressively on my door.

I curled up in my bed, violently shook, and envisioned what would happen to me if he got into my apartment.

"Come on, Apryl!" BANG. BANG.

That October night never ended, the last nine months collapsed, and I prepared to live through that nightmare with Jared all over again.

BANG. BANG! "Damn it Apryl, open the door! Come on!" BANG! BANG.

After what felt like an eternity, Jared eventually left. I peeked out of my bedroom window and watched him walk away from my apartment building, but I couldn't go back to sleep that night. My heart pounded for hours, and I felt the tingle of every erect hair on my body.

As I left my apartment the next morning, I saw that Jared had left me a little note—DAMMIT APRYL—scratched into the cork of the announcement board by the front door of my apartment building. This eyesore horrified me, and I desperately hoped that nobody else had seen it yet. I pulled one of the thumbtacks out of the corkboard, wondered if it was the same one Jared had chosen to create the message, and attempted to scratch out the words.

I always wondered if my friends or neighbors could read the words that were scrawled into that corkboard, as I occasionally noticed someone curiously looking at it. When I got so sick of seeing the scribbled mess that was my name, I placed a Chinese delivery menu or nail salon advertisement over that area of the corkboard. Even though I furiously scratched out the words, focusing mostly on my name, I always clearly saw "DAMMIT APRYL" written on that corkboard and etched into my mind every time I left my apartment and every time I came home. Jared really did like to leave his mark wherever he went.

I suddenly began to have serious panic attacks that even my Paxil couldn't help. Over the course of a couple days, I became increasingly suicidal for reasons I didn't understand. Leaving my apartment terrified me, but staying there scared me even more. The universe pulled my soul in opposite directions, either of which would surely lead to excruciating pain.

Lance and I spoke on the phone while he was on vacation with his family. I didn't say anything about feeling uneasy, but he called my mom when he sensed something wrong. My mom walked into my apartment as I held the knife to my wrist. The knife was dull; I sawed back and forth and back and forth across my arm. I didn't understand why I wanted to kill myself—my life seemed better than it had ever been, but now that Jared knew where I lived, I wanted to kill myself before he had a chance to come back to my apartment to take over my body again. I knew I couldn't survive another experience like that, but it felt so inevitable that it would happen again. I re-lived it every single day in my mind and body. I still felt his hands on my ribcage, I still felt my forehead bashing into the bed frame, and I still felt the deep pain in my vagina as if it'd just happened a day ago instead of almost a year ago. I felt like a prisoner in my own body, but nobody else could see this cage.

This was in 2004, right around the time the FDA issued their black-box warning that Paxil could lead to suicide in children and teenagers. My mom told me that the Paxil caused my suicidal ideation, so we made another doctor's appointment for the following week. The doctor took me off Paxil, and instead of switching to a different drug, I decided to see how I'd do without any medication. I started drinking again, and aside from a week of some strange withdrawal symptoms from the Paxil, I felt perfectly fine. I made it through several months without feeling overly anxious. I liked that I didn't need any medication to feel "normal," but I had no idea how much I needed alcohol to feel normal.

I wanted so badly to walk across the street to the liquor store to buy my own booze without having to wait for one of my older friends to make a trip there or having to ask someone to buy it for me. I investigated how to get a fake ID like the one Jared had, and found a website that claimed to make them for a small fee. I must've recognized this as a scam, but I didn't have anything to lose. I sent them my name, address, phone number, and picture for them to put on my new Illinois state ID, and they asked me to wire them $400 through Western Union.

My shift at work started in fifteen minutes, so I rushed over to the grocery store to place my money order and when the cashier, who happened to be an old tennis teammate, asked me to confirm the name of the payee, I totally forgot to whom this money went. Somebody in Russia. My face heated up, and I thought she'd call the cops on me, but then somehow I remembered and blurted out "PETERSEN CARSTEN!" When I left the grocery store, I looked over my shoulder for any cops. A major cloudburst interrupted the otherwise sunny day and left me drenched for work. I thought maybe this was God's way of telling me I just did something stupid.

After several months of constantly checking my mailbox, I conceded that I wouldn't receive my ID after all, and I let my older friends and coworkers continue to buy me alcohol. I had enough friends that I never had to ask any one person too often anyway, and with every empty bottle of liquor I collected on top of my refrigerator, the mask I created for myself grew stronger and more permanent.

I started college in August 2004, majored in music, worked at Little Caesars as a shift manager, and claimed my independence in my new apartment. I went to church twice a week, and hung out with my friends. We went to concerts, pumpkin patches, movies, played flashlight tag in the park, played video games and board games, went bowling, colored Easter eggs, had parties, went to parties, laughed, danced, made gingerbread houses, played badminton, and went to amusement parks. I had something to do almost every night. Lance and I traveled to Mexico and Jamaica and Canada and a road trip to the East Coast. It was everything I wanted for my life, but something always felt...wrong. I knew I had a privileged life, and I felt grateful to have such nice friends, so I considered myself selfish for being so miserable. Without Paxil, I drank to regulate my anxiety and to enjoy these activities—or to at least make it look like I enjoyed them. I feared my friends wouldn't want to be around me anymore if they saw my natural instincts to cower to the ground every time the doorbell rang or throw things against the wall when I felt angry, so I placated myself with booze.

I had no idea how much Jared affected every part of my being. I didn't associate that event with why I bolted out of bed terrified every single morning, not knowing where I was or what day it was or why I threw punches at anyone who tried to wake me from my sleep. I didn't know why it took me three or four hours to get ready to leave the house in the morning. I didn't know that constantly fighting for my life, just trying to survive each day, wasn't a healthy feeling.

In some odd twist of fate, I did an Internet search for "what is rape?" At the end of one of the countless days where I couldn't stop thinking about what'd happened with Jared, I somehow knew "non-consensual sex" didn't quite describe it. So I shut myself in one of the bedrooms at the Halo House while the guys played a game in the living room. My heart pounded and my palms sweated as I checked the door to make sure nobody would catch me reading about rape on the Internet. I didn't know what'd happened to me, but I hoped it wasn't rape. I found my way to a support forum and read a story about a girl who was drugged and raped by a friend, and her account was similar to mine—almost identical, even down to her friends abandoning her. And then I read another just like it. And another.

I realized that I was raped, that this happens to way too many girls, and that we were all so fucking confused about what had happened to us or what to do about it. I thought that maybe I'd also been drugged, which explained why I suddenly got so sick that night and woke up paralyzed. That made me feel a little better, like it wasn't as much my fault. Maybe getting raped was beyond my control. Calling what'd happened to me what it was—rape—planted some sort of seed that allowed me to begin to move on. The naming of this thing marked a small step, but a crucial turning point in my recovery.

That summer, after my first year in college, I felt ready to talk about what'd happened. After I read those stories online, I practiced saying "I was raped" in my head for months, in preparation to say it out loud. I went over to my mom's house to have dinner and play cards with her and Jim. They mentioned how much happier I seemed now that I'd graduated high school, so I saw that as my opportunity to bring up the issue.

"Well…the reason I was so miserable in high school was because I was raped right after senior year started." My legs and shoulders trembled as these words came out of my mouth, so I took a big swig of champagne.

"What happened was…"

"What?? Why didn't you tell me this? I thought we told each other everything," my mom immediately interrupted.

She was so hurt and disappointed that I didn't tell her sooner. She thought I trusted her, that I was always honest with her.

"I could've helped you if you would've told me."

I thought telling her now should've counted for something, but I never got to finish my story, and we didn't even finish our game of cards.

I know that parents can feel their children's pain, but this response from my mom didn't divide the burden at all—it just created even more pain. I finally opened up to my mom, only to make her feel hurt and disappointed. I felt like I'd done something terribly wrong all over again—I didn't want to hurt my mom. When she said that she could've helped me if I would've told her about being raped right away, I realized that it was too late now for me to get help, so I decided it would be best to never talk about this again with anyone.

That summer, a few girls from a small town fifteen miles away were home from college for the summer and started hanging out at the Halo House. For a year-and-a-half, I had been the only girl who regularly spent time there, and for some reason, I felt threatened by these girls. I didn't want to be friends with girls, but I did like that they didn't know anything about me or my history. It didn't take long before I bonded with them and made some great new friends.

Ashley quickly became my new best friend, and I spent almost as much time with her as I did with Lance. Like the other girls, Ashley was the same age as me, but she also went to EIU, so she stuck around the Halo House at the end of the summer when the other girls went back to their colleges. I went to a party with Ashley and ran into Elizabeth, who'd been my lab partner in chemistry class the previous semester. We realized that we all had mutual friends, and the three of us hung out all year.

Ashley and Elizabeth were almost polar opposites. Ashley stood a foot shorter than me, had long auburn hair, and majored in marketing. Elizabeth towered several inches over me, had short blonde hair, and majored in family and consumer sciences. I loved them both, and having girlfriends again made me immeasurably happy. I didn't know why, but I felt so much more connected with them than I did with any of the guys, which was probably precisely what scared me about having girlfriends.

FOR ALL THE WORLD TO SEE

DUSK
AUGUST 2005-MAY 2006

AFTER ONE SEMESTER in the music program, I stopped taking music classes. My music theory class bored me, as I'd been learning that stuff for years in private lessons, and I found that I couldn't play the piano anymore. I didn't understand why, but the emotions I felt when I played the piano scared me. Usually, the second I sat down at my bench, my fingers automatically met the keys in perfect union, but now when I sat down at the piano, I just clammed up.

I took a genetics class in the EIU Biology Department to fulfill my required science general education credit in my first semester, and unexpectedly fell in love with science. The professor taught science in a way I didn't know it could be taught. She made it fun, and I'll never forget her use of foam pool noodles to demonstrate meiosis and mitosis. I'd never been exposed to the inner workings of the human body before, and couldn't believe I'd been living with my body for nineteen years without any idea how it worked. I had to figure it out, so I signed up for a general biology class the next semester.

The intricacies of the organ systems and molecular mechanisms that control every movement, thought process, emotion, sensory interpretation, and environmental response within a person left me in awe. The deeper my understanding of the elegant structural and functional complexity of the human body became, the closer I got to answering a question I hadn't even fully formulated yet. Memories and emotions and what makes a person an individual especially intrigued me.

In my second year of college I officially declared my biology/pre-medicine major and took every class related to human biology offered. Elizabeth and I happened to be in another semester of chemistry class together and became lab partners again. Chemistry lab with Elizabeth was one of my best school-related memories—we had so much fun doing experiments, narrowly avoiding chemical burns, and getting to know each other. We each "borrowed" a small Erlenmeyer flask from the lab to take shots out of on the weekends. We were real mad scientists.

I also decided to start a Myspace blog about my journey through college to entertain my friends, but I now wonder if it was a more of a way for me to communicate something to myself. I wrote my inaugural blog during the first week of my sophomore year in college.

* * *

BLOG: AUGUST 26, 2005 —
"I've actually never done this blog thing before because I always felt weird about different people I know, and people I don't know reading it... Umm...I don't remember why I came on here in the first place, I feel like I had something to say, but I don't remember...I'll probably erase this in the morning. But, umm...goodnight! And don't drink, drinking is bad...just because I can't stay away from it, doesn't make it a good thing...do your homework!"

* * *

Lance and I had since lost our "official" title due to his usual reasoning that he didn't want to be tied down in a relationship, but we were still best friends and saw each other every day. Lance basically lived at my apartment, although he still sometimes left in the middle of the night to go sleep at his parents' house. Our relationship hadn't changed at all emotionally or physically, but he wouldn't acknowledge our relationship to me or anyone else. I lived two lives with Lance: in one life—our public life—we were best buddies, like brother and sister. In the other life—our private life—

we were basically married. In public, Lance didn't want to show any physical displays of affection or do anything that might reveal that we were more than friends, and I felt so damaged that I understood why he wouldn't want anyone to know he was with me.

But when we were alone, we held hands, cuddled, took naps together, and kissed. Except Lance didn't want to kiss with our mouths open because it might make him sexually aroused. Other than the moment in the car two years earlier when Lance suggested we have sex, he stayed committed to remaining a virgin until marriage. At this point, I was completely in love with Lance, and knew I'd be comfortable and safe having sex with him, but I respected his wishes. We were like Lucy and Ricky Ricardo in our black and white lives with separate beds. Or maybe we were a little more like Bert and Ernie. Still, I enjoyed my life with Lance, and he provided a little structure and balance in my life, even though it never quite felt like a romantic relationship.

*   *   *

BLOG: MARCH 8, 2006 —
"So things have been going pretty well lately...I've kind of been in a permanent bad mood for the past several months, but now I'm getting things straightened out. I'm setting my priorities and being productive...well at least productive enough to get things done, but not too productive to not have a life. I've finally gotten used to this semester and having class at 8 am and spending 10 hours a week writing lab reports, and I'm okay with that. I've pretty much figured out what I want to do with my life, which is a bigger relief than you can imagine. I've been drinking much, much less than normal, and I'm perfectly okay with that, too. I've been playing lots of racquetball which makes me happier than it probably should, but I love it. So basically, I'm doing pretty well right now. I think it's weird how you can have feelings towards people when you don't even know their name or you've never even talked to...there are these two girls I have three classes with and I just think they're hilarious, everything they do cracks me up, but I have no idea who they are. Hmm."

*   *   *

Since we were almost always together, Lance saw the spectrum of the chaos in my life—he saw the constant anxiety, restlessness, emotional numbness, and irritability. He got the brunt of my aggression—I threw my phone at him, charged at him with my fists, and one time threw a spatula at his head in front of a lobby full of customers at Little Caesars. These outbursts didn't happen often, but when they did, I entered into a full-on state of rage and anybody who got in my way was bound to get hit by some shrapnel.

Even though he knew I'd been raped in high school, he, like me, didn't know this had anything to do with why I woke up in such a panicked, disoriented state every morning or why he terrified me in bed sometimes. My story lived on in my mind and spilled over into Lance's life, but I had no idea it was out there for all the world to see.

The summer after my second year of college, I received a text message from Colin who told me that he'd Googled my name and found a story about me on someone's blog. He told me I could easily find the blog if I searched for my first and last name, and he asked whether or not the story was true. I performed an Internet search for my name that yielded a link to Adrianne's blog, on which she'd written a paragraph that described the end of our friendship after I decided to get drunk and high and lose my virginity to her ex-boyfriend with whom she was still in love at the time. Seeing this blog made me want to die, not only because I had to read Adrianne's skewed depiction of this story in which I wanted to stay at Jared's and then maliciously send her a graphic email describing my night with him, but also because Colin had read this story.

Colin, my oldest friend, who'd known me as a toddler, in whom I took solace knowing that he didn't know anything that'd happened to me in high school, had read about the loss of my virginity. And if Colin stumbled upon this story so effortlessly, who else might've also seen it? My friends? Professors? Classmates? People at church? Family members? I told Colin the story was a lie, and he never questioned me about it again.

Shortly after that, one of the guys at the Halo House also found that blog on the Internet (did everyone Google my name?), and I also told him the story was untrue. He didn't inquire any further about what'd happened, but he told me that I could contact the website that hosted Adrianne's blog to report the libelous use of my full name, a violation of the website's code of conduct policy.

I checked that blog almost every day, waiting for my name to disappear, and the site finally removed my last name several months later. But even without my last name, the blog was still accessible to the public, and the uncommon spelling of my first name left a distinct identifying characteristic linking that story to me. I often wondered who else had read that blog and if they connected it with me. It disturbed and sickened me that, after two-and-a-half years, false rumors still circulated about me.

More than six years later, I sat in the HR office of my PhD program department to find out how a building maintenance man got my personal email address and why he kept sending me requests to meet him for coffee. He started to scare me, especially because I sometimes worked in the building alone at night. Our HR administrator wondered if he got my name from my security badge and searched for my email online. She did a Google search for my name, and among descriptions of my research on university websites, papers published under my name, and pictures of my art that were featured in an international art competition, Adrianne's blog stared me right in my beet-red face. My heart pounded as I did anything I could to distract her from clicking on that search result. I knew that if she read that story about me, she'd think I was asking for it from the maintenance man. Or that if she knew I'd been raped, she'd think I'd just over-reacted to an overly-friendly person. I could never escape this.

DÉJÀ VU

THE SUMMER AFTER my sophomore year in college, I ran into my cousin Heather at a party. We'd lost touch throughout junior high and high school, mostly because I became so devoted to my youth group. But we both attended EIU now, and unexpectedly running into her at a party was a great surprise. We caught each other up on the past several years of our lives, reminisced about our Lauryn Hill first-concert experience, and then hung out that summer and went to parties together.

One evening that summer, Heather's roommate invited us to go to a house party near campus. Heather and I didn't know anybody at the party, but they had a lot of beer that we'd chipped in money for, so we stuck around. We were both twenty-years-old, so we couldn't buy our own alcohol anyway. I could get alcohol from Lance or some of the other guys at the Halo House, but I never wanted to bother them too much for it, so any time I got a chance to imbibe, imbibe I would.

We met some cool people, played some games, and hung out on the porch of the house. One guy, Jason, was particularly chatty. Tall and stocky, he had blonde hair and even blonder eyebrows. He reminded me of a Viking minus the beard—a baby-faced Viking. Jason, Heather, and I sat on the porch and talked for a long time, and we all drank a lot. At one point, Jason and I caught each other alone in the kitchen, and he moved in to kiss me. I thought it would be okay if I kissed Jason because Lance's lack of commitment after two-

and-a-half years of "dating" irritated me. But Jason had a short, pokey little tongue, and kissing him didn't exhilarate me at all.

We joined Heather back on the porch and continued our conversation. I don't know what all we talked about, but I thought Jason was a pretty cool guy—someone I could hang out with again. Throughout the night, Jason snuck kisses if nobody looked—it didn't excite or bother me, but I didn't mind the attention. Then, he asked me if I wanted to go home with him. His bold inquiry took me by surprise, and I told him that I came with Heather, and needed to leave with her. Plus, I needed to get up early in the morning, so I wanted to get home and sleep.

"Oh, come on, I promise not to keep you up the whole night. I'll even make you breakfast in the morning," he pleaded.

Breakfast in the morning? Why would he make me breakfast in the morning? And why would keeping me up the whole night even be a possibility? I was confused. I laughed and told him I'd think about it, not knowing how to respond, and hoped he'd forget about his offer. The night had just begun, and we had no plans to leave anytime soon anyway. I actually considered what it would be like to go home with someone I'd just met. I didn't know people actually did that in real life, and I wasn't entirely sure what he meant by "go home" with him but I figured it had something to do with sex. Lance and I never had sex, so I still hadn't found out if I could have sex normally—without fear or pain—like I wanted. I received Jason's advances as I debated whether or not to go home with him. I tested out the water to see if this felt safe.

He asked more persistently and more often if I'd go home with him, and I kept saying, "I don't know, I should just go home tonight." We kissed in an empty bedroom next to the kitchen, and he tried to reach down my pants. I grabbed his arm and pulled it away. Then he tried to unbutton my pants, and I quickly left the room to go back to the party. I started to get uncomfortable, but as far as I could tell from my limited interactions with men, all guys acted like this. I returned to Heather and didn't see Jason for a while, but when I ran into him again, he asked if I wanted to go outside to smoke a cigarette. I agreed, and we walked around to the side of the house and kissed briefly, but I didn't want to stand outside in the rain.

Jason suggested we hop in his car as he pointed to his boxy red Jeep in the driveway.

He got in the driver seat, I got in the passenger seat, and he leaned over to kiss me. I remembered being in the minivan with Josh a couple years earlier and wondered why I thought it was a good idea to get into this guy's car.

These are the kinds of stupid things girls do to get raped, echoed in my head as before. I opened the car door and told him I wanted to go back into the party.

"Wait. I can't go back in there now," Jason guffawed as he pointed out the erection in his pants.

Gross. I decided I definitely wouldn't go home with Jason. I didn't want anything to do with his, or anyone's, penis. Later, back in the party, he asked me again if I'd go home with him. I told him no, but if he wanted to hang out sometime, I'd give him my number and maybe we could do something next weekend.

"Or how about you just come home with me tonight, and then I'll get your number in the morning," he proposed.

"No. I'm going home alone tonight, but call me sometime and I'd love to hang out," I said with earnest intentions.

Jason refused to take my number unless I went home with him, so I told him that was his loss. His persistence irritated me, especially after I already told him no, and that he wouldn't even take my phone number when I offered it insulted me. Was I only good for that night? I was drunk and ready to go home. I found Heather, and we decided to tell people goodbye and head home. Jason lingered in the kitchen, and I told him it was nice to meet him and maybe I'd see him around sometime.

"Okay if you're not going to come home with me, at least give me a goodbye kiss," he said.

This annoyed me, but I just wanted to go home without being harassed so I kissed him. Jason kissed more passionately this time, and when I pulled away and said I needed to go, he pulled me closer to him. He tried to reach down my pants again, and I pulled his arm away. I told him that Heather waited for me, and he pulled me closer to his body. I thought if I kissed him the right way, he'd let me go. I kissed back a little more. He pulled me into the empty bedroom we were in earlier. He shut the door. He locked the door.

Jason shuffled me against the wall and reached down my pants. I tried to get away. My eyes darted around the room, looking for an exit. The room was completely dark and completely empty, and the only door was the one through which we'd entered. Why couldn't he let me go home? In a smooth maneuver, Jason scooped me up and laid me down on the floor. He lay on top of me, and I felt how heavy he was.

I cannot believe this is happening again. I cannot believe this is happening again.

I was in shock. I was seventeen-years-old again, back in that frat house. In place of the cluttered fraternity dorm room was an empty bedroom. In place of the dark-haired man on top of me was a blonde-haired man—the Bevis to Jared's Butt-head resemblance. Like Jared, Jason never took off his dirty white t-shirt. It was a parallel mirror universe. I was re-living what I'd re-lived in my head for two-and-a-half years, but this time it was actually happening again.

Jason worked quickly to remove his clothes and my clothes, and immediately thrusted into me. In and out so fast, like a jackhammer. I didn't fight back. Or scream. Or answer my phone when Heather called. I just wanted it to end as quickly and painlessly as possible. The damage had already been done. A hole had been dug in me two-and-a-half years earlier and was now being excavated into a grave. Now there was nothing alive in me worth fighting for. As I lay on the hard floor, the same phrase repeated itself in my head. *I cannot believe this is happening again* filled my head over and over, drowning out the vivid snapshots of the night Jared raped me until my whole existence was completely contained within that phrase in my mind.

I became detached from my body so I could no longer feel the pain in my vagina and on my forehead and on the sides of my ribs that still lingered from Jared and was now compounded by Jason. It all ended in about five minutes. Jason rolled off of me and stood to put on his clothes. A trail of semen hung from his half-erect penis, dripping all the way to the floor. I wanted to vomit. At least I didn't have to worry about getting pregnant this time, as I still took birth control.

"Wow. Thanks. That was the best orgasm I've had in a really long time," Jason said.

I became infuriated, and the heat rose in my face. I'd actually considered going home with this guy a couple hours ago. If I'd known that I'd have to have sex with him whether or not I chose to, I would've just gone home with him and done it the right way. In his bed. With breakfast in the morning. Not on the floor of an empty bedroom. I felt so powerless.

"Wait, what about me?" I said as I crawled over to him.

I decided that since he got to have sex with me, I should get to have sex with him too. I desperately needed some kind of control over this situation. I needed to try to make myself think what just happened was okay—that I wanted it.

"Nah. I'm spent," Jason said, and he put on his clothes and left the room.

I cannot believe that just happened again.

I slowly stuck the clothes back on my body—each article of clothing weighed a thousand pounds, and they didn't feel like my clothes anymore. Or maybe it was that my body didn't feel like my body anymore. A black hole grew in the pit of my stomach and sucked my very existence into itself. I stood in the dark bedroom for a moment and felt the thick, heavy, black air push down on my body. I felt like I was drowning. I wished I was drowning. I walked back out to the party. I didn't know these people, but it felt like walking through the halls of my high school again with everyone staring at me. I found Heather, and rushed her out the door. I wanted to get home immediately, and Heather asked me what was wrong.

"Nothing. I just want to go home. Jason basically pinned me to the floor in that bedroom, and forced himself on me," I confided in her.

"WHAT! He pinned you to the ground?" Heather was livid.

She wanted to call the police, call the FBI, and send in the troops! I just wanted to go home. Nobody would believe that Jason raped me, and I didn't even know if that counted as rape since I let him kiss me earlier. Or maybe I just didn't want to believe that I'd been raped again. Everyone had seen us kissing earlier. And we were both drunk. And I didn't scream or fight back. Plus, I didn't even know anybody at that party, so nobody would take my side over their buddy Jason. I probably wouldn't have let him kiss me in the first place if I hadn't been drunk. This was all my fault. This doesn't happen to a person twice in just over two years. This felt like a punishment. Was I being punished for not taking that damn True Love Waits pledge in high school? Was I being punished for thinking about women? Somehow in the brief time that all these things went through my head, Heather had called her roommate who told her that Jason had already left the party. He must've left the party as quickly as he'd left me. Heather found out where Jason lived and raced over to his house.

"No. No. NO. Stop. Don't go over there. No! Let me out of the car! NO!" I panicked.

I didn't want to see Jason or him to see me. I didn't want a confrontation. I didn't want to get the police involved because I knew they'd tell me I was asking for it. I didn't want Heather to scream at Jason as I could see she planned on doing. I didn't want to be that girl who gets drunk at a party, has sex with a guy, regrets it, and then tells everyone she was raped. I'd already been raped once, and I didn't want to make a habit out of it. Heather found Jason's house and got out of the car to go inside. I told her I wouldn't go in there, so she told me to wait in the car.

I sat there for about five seconds, and then thought if Jason knew I was outside, he might come after me. Suddenly, Charleston became a war zone, and bombs dropped all around me. I ducked out of the car and bolted down the street. We were only about two blocks from my apartment, but I was so scared, I didn't know where I was or where to go.

I ducked behind trees and bushes, ran in between houses, tried to stay out of view. I heard the bombs fall all around me. The whole world felt like it was caving in. I ran around the block, tried to step lightly so I wouldn't make too much noise. I pretty much went in circles so I never made it far from Jason's house, and I saw Heather's car take off down the street a few minutes later. Then I saw Jason run out of his house, slamming the door so hard it overpowered the sound of the bombs I already heard. He looked so angry, and twice the size he did earlier—like the Incredible Mr. Hulk, but with a fairer complexion. He got in his car and squealed away. I was terrified, shaking. Once Jason and Heather were both out of sight, I came back to reality. I realized I was right next to the Halo House—my safe house.

I went inside, and a few of the guys were there sitting around. Out of breath and sweating, I got a glass of water and sat with them. I sent Heather a text message telling her I walked home. The guys asked where I'd appeared from and what I'd been up to.

"Oh not much, I went to a party with my cousin. I just wanted to see what you guys were up to on my way home," I slurred, out of breath.

I felt so relieved to be somewhere safe. I finished my water, talked with them for a short time, and then walked home. I thought about how my friends at the Halo House had no idea what'd just happened to me. I knew I couldn't tell them because I didn't want them to think about me in any sort of sexual way—I just wanted to be one of the guys. But I also knew I didn't want to keep this bottled up inside me like I did the first time. I needed somebody. I needed my best friend—Lance. I lay on my couch for a while when I got home and tried to think of what to say to Lance. I couldn't formulate any complete thoughts, so I called him and I told him I'd just been raped.

"Are you sure you were raped, and you didn't just get drunk and sleep with the guy?" was Lance's first response when I finished talking.

Am I sure I was raped and not just drunk? How could my best friend be so patronizing? Lance's response echoed what Rebekah said to me when I told her I was raped in high school. Oh, my God, I really *am* re-living this nightmare all over again.

I told myself I should've been more firm in telling Jason I didn't want to go home with him instead of leading him on. I should've left the party as soon as Jason made me uncomfortable. I should've screamed and fought back when he lay on top of me. But the truth was that I didn't want to run away screaming from every man who made me uncomfortable—that would mean that my fear had won, and that what Jared had done to me still controlled my life.

I didn't want to believe that any and every man could rape me. I wanted this situation to turn out differently. If I could ease my way out of Jason's grasp without having an all-out fight-or-flight response—if I could make him let me go—then I'd know that not every threatening situation was actually so dangerous. I'd know that what Jared did to me was a one-time anomaly that wouldn't ever happen again. I thought if I experienced a different outcome in this present situation, then it would somehow erase what'd happened with Jared. But I didn't experience a different outcome, and once I realized that Jason was raping me, I froze. I was helpless, hopeless, and dead. I knew that I could never protect myself.

My first blog post after that night didn't detail this time I hung out with Heather, but the next party we went to.

*   *   *

BLOG: MAY 5, 2006—

"I started feeling really out of it so I laid on the couch for a while and thought about aliens and such and then I stumbled into the bathroom and vomited a little, so then I decided that I needed to go home because I didn't want to make an ass of myself at someone's house I didn't even know so I started to try to walk home because I only live like two blocks away, but I was having trouble getting oriented in the outside world so I tried to call Ashley while I was wandering around in the road because she's probably the only person I trusted my life with in such a fragile condition, plus I didn't really want any other sober person to see me like that...but I was having trouble dialing her number, I kept hitting 3 or 4 random numbers and pushing send, but after about 15 minutes I finally got her number and she said she would come get me, so she did and she took me home and I passed out on my couch and woke up this morning. I fell pretty shitty today and my nose is bleeding and so is my arm, but that's the price you have to pay to live a rock n roll lifestyle. That night reminded me of how I spent much of my summer last year...getting very fucked up and passing out and waking up and feeling like shit and then doing it all over again...it's fun for a while, but it really wears me out physically and mentally after some time of that...so I don't know if I'll be doing a whole lot of that to a large extent this summer...plus, I don't want to develop some crazy drug addiction, which has been known to happen. But yeah, even though I got really fucked up really fast last night, I had a good time and hopefully I can hang out with Heather more this summer...just like the good old days...kind of, hehe. Umm I don't think I feel like blogging anymore so I'll save the other stuff I was going to say for another issue...goodnight!"

DAY 2

THE GREAT TRIBULATION

PURGATORY

WHENEVER I SAW a stocky, blonde-haired man in town, I wondered if he was Jason and if he recognized me. A guy who worked at the liquor store I frequented almost every day looked a lot like him, and Heather's old ID that I used to buy alcohol gave me a little comfort that he wouldn't know my real name. I could never escape the feeling that Jason lurked somewhere in town, watching me. I was buried alive. Jason killed the last remaining part of me that still had some life, and only my vital functions were still operational. I wasn't even worthy of the finality of death—was this purgatory? I had nothing left to live for. If my inevitable death would be prolonged, I would try my hardest not to feel any pain.

Regardless of how miserable I felt, alcohol always provided me with a comforting, consistent feeling of familiarity. Drinking didn't necessarily make me feel happy, but it always made me feel exactly the same. I counted on that cloud of thick, foggy, numbness that allowed me to move through my day without the distractions of my own mind.

If I wasn't drinking, I stayed on high-alert and constantly felt like something horrible would happen to me any second. Any unexpected noise or movement startled me immensely, which left my heart racing for hours afterward. Every muscle in my body tensed all the time. I couldn't have my back to a doorway. I couldn't be in large crowds of people. I couldn't be in any situation without an easy exit. Falling asleep was rarely a peaceful experience for me.

Sometimes, right as I fell asleep or awoke in the middle of the night, my entire body felt like it was being electrocuted. It started at the top of my head with chattering teeth and moved all the way down to my toes. Everything around me sounded amplified and garbled—the ticking of the clock in the room sounded like a wrecking ball, cars driving by outside sounded like space shuttles taking off, voices outside sounded like screams. The screams were the worst, and the sounds echoed, so the longer it went on, the louder and more layered it became. My body felt like it was falling and spinning in an endless spell of vertigo, accelerating faster and faster, the screams getting louder and louder. I was being held underwater, quickly running out of oxygen. I knew that I was falling asleep, but my body remained completely paralyzed as I tried to get up, and my vocal cords produced no sound as I tried to scream.

It didn't take me long to realize that if I didn't fight back, if I didn't resist the uncontrollable mayhem my mind and body experienced, then I'd get used it. I became accustomed to the chaos because I knew it couldn't possibly get any worse—unless I struggled. If I tried to escape, I'd invariably fail as my screams went unheard and my attempts to get out would leave me in the same horrifying situation.

And that's real terror—knowing that you can't escape the pain, at least not without first making it worse. Even when I wasn't paralyzed, waking up terrified me, and for the first ten minutes of every morning, my head inflated with escalating questions of *What's going on? Where am I? What day is it? What happened last night?* Drinking made all of these feelings disappear, so I could relax and live a semi-functional life, but I started to realize that drinking caused problems of its own.

* * *

BLOG: JUNE 3, 2006—
"Well last night was the birthday party at Ashley's, and it was pretty fun...I just got so drunk, so fast though that it kind of ruined it. I've been putting the pieces together over the past few years and I think

I've finally come to the conclusion that I actually have a better time when I'm not drinking...seriously, I just have a lot more fun when I'm not wasted. So will that stop me from drinking?? Probably not. But maybe I can cut back a little, or a lot, or not at all...who knows."

*   *   *

I learned countless times that my desire to be clean and sober couldn't overpower my inability to tolerate the traumatic memories and pain and confusion that completely flooded my mind, which could all be ablated with alcohol. By the end of my second year of college, that $30,000 bond I used to pay for tuition ran out. I became eligible for low-income financial aid, and secured some grant funding to continue to pay for school. I still needed money for my bills, which mostly included alcohol, so after almost four years, I quit Little Caesars and took a higher-paying job at the telemarketing firm where my friend Sam worked. The people at this job smoked even more cigarettes than those at Little Caesars, and I quickly began smoking a pack-a-day. I figured that smoking cigarettes was the least of my problems.

I finished the first semester of my junior year of college, and got my first and only C. Organic Chemistry II, which everybody considered one of the most difficult classes on campus, wasn't much of a struggle for me, but I stopped trying. I just didn't care anymore. And I stopped blogging for an entire year.

On May 4, 2007, my twenty-first birthday, I finished my junior year of college, and all my intentions of cutting back on drinking went out the window now that a whole new world opened up for me to explore: the bar scene. While I'd been using Heather's ID to procure alcohol, I only used it sparingly so I didn't get caught, and I couldn't go to most of the bars in town because my mom knew many of the owners. But now, the whole world of liquor belonged to me.

I found out that Lance had been seeing other women and lying to me about it. I could look past his indiscretion if he committed to our relationship. I thought he probably went out with other women because I became an alcoholic, so I didn't blame him. We'd been together for four years, spending every day with one another, cooking dinner together, celebrating every holiday and every accomplishment together, and wallowing in every heartache and stomach ache together. We took care of each other when we were sick—Lance bought adult diapers for me and carefully wrapped me up in them when I had food poisoning. I gave him an enema before his colonoscopy. If that wasn't love, I didn't know what was, but Lance still wouldn't acknowledge that we were more than friends.

We'd never had sex, but we had a sexual relationship. I was in love with Lance, and wanted to discuss our future together. He held me in bed and I felt safe enough to ask him, again, if he saw us together in the future—like as real adults. Silence. I told him I didn't want to get married right now or anything, but I wondered if he envisioned us together the way I did—picking up kids after school and doing our taxes together. After many stretches of silence between us, and my increasing persistence, Lance finally told me that we'd never get married, and that initiated the end of our relationship.

I spent the first two months of my senior year of college trying to get sober, hoping that Lance would see me as more of a long-term commitment. But even though I glued my nose to my father's 1976 Third Edition of the *Big Book, New and Revised Basic Text of Alcoholics Anonymous*, I only made it through a few excruciating bouts without alcohol. In his child-like handwriting, my father had scrawled his name on the inside cover of the *AA Big Book*, using for a bookmark an illegible Memorial Hospital prescription dated 9-2-80, six years before I was born. I wondered if my father had also locked himself in his apartment on Friday nights, not accepting any calls of temptation to go out, to read about how alcohol is the ultimate destroyer.

I couldn't stay sober for any length of time, and while Lance went out with other women, he didn't notice that I writhed in pain on my living room floor—frantic and alone and looking only to him and alcohol for solace. I thought Lance was the only man that I could be happy spending the rest of my life with—pursuing women never occurred to me as an option. But my most desperate and genuine attempt at sobriety only brought my pain, not Lance, closer to me.

So I let the pendulum swing the other way and spent the next six months trying to separate myself from Lance in preparation to leave him. At first, I slowly inched away from him, going out more often without him, staying at friends' houses so I could try sleeping without him next to me, holding back on all the times I wanted to call him. One night at my apartment, I asked him if he wanted to have sex with me for the first time.

"I think I would if you weren't drunk right now," tumbled out of Lance's mouth in the most devastating way. My heart sank.

And that's when I knew that I could never be in a real human relationship because I'd committed to my relationship with alcohol. But after developing an insanely high tolerance for alcohol, I wanted more. More numbness, more nothing. Sam and I began experimenting with drugs.

Sam was a year younger than me in high school, but we didn't become good friends until college, especially after we'd started working at the telemarketing place together. We had a lot of mutual friends, and he liked to party as often as I did. Unlike Sam, I didn't enjoy smoking pot—it made me feel even more anxious than I felt already. But Sam always had large quantities of marijuana, and he always hung around with people who also had access to a variety of other substances. When Sam came across some drug he hadn't done yet, he knew I'd be eager to try it with him. My favorite text messages from Sam were those asking if I wanted to split a gram of cocaine with him.

Aside from my life-sustaining alcohol, cocaine was my drug of choice. Alcohol made me feel numb emotionally, and cocaine made me feel numb physically. The perfect combination — the perfect storm. Using cocaine started out innocently, I thought. At first, we couldn't acquire it often, and when we could, Sam and I would only buy a small quantity to split.

We felt like rock stars as we snorted a couple lines before going to a party. But it didn't take long before a couple lines of coke before going out turned into a couple lines in the bathroom at the party, too, and then a couple lines at home after the party ended. Splitting a gram of coke with Sam on the weekend progressed into splitting an 8-ball (3.5 grams) with Sam, which progressed into me buying an 8-ball for myself. At that time, a gram of coke cost $60, and I set the "fast cash" option at my ATM to that amount so I could automatically get $60 instead of going through the whole money-retrieval rigmarole every time I went to get cash for coke. Aside from the large amounts of money I wasted, I didn't see any problem with my drug use.

Cocaine made me energetic and talkative, and curbed the effects of the alcohol so I wasn't such a sloppy drunk. Sam and I were like celebrities. We were untouchable. We could do whatever the fuck we wanted and nobody could stop us. I transformed into an entirely different person, away from the curious and creative girl I used to be—and I loved the idea of this. If I could be somebody else, then whatever happened to me didn't actually happen to me.

We had parties to go to almost every night, and everybody loved us, mostly because we entertained people. We always did ridiculous things like put out cigarettes on our arms or set something on fire or throw microwaves off of balconies. I didn't have to hide my drug use around Sam and his buddies, but I definitely didn't want my friends at the Halo House in on the secret. They didn't understand that doing a little coke wasn't that big of a deal, and I couldn't risk losing the only people I truly felt safe with—the only people I could still be myself around.

I went out for a couple beers with my friends from the Halo House, but I was busy sending text messages trying to find some coke. I completely disengaged from the group and had no idea what my friends were even talking about. I had one goal for the immediate future—to score a bag of coke. When I finally found what I wanted, I quickly excused myself from the table and told everyone I'd be right back. It was raining so my friend Corey offered to give me a ride to wherever I needed to go. I sensed the suspicion in his voice and immediately saw him as a threat. I don't know how much my friends knew about my drug use at that time, but they knew of the people I'd been hanging around with more and more often, and made their own assumptions.

I defensively declined Corey's offer for a ride, reassuring him I had an umbrella and just needed to run across the street for a minute to Sam's apartment. If anybody at the table wondered why I wanted to leave so abruptly, it was obvious now—Sam's apartment was a well-known drug hub. But Corey insisted on giving me a ride, and I hated going out in the rain anyway, so I decided to let him drive me over to Sam's apartment. I figured that if he knew I planned to buy drugs anyway, I might as well take the ride.

When he got out of his car to go into the apartment with me, I told him to wait there. Persistently, he said he hadn't seen Sam in a while and wouldn't mind catching up. Irritated, I sent Sam a quick text message letting him know Corey and I were both coming up and instructed him to leave the coke in the bathroom in the tissue box, and I'd leave the money there.

I hoped to do a line or two with Sam before I met back up with my other friends because I knew I'd be doing it by myself in the bathroom at the bar the rest of the night (Sam wasn't twenty-one yet, so he couldn't go to the bar with me). It always felt better, less isolating, to do drugs with other people—the camaraderie (or commiseration?) made this lifestyle acceptable.

The tension between Corey, Sam, and me hung thick as molasses in the air. We all knew what was going on, and Corey was determined to stop it. We bullshitted around for a couple minutes with some small talk, but I just wanted to get my drugs and get out of there. When Corey wouldn't even let me go into the bathroom, insisting I could wait until we got back to the bar, I grew immeasurably angry. Heat spread throughout my chest and rose up to my face, and I envisioned myself pushing Corey down for a second so I could run into the bathroom and at least get a little coke in my nose before he could stop me. I wanted to bash his head in with something in the pile of dirty dishes that were strewn around the kitchen.

I found a brief moment of clarity where I recognized my irrationality—Corey was my friend, and he was trying to look out for me. For a moment, I appreciated him for that and told myself that he just didn't understand that doing a little coke wasn't that big of a deal. So I let Corey threaten Sam, we went back to the bar, and I decided to go back to Sam's later.

"If you ever try to give Apryl drugs again, I'll mess you up," Corey said to Sam.

I cared about Sam as much, if not more, than any of my other friends. To me, he wasn't just the guy who had access to all the drugs like he was to most of the other junkies that hung around us. In my eyes, being a drug addict didn't negate the fact that Sam was a kind, honest, and genuine person. Sam and I started on this journey of self-destruction together, and I planned to see it through with him. At that moment, I decided that I needed to keep my "real" friends separate from my "party" friends—my "real" life separate from my "party" life.

Again, as with Lance, I lived two lives. I had my party life, my normal college life, my life as friends with Lance, my life as more than friends with Lance, and although my attendance had become progressively less frequent, my life at church. The volatility of living such a fragmented life was bound to blow up eventually.

Hiding my drug use from Lance was impossible since we still saw each other every day, and he knew my normal demeanor so well. Like Corey, Lance had also threatened Sam for supplying me with drugs, and he'd flushed my cocaine down the toilet on a couple previous occasions. When Lance found my latest vial of coke in my purse and flushed it down the toilet, my anger completely consumed me. I didn't know that I harbored such a desperate rage in my body. I was like a rabid animal.

"You do not have any right to go through my purse! That is my vial and I paid for it with my money and you have NO RIGHT TO TOUCH IT!" I screamed in a way I'd never screamed before, eyes bulging, saliva pouring out of my mouth, on the verge of convulsing.

I was psychotic, and I think the only thing that kept me from seriously injuring Lance was the fact that he'd already flushed my coke down the toilet, and hurting him wouldn't bring it back. I realized that my life had completely spiraled out of control. How could I have so much animosity toward someone I loved so much? I cowered into a ball on the floor of my apartment and decided I needed to change my life or I'd lose the only people who cared about me. I eventually calmed down, told Lance I'd never do drugs again, and thanked him for trying to take care of me.

A couple weeks later, when Lance came home to find me passed out, flat on my back on my kitchen floor with my nose completely caked in white powder, he did what would most effectively get my attention—he called my mother. It was two o'clock in the morning when my mom and Jim got out of bed to come to my impromptu intervention. I didn't know what to do or say, I felt so broken. Nobody understood what could possibly be so difficult about my life that I wanted to risk destroying it with drugs. My mom told me that I had so much to lose with my academic potential and good looks ("you've seen those 30-year-old women who look like they're 60…"), but I felt like I'd already lost everything that mattered—my control over my own body, my self-respect, my safety.

I cried for the first time in my adult life, not because I felt ashamed, but because I knew that nobody would ever understand the constant agony I endured. From across the room, my mom and Jim watched me sob and melt into my computer chair. We sat in my dark living room and stared at each other for the longest time without saying anything. Again, I promised I'd never do drugs again, my family left, and I went to bed alone.

I took a human anatomy class that fall 2007 semester, and at the end of the year, the professor asked me to be an undergraduate teaching assistant for the anatomy lab the next semester. I enjoyed my first teaching experience, but balancing teaching, going to school full-time, and working 30 hours a week strained me, so I decided to leave my telemarketing job and took out my first student loan. I used a large sum of the loan money to pay off the credit card that I'd used to take a trip to Europe, but I then used it to buy $400-600 worth of alcohol and cigarettes and drugs each month.

I enjoyed teaching, and hoped the extra responsibility would help me keep my shit together. I loved helping students understand the elegance of the human body, helping them identify structures on models, and then showing them the real thing on our human cadavers. I got my first experience writing and grading exams, holding review sessions, and connecting with students, and I realized my passion for learning extended beyond my own curiosity—I wanted to inspire other people to gain a deeper understanding and appreciation of life. As in my elementary school days, this extra responsibility made school more interesting for me. While my upper-classman pre-med course load challenged me more than anything I'd encountered before, school was still just a matter of doing the assignments and studying to get an A.

I resumed blogging again after a one-year hiatus. It was a long blog that recapped the highlights from the previous year, February 2007-February 2008.

*   *   *

BLOG: FEBRUARY 12, 2008 —
"There was spring break during which Ashley turned 21…Then there was St. Patrick's Day and everyone wore green and I discovered how awesome Irish car bombs really are…Then there was Easter and we colored Easter eggs at my house and I met the Easter bunny at Richard's farm. His tail fell off…Then the semester was finally over and I got all As for the first time since high school so that was cool. I put my Dean's List certificate on the fridge next to all my written warnings from the police. The last day of school in the spring I turned 21 and it was everything I thought it would be…A couple weeks later we went to Nashville to see Ben Gibbard…Then I went to Europe. We were there for about a month and we went to England, France, Spain, Switzerland, Italy, and Ireland….Everybody in Europe loves ice cream. After Europe, it was pretty much a normal summer in Charleston…we went camping…it rained on 4th of July…I made pistachio pudding and put vodka in it. It seemed like a good idea at the time, but no. It wasn't. I went on a work bar crawl, and I apparently sang karaoke which is embarrassing. Me and Heather went to Lollapalooza in August…I went paintballing with Colin…Then school started and I had to write a 50-page paper on depression, which was really depressing…Homecoming was fun. I went with Rebekah and Aaron to the War on Sobriety…Me and Lance and Elizabeth saw Ryan Adams in St. Louis…Then there was Halloween and I dressed up like an alien…Then there was Christmas break and I went skiing…We all started going to Bingo at the Moose on Thursdays."

*   *   *

My life revolved around holidays. I loved holidays because then I wasn't the only person partying. When Lance and I went to a St.

Patrick's Day 2008 party at the Halo House, I decided that since it was a holiday, I could get some coke just this once. I inhaled a large amount of cocaine and drank an even larger amount of liquor over a short period of time that night, and I got edgy and delusional. I locked myself in the bathroom of the Halo House, snorted coke off the back of the toilet, and listened to my friends having innocent fun on the other side of the door. I left Lance at the party and went home alone.

Lying on my back on the floor of my unlit apartment, my frenzied mind knew that I couldn't live like this anymore. Darkness caved in on me and I knew that night would never end—I fell backward into a bottomless pit, and saw the outside world quickly disappear in the hole's shrinking entrance. I literally crawled into my kitchen and sawed on my wrist with the same dull knife I'd used three years earlier. I needed to take some form of action, and if it happened to end with my death, that was fine with me.

When Lance came home and found me in the kitchen, he didn't know what to do—he just cried. I muttered Elizabeth's name, and Lance called her on my phone. She told me that she didn't want me to die, and I went to bed and fell asleep. The genuine pain I saw in Lance's eyes and heard in Elizabeth's voice sunk in that time. I felt the pain I caused them—the pain I caused everyone who cared about me. I never wanted to hurt anybody but myself, but instead of changing my behavior, I finally ended things with Lance. After six months of trying to learn how to live without him and realizing that I couldn't live with or without him, I finally told him to return my apartment key and take whatever stuff he had at my place. I continued to downplay my dire situation.

*   *   *

BLOG: MARCH 28, 2008—
"Only four more weeks left of school...I'm pretty sure I don't want to graduate. I had somewhat of a cataclysmic breakdown a couple weeks ago...so I went to Elizabeth's. It was nice. I think I like Elizabeth. And the only place to go from here is up. Yay! I got a few

new albums: Sufjan Stevens--Illinoise, The Raconteurs--Consolers of the Lonely, Counting Crows--Saturday Nights & Sunday Mornings, and Modest Mouse--The Moon and Antarctica. I love them all!"

DENIAL AND DISTRACTION

DAWN
MARCH 2008

I HAD HIT ROCK BOTTOM, so I thought I had nowhere to go but up. I cut back on coke, and mostly stuck with alcohol. I felt good about this positive life change, but I still went out almost every single night, no matter how exhausted I felt or how much homework I had.

I continued to do well in school anyway, steamrolling closer and closer to my bachelor's degree. I mostly stopped going to lectures, but enjoyed the lab portions of my classes. The night before an exam, I pulled all-nighters at the library, alternating energy drinks with swigs of Jim Beam from my travel mug. One morning, when I stumbled into the biology building to take an exam in my immunology class, my nose bled from all the coke I'd been doing the night before. The professor got up and handed me a tissue.

"Been partying a little too much?"

His comment shocked me. I didn't think anybody pegged me for a drinker, let alone a cokehead. I tried to keep a professional demeanor when I went to class, so nobody would suspect I was less than the top-of-the-class student I always appeared to be.

Some days I told myself I wouldn't drink that day, but I struggled so much the entire day with not being able to drink—and knowing that I couldn't drink if something came up and I needed to calm down—I felt like I lived in a war zone fending off enemies. I ran around all day, dodging bullets, engaging in hand-to-hand combat, pushing over barricades, busting down doors simultaneously looking for the alcohol that was nowhere to be found and desperately trying to keep it out of my mouth. I never won that white-knuckle battle. It exhausted me mentally and physically so much that I always gave in by nighttime to have a drink (then two, three, four…) to feel the sweet relief wash over me and relish in the comfort that everything would be okay because I tenderly held my bottle to my chest once again.

It was a primal feeling of imminent death turned to immediate comfort, much like what I imagine a baby feels with a pacifier or bottle or blanket. It didn't take long for me to realize that putting up that fight wasn't worth it if I would lose at the end of the day anyway, so instead of trying to completely abstain from alcohol, I tried to set limits on my drinking.

I could never keep track of the number of drinks I had, which always surpassed ten or twenty, sometimes thirty. But I could count on lighting the wrong end of my cigarette, and that's when I knew to stop for the night. And I could count on the ceiling spinning in faster and faster accelerating circles if I tried to stare at a fixed point, and that's when I knew to stop for the night. Soon enough, my limits became my goal. I wouldn't stop drinking until I got to the point where I lay on the ground with the rotten smell of a burning cigarette filter in my nose and the world falling down on top of me.

Lance finally accepted that I'd actually left him, and he desperately tried to win me back. He had five-dozen roses delivered to my apartment, and then two-dozen more roses and chocolates delivered to a friend's apartment that I visited in Wisconsin—how he even knew I was there and what address to send the flowers to frightened me. He told me, for the first time in our four-and-a-half year relationship, that he loved me. He told me that he planned on marrying me. These gestures would've meant so much if he'd done them any time in the last four-and-a-half years, but now it seemed like a frantic attempt to control me. Even with everything else I'd lost, I refused to let anyone take my stubbornness from me (funny how that works).

That I'd already made up my mind to leave Lance left him no chance. So he resorted to more extreme behaviors like trying to run me over with his car when I wouldn't get in the passenger seat to talk and throwing my phone against the wall when I tried to call 911 because he refused to leave my apartment. He smashed Ashley's foot in the door when she came over after I sent her a message desperately asking for help with getting Lance out of my apartment. He pinned me down on the ground and screamed at me to tell him why I didn't love him anymore. It shocked me that this monster lived inside a man I thought I knew inside and out. I wanted to try to remain friends, but after hours and weeks of exhausting circular conversations between us, and Lance's quickly-accelerating erratic behavior, I decided I needed to break all contact with him for a while.

Our arguments got nowhere and I actually became afraid of him, so when Lance showed up at my apartment in the middle of night pleading for me to talk to him, I couldn't answer the door. Instead, I ran into my bedroom to hide under the covers with the same fear I'd had when Jared banged on my door nine months after he raped me. I didn't understand how Lance could make me feel the exact same fear for my own life that Jared did. It was like re-living the whole experience again. I physically felt both Jared and Jason's bodies simultaneously pressing down on me—all because Lance wanted in my apartment where he'd spent nearly every day of the last four-and-a-half years.

I didn't reply to the hundreds of desperate text messages and phone calls he sent me. He didn't understand why I left him after all those years, and I didn't know what to tell him except that our relationship was going nowhere. The fact that Lance got in the way of my partying lifestyle also played a part in why I left him, or at least that's what I told myself to get over him more easily. With Lance out of my life, nobody could stop me from doing whatever the fuck I wanted and becoming the person I wanted to be—anybody but me.

NOT TONIGHT

ON MY TWENTY-SECOND birthday, I realized I'd die without ever having had my ears pierced. I perused the mall with Ashley (and a water bottle full of vodka) when I decided to make a spontaneous pit stop at a boutique to get a piercing for the first, and what I thought would be the last time.

Now that Lance wasn't on my arm anymore, I suddenly got a lot more attention from guys, something I'd never experienced before. At the bar that night, I ran into Josh—the man with the minivan from five years earlier—and he followed the after-hours crowd back to my apartment to continue celebrating my birthday.

I knew Josh had always been interested in me, so his kiss didn't surprise me. We were the only ones in my kitchen when he pulled me toward him, kissed me, and then reached down my pants and stuck his fingers in my vagina. I didn't understand how guys managed to do that with such casual forwardness, but I immediately remembered two years earlier when Jason kept trying to reach down my pants in that kitchen, and that situation obviously didn't end well for me.

In this moment at my apartment, I wasn't even aware that I stood in my own kitchen and not the kitchen back at that party house two years earlier. I felt exactly the same way I had the night Jason raped me—I couldn't separate the emotional response I presently had with Josh from the traumatic experience I'd had with Jason. I remembered thinking that if I'd known Jason would rape me, I would've gone home with him and done it the "right way." In his bed. With breakfast in the morning. Not on the floor of an empty bedroom. I decided that if this night would end with me having sex with Josh whether I wanted to or not, I might as well take control of the situation right at that moment.

With all of my friends still hanging out in my living room, I led Josh into my bedroom where we both quickly undressed and had sex. This marked the first time I "consensually" had sex, and it was a pretty benign experience—probably due to the large amounts of alcohol I'd consumed and the fact that I tried to focus on anything other than what was actually happening. I imagined myself as somebody else—an actress, a porn star, Lindsey Lohan, anybody but me. I wasn't attracted to Josh, or men at all for that matter, and I didn't feel especially sexually aroused, but I took pride in the fact that I could at least have sex without being in fear or pain. This was good, right? I thought this was how sex was supposed to be.

I woke with a strange feeling in my stomach that I couldn't explain, so I started drinking and floated away from my discomfort. That day, I ignored Josh's phone calls because I didn't want to have sex again—I assumed that was the only reason he wanted to spend time with me, and keeping him on the other end of the phone line and out of my apartment was the only way I knew to protect myself. Lance still made futile attempts at trying to get back together with me, but when he found out that I'd slept with Josh, Lance told me that he wouldn't take me back anymore.

"I wouldn't get back with you now, you've been tainted," Lance said to my face.

A few days later, I met a group of my friends at Lake Charleston to cook out and drink. Once the sun went down, we all decided to go to a party back in town, and I got a ride with a guy who'd come with one of my friends. I'd never met this guy before, but his dark goatee and multiple facial piercings made him mysteriously intimidating. The party was a couple houses down the street from my apartment complex, so we parked in my parking lot, but it was a little too early to go to the party, so I invited him up to my apartment for a drink. We never made it to the party, and none of my friends called asking where I was. I had a reputation of "peacing out" in the middle of an outing with my friends without saying goodbye, and I always somehow made it home, so people stopped asking after me. Oh, that's just what Apryl does...the old Irish Goodbye.

I was in no way interested in this guy, but when he kissed me, I didn't know what else to do alone in my apartment with him besides have sex. As far as I could tell, I didn't have a choice—if he wanted me, there was nothing I could do to stop him. The only shred of power I could hang onto was not saying no.

He twisted and threw my body around in whichever ways he pleased, and among many other backhanded terms of endearment, he called me a whore. I felt like a whore. I didn't even know his real name—only his nickname, Butter. He even had custom sneakers with Butter sewn in cursive yellow leather letters on the side. I thought Butter was a stupid nickname, so I always referred to him later as Mr. Piercings.

After this encounter, I conceded that I simply didn't enjoy sex, but based on what I'd seen in the movies, that wasn't so strange. Women were always portrayed as the evil with-holders of sex from men, they were portrayed as loathing giving oral sex, men were never satisfied with the amount of sex they had in their lives and always had to beg women for it, so women just saw it as a chore, a duty, something to keep men placated or something to reward them with for good behavior—and this made complete sense to me. Why should women enjoy this? It was messy, painful, sweaty, and completely exhausting.

But more than anything else, I wanted to prove to myself that being raped didn't have any effect on me. I always thought of rape victims as people who would never be able to have sex again without having horrific flashbacks, so I thought being able to have sex was a step in the right direction for me. I thought having sex "on my terms" would erase what Jared and Jason had done to me, but it actually initiated my transformation into a person I didn't recognize.

I ran into Mr. Piercings at the bowling alley the following week, and he came home with me again. I thought since we'd already had sex once, he'd expect me to sleep with him again, and at that point, after having slept with two different guys in the same week, I completely disowned my body. Maybe Lance was right, I was tainted. I was trapped in a contaminated, filthy body unworthy of any respect so I completely detached my mind from it. My body wasn't me—my body had died years ago.

I didn't realize it at the time, but I probably often entered into a dissociative state when I had sex, with my mind in a far-away land. I never enjoyed sex, certainly never had an orgasm, but it wasn't necessarily a negative experience. I didn't feel anything at all, physically or emotionally.

This trend of having sex with guys I barely knew became routine for me. Any time I sensed that an interaction with a guy might head in the direction of sex, I took control of the situation. If we were going to have sex, I wanted it to be on my terms. After having slept with two guys, I kept telling myself, "What's one more?" As long as I could make myself think that I stayed in control, I felt safe. As long as I said yes, then I wouldn't be raped.

I told myself I was glad I could at least join in on my friends' conversations about boys and sex now. This is what single college girls are supposed to do, right? They go out with a lot of guys and have a lot of sex, like *Sex and the City*. I always told stories about my ridiculous, drunken encounters with men and my "walks of shame" home in the morning (or afternoon) with my pants on inside-out or one shoe missing. Talking about sex with my friends certainly helped me maintain my image as a straight girl, and I desperately tried to convince myself I could be straight, too. I wanted to prove to myself that being raped hadn't made me gay, something I'd heard over and over—women are with women because too many men have hurt them. I just didn't want to be a lesbian. I didn't want anything to make my life more complicated than it already was, and all the years of internalized homophobia I garnered from church filled me with so much self-loathing. I hated myself. I just wanted to be a "normal" person, and to me, that meant heterosexual.

But all of my after-hours encounters just filled me with another kind of self-loathing. I wanted to believe that women were sexually liberated and could have "casual sex" without being called a slut, but people did call me a slut. And words like "tainted" and "walk of shame" were filled with connotations of being infected and dirty.

Josh was the only man after Lance that I ever pursued. Maybe it was because I marked him as my "first" and thought he had something special of mine—or maybe it was because I thought if I got into an actual relationship with someone, I could get other guys to stop sleeping with me. I wanted to get to know Josh, I wanted him to know me, I wanted something like what I had with Lance (but more romantic, physically). But he left my pursuit wholly unreciprocated.

Josh and I lived three hours away from each other, and when I made the trek to Chicago to stay at his house for a couple days, the only time I saw him was when we had sex—he spent the rest of the time working or at the bar without me. This went on for about a year, and I'd only see Josh about every two months. I thought this was a relationship; this was how dating was supposed to be. I told myself I liked it this way because I had someone who liked me enough—or wasn't repulsed by me too much—to have sex with me, but I could still do whatever I wanted without him controlling me. It was basically the opposite of my relationship with Lance.

But this relationship with Josh wasn't a relationship at all—not enough that I could tell other suitors to leave me alone because I had a boyfriend. I had no idea how to say no to guys or that I even had the right to decide who got to touch me. Instead of telling a guy that I wasn't interested in him or didn't want to have sex, I'd try to make him lose interest in me, which usually involved stuffing my face with odorous food.

I'd discovered this trick during one of the only times Josh and I actually hung out, about a year-and-a-half before our first sexual encounter. Josh came over to watch a movie, and I knew he hoped for more than just a movie as soon as he walked into my apartment. I figured I'd be safe for a little while longer at least if I could get him out of my apartment, so I asked if he wanted to go get something to eat. He told me he'd already eaten dinner, so I asked him to come with me while I grabbed some food.

I dragged him to the grocery store where I went straight for the fish aisle and picked up one-pound of fresh farmed Atlantic salmon. We got back to my place, and I cooked the whole plank of salmon. My entire apartment smelled like dead fish. I sat next to Josh on the couch and ate my buttery salmon, periodically asking him if he wanted a bite. He looked at me with disbelief and told me he thought I'd just grab a sandwich, and then he left. I felt so proud of my accomplishment that I even blogged about it.

*   *   *

BLOG: OCTOBER 16, 2005 —
"Today I cooked some salmon and ate almost a pound of it...it was really good!"

*   *   *

Another friend who lived a couple blocks away asked if I wanted to meet at the bar in between our apartments for a drink before going back to his place to watch TV. I walked to the bar and found him at a tiny table near the door. I asked if he wanted to order dinner, but he said he'd already eaten and just hoped to get a drink and leave—so I ordered a huge basket of onion rings. I ate each greasy onion ring slowly and methodically, pulling the parasite-looking tape of onion from its crispy battered shell while oil dripped from my chin. He looked at me with the same incredulous face that I'd seen on Josh as he flagged down the waitress and scurried me out of the bar.

I told my friend Greta that a guy asked me to go bowling, and I wanted to go but didn't want to have sex with him. When she asked why I thought going bowling meant I had to have sex with him, I told her that I'd already had sex with Andy once—on the floor of a dark, empty classroom in Ashley's former elementary school-turned-BYOB-strip-club called The Schoolhouse. And I thought if I said yes to sex once, that was a free pass for that guy for the rest of my life. So Greta came to my apartment and we sat in her car while she pretended to be Andy asking to come up to my apartment after bowling. She taught me to say "not tonight" with a little wag of my finger and quick hop out of the car.

The next night, when Andy asked if he could come up after bowling, I sputtered out my rehearsed reply, "Not tonight." I trembled as I got out of the car, my legs shook with each step up to my second-floor apartment. When I got into my apartment, I quickly locked the door and ran to the window, expecting to see Andy screaming and throwing punches at his steering wheel, growing larger and larger like the incredible hulk—like Jason. I expected to see him punch through his windshield, climb out of his car covered in glass and blood and kick down my apartment door with one swift fateful blow. Instead, I watched his car pull out of my parking lot, politely signaling as he turned out of view. I couldn't believe "not tonight" actually worked, and I felt an immediate surge of empowerment, followed by an equally intense upwelling of guilt. I felt guilty for thinking of the horrible things Andy could do to me when it turned out he was one of the nice guys. Now I felt like I owed it to him to have sex. How much longer would "not tonight" work anyway?

I dated Andy for the next several weeks, and he really was one of the nice guys—he was one of the only men who ever truly treated me with respect, and perhaps not coincidentally, the only man I'd ever orgasmed with. But he came over to my apartment a couple months after our initial encounter at the strip club to tell me that he couldn't hang out with me anymore because I was drunk all the time and it was too hard for him to stay committed to his sobriety.

THE END OF AN ERA

DESPITE MY HEAVY drinking, I ended up finishing my bachelor's degree in biology/pre-medicine, graduating from The EIU Honors College. Succeeding in school was the only thing that relieved me of some of the guilt of partying so much and gave me some control over my life. In a mid-sized college town with nothing to do but drink, I could always find a party. I championed front-yard games of beer pong, and while other girls only pretended to take the fifteen drinks doled out to them in a game of Fuck the Dealer, I lost the game on purpose just to give myself a reason for drinking as much as I already was. I lived "the single life" (read: destructive life) and got completely trashed every day.

The activities I did with my friends moved away from board games, video games, crafts, and movies to more alcohol-centered things like going to sporting events, concerts, barbeques, fishing, and parties. I kept busy doing something all day, every day, but most of the time I got so drunk that I'd pass out or not remember half of what I did.

I passed out during every movie I watched. Sometimes I went to movies by myself because it was one of the only times I could sleep—something about the anonymity of the dark theatre and the fact that I couldn't see how quickly I drank from the pint of whiskey I'd poured into my seven-dollar fountain drink put me right to sleep, usually before the movie even started. I couldn't finish any board game I played with my friends because I'd be too drunk before the end. I spent hundreds of dollars on concert tickets to see my favorite bands only to spend the night doing coke in the bathroom or glued to a barstool.

I found other like-minded people who challenged me to do things like the "red light game" where I poured beer down my throat as I drove down the main drag in town, until a light turned red, and then the passenger took a turn to drink. One time during this game, I accidentally drove my car up on the front lawn of EIU, swerving around in front of our trademark stone castle and weeping willow trees. Welcome to college. It never crossed my mind that I could potentially hurt someone or that anything was wrong in my life. The denial continued.

* * *

BLOG: APRIL 30, 2008 —
"So I guess this is it. I just finished my last real final of my undergraduate career at Eastern. I'm pretty sure I'm going to end up remembering this as the best four years of my life and I'm not ready to move on. I wish I could just repeat the last four years...I'm not ready to enter the real world or even go to grad school yet. I wasn't sad at all after I finished high school...I was actually really, really excited. But that's probably because high school was pretty much miserable."

* * *

Five years later, with my sober mind, I saw myself playing that red light "game" and the possibility of running over a child on the sidewalk, and I knew the persistent, lingering shock and horror at what my life had been deserved its home in my chest. I shouldn't even be alive right now.

But for the time being, I continued on my path of destruction.

* * *

BLOG: MAY 21, 2008 —
"…Needless to say I drank a lil too much and dropped my phone in a glass of beer at the Black Rebel Motorcycle Club concert, so that was the end of that…"

BLOG: JULY 3, 2008 —
"…it's mid-summer now…so far it's been an awesome summer. I've just been pretty much doing whatever the fuck I want and having a great time. However, I've been spending way too much money, but that's the price you gotta pay to be a rock star…"

BLOG: JULY 28, 2008 —
"…I went to the fireworks with Ashley. I was pretty drunk at that point and I basically slept through the fireworks…then we went back to the Uptowner where I got pretty much sloppy drunk, so sorry to everyone that had to deal with me that night…"

*   *   *

My last blog post of that summer took the form of some oddly-syllabled quintain.

BLOG: SEPTEMBER 12, 2008 —
"I just bailed myself out of jail.
     I got a DUI.
     I'm sorry to anyone I could've potentially hurt.
     Now I'm pretty much fucked.
     End of story."

ARRESTED DEVELOPMENT

SINCE I'D FINISHED SCHOOL, I decided to go back to work at the telemarketing job with Sam. I needed the extra money and definitely needed some extra responsibility to keep myself from drinking all day long. My supervisors invited me to go out with them after work one Thursday (Thursdays were the new Fridays), and I agreed to go. They wanted to go to a bar in a neighboring town ten miles away that sold ten-cent chicken wings.

My friends called a shuttle bus to take us all to the bar, but I didn't want to get trapped there, so I picked up Sam and Elizabeth and drove my car to the bar. I drove myself everywhere I went because if I didn't have an easy escape route or had to rely on someone else to get me out of a situation I didn't want to be in, I grew so anxious that it became pointless for me to even go anywhere at all. Having my car made me feel a little more in control of my destiny. Since I had to drive my friends home later, I planned to take it easy on drinking until we got back to town. By the time the bar got ready to close, the three of us had split a couple pitchers of beer and each had taken a couple shots. But my co-workers had a lot of beer they needed to finish in the thirty minutes before the bar closed, so we decided to help them out.

We all played Quarters, a game that involves bouncing quarters off the table into cups of beer, and I ended up drinking several more glasses of beer, doing several more shots, and eventually I drank straight out of a pitcher of beer. The bar closed, my coworkers got on the shuttle, and I got in my car with Sam and Elizabeth.

I decided to take the country roads home because I didn't want to drive drunk on the highway. I knew I was legally too drunk to drive, but I thought I was in control enough to get us home safely. The night was dark and rainy, and I found out later that I was driving about sixty miles per hour on the slick, narrow country roads. I didn't see the sharp turn in the road, so I kept going straight. The sudden jolt of my car flying off the road and over the ditch terrified me, and my car went at least another fifty yards before it came to a stop in the wet grass next to an unplowed corn field.

After the car stopped and I thought everything was fine, the airbags deployed with a huge BANG, shattered my windshield and left Elizabeth and I with bruises. Sam sat in the back seat, silent. I assessed the damage—Elizabeth and Sam were okay, and aside from my airbags and windshield, my car appeared to be fine as well. I decided to drive my car back up to the road and go home—shattered windshield and all—no big deal. We all laughed and even took some pictures of the three of us in my car. It was just another comical calamity in my outrageous life, or at least it was easier to think about it in that way rather than process the stark reality of what'd just happened.

Unfortunately, my car wouldn't start, so I called Ashley to come pick us up. When Ashley finally found us on the side of the road, she called me to say she didn't want to stop because the cops were already there. I saw the flashing lights in my rearview mirror, but the cop car had stopped farther down the road, so I thought they must've been arresting someone else. I hadn't even thought about the possibility of being found by the police—we were in the middle of nowhere. I had some bright ideas for ensuring that I didn't get a DUI.

First, I took the keys out of the ignition—nobody could prove anybody drove that car if there weren't any keys, right? Then, I chugged a couple warm Dr. Peppers that were in my car—that should bring my blood alcohol concentration down. Before we could implement my plan to run into the cornfield and hide, the cop car with its flashing lights slowly pulled up on the top of the ditch beside my car. I told everyone to be quiet and duck, and we all crouched down in my car. Maybe the cop would think my car had been abandoned. Then I remembered Sam was in the backseat, and I panicked. I asked if he had any drugs on him, and when he said he just had a little weed, I told him to throw it in the corn field immediately.

By the time the police officer walked down the ditch toward my car, I figured enough time had gone by since my last drink that I could pass any kind of sobriety test, so I hopped out of the car.

"Heeeyyyy officer! Soooo I guess I didn't see that curve back there. I just kept going straight. It's dark." I was off to a great start.

"Yeah well your car made it pretty far past the ditch. You must've been going fast. Have you been drinking?" inquired the cop in a tone that was more of a statement than a question.

"I had a couple drinks earlier, but that was hours ago," I admitted. I figured my blood alcohol concentration on a breathalyzer wouldn't show up as zero, so I should at least admit to having something to drink. I still thought I'd be under the legal limit for driving at that point.

"A couple? How many is a couple?" asked the cop.

"Oh about four…" I said. My tone must've been incredulous as I pondered whether four drinks seemed like a reasonable amount a normal person would have after work.

"About four?" the cop probed. "Four of what?"

"Beer. Four or five beers. Over the course of several hours. And it was way earlier in the evening," I rambled.

It was two o'clock in the morning, and the cop sighed and leaned into my car to look at Elizabeth and Sam. Upon seeing Sam, who looked like a typical stoner kid, the cop perked up. He asked if there were any drugs in the car, directing the question at Sam, who looked like a deer in headlights. Sam stared at the cop for what felt like five minutes before Elizabeth assured him that nobody had any drugs.

By that time, a second cop car arrived, and I heard the dogs barking at the top of the ditch—these guys weren't joking around. I panicked because when I asked Sam to throw his weed in the cornfield, he threw it directly underneath my car. If the dogs came down to my car, they'd surely find the drugs underneath it, and I tried to think of a way to explain how my car just happened to land on a small bag of marijuana after flying off the road at sixty miles per hour in the middle of the night.

Miraculously, the cop didn't bring the dogs down, but he did call the second officer over to my car to bring a breathalyzer. After I breathed into the machine, the two officers looked at the result, and told me to get back into my car while they went back up to their cars. Since they told me to get back in my car, I felt confident that I passed the breathalyzer and told Elizabeth and Sam that everything would be fine. When the cop came back to my car and asked me to follow him up the ditch, I figured he needed me to sign something to be on my way. One of the officers had apparently called a tow truck because it had just arrived.

It rained a little harder, and I saw the diagonal drizzle in the blinding lights of the police cars—I felt like an actor on a movie set. The cop told me he needed me to do some field sobriety tests, which I thought meant that I'd passed the breathalyzer test and they needed another way to bust me. Plus, I was confident that I'd be able to complete any field sobriety task. I followed the cop's finger back and forth, touched my nose, walked in a straight line, and stood on one leg.

"Okay, one last thing: turn around and face the car with your hands behind your back." I didn't know what this test would be. "I'm placing you under arrest for DUI," said the cop as he handcuffed me and recited the Miranda rights.

The arrest absolutely shocked me. I thought for sure that I'd be headed home with Elizabeth and Sam any minute. Ashley still lingered in the area, so she picked up Elizabeth and Sam as I rode back to town in the back of a cop car. I felt trapped and helpless and anxious in that car, and not knowing what would happen to me in the next five minutes, I knew I would die.

Oh, my God, I'm stuck back here with my arms handcuffed behind my back. These doors are locked from the outside. I wouldn't even be able to get out if I tried. I wonder if this cop is a good guy or a bad guy. He could just pull over to the side of the road right now and rape me and nobody would ever know. Nobody would believe me if I was raped by a cop. I've got to get out of this car. I can't even move my arms. These doors are locked from the outside. It's so dark out here in the country. I can't move my arms. Oh my God, oh my God, oh my God. Get me out of this fucking car!

My heart pounded, adrenaline pulsed through my veins, my eyes darted around to find an exit, I wanted to bash my head against the window, but I stayed completely frozen—I couldn't have moved even if I did find a way out. I felt as powerless as I had when I was raped.

"You're one of the calmest DUI arrests I've ever made," the officer acknowledged, "Especially for a college girl—they usually cry."

I didn't cry. I couldn't cry—my hell was entirely internal. I sat anxiously paralyzed with the threat of what this cop had the power to do with me alone in the country in the middle of the night, and I just wanted to get home without getting raped. I just wanted to survive.

When we finally got to the police station, an officer at a desk instructed me to stand by the wall for my mug shot. I thought I probably looked like a mess with my smeared mascara and wet, frizzy hair from standing out in the rain. I'd taken off my button-up shirt right after my car went off the road, so all I had on was a thin, low-cut, spaghetti-strap, sequined camisole. I thought I probably looked like a prostitute.

Conflicting thoughts ran through my head about whether or not I should smile for the picture. I wasn't particularly happy at that moment, so the smile would look fake. But if I didn't smile, I'd probably look like even more of a mess. If I smiled too much, though, it might look like I wasn't sorry for whatever I did. I remembered Lindsay Lohan's mug shot from the previous year—she had this pouty-lip look going on, which I thought was pretty hot, so I tried that. I had no idea when the officer took the picture during this thought process, and I never got to see my mug shot, but I like to think I looked like a wet Lindsay Lohan mixed with a little bit of Julia Roberts circa *Pretty Woman*.

After waiting at the police station for an hour, during which time all I could think about was how badly I had to pee, the cop finally called on me to take my official breathalyzer test—the results of which would be used in my court hearing. I still held onto hope that my blood alcohol concentration might be under the legal limit to drive by the time I took this breathalyzer test.

It was four o'clock in the morning, over three hours since my last drink, and my blood alcohol concentration was 0.186, still over twice the legal limit to drive. The police report stated that I smelled strongly of liquor, had bloodshot eyes, slurred speech, inability to walk in a straight line or stand on one foot, and lack of knowledge of the current date or my current location. On the upside, I was polite and compliant with the police officers. I called my mom to pick me up from the police station, and when she answered the phone, she didn't sound surprised at all.

"I wondered when I'd be getting this call from you."

At this point in my life, I readily admitted that I was an alcoholic, but I thought it was okay to be a functional alcoholic. After all, I performed extremely well at school and work—what else mattered? I thought that I was in total control of how much I drank but that I always chose to drink way too much every day.

The next day, I went back to the spot where I drove off the road, and saw that my car had missed hitting a telephone pole by only a couple inches. Oh, my God, I could've killed my best friends.

I finally realized the seriousness of my self-destructive behavior. I didn't care what happened to me, but I hadn't taken into account that my conduct affected those around me. I didn't want to hurt anybody but myself, and I couldn't bear the thought that I could've been responsible for killing the people I cared about most. That was when I realized I wasn't in control of my drinking habit or of myself when I drank, and this scared me to death. I couldn't face the reality of what'd just happened, and I definitely couldn't face the idea of what it would take to undo all the damage that had already been done. It was easier, safer, to pretend like it wasn't that big of a deal.

I wanted this nightmare to end so badly, but if getting a DUI wasn't enough for me to get help for myself or for anyone else to help me, I was scared to find out what it would take for something to change. Instead of making a resolution to change my cataclysmic behavior, I resigned to the fact that I was completely out of control. I lost my driver's license, so I figured I could drink as much as I wanted since the risk of injuring someone driving drunk was no longer an issue.

My mom bought me a bike since I couldn't drive anymore, and I rode my bike to and from the bar. But I constantly fell into the street, so I usually ended up walking it home or leaving it outside the bar until the next morning when I called my mom to drive me to pick up my bike. An endless rotation of bruises and cuts and scrapes from falling off my bike or hitting my head on my coffee table or falling down stairs covered my body. I stopped giving myself limits on how much I'd allow myself to drink because I knew I'd fail at implementing such limits, as I usually failed in the past. I decided that I'd rather succeed at being a functional alcoholic than fail at attempting to achieve sobriety. I couldn't imagine having to endure my painful, messy life sober anyway.

I wasn't aware of how physically addicted to alcohol my body had become, but the compulsion to drink was so strong most days that it was easier to give in to the urge than to try to deny myself a drink. If I tried to fight the urge to drink, I'd be completely unproductive the rest of the day because I couldn't focus on anything else aside from trying not to drink. But if I'd just let myself drink, I could go about my usual business with general efficiency. I told myself that as long as I didn't let my drinking habit interfere with my performance at school, I could drink as much as I wanted. And since I'd finished all my biology/pre-med coursework, leaving only a seminar in British film – required by the Honors College – that met only once a week, it wasn't hard to keep alcohol from interfering with school. As illustrated by one of my blog posts, I'd eat, sleep, and breathe alcohol—it was my lifeline.

* * *

BLOG: OCTOBER 7, 2008—
"Friday I had my DUI assessment...they determined that I did not have a drinking problem, lol. Yes, that's a laughing matter. Last night I had a dream that I was outside in the rain with my umbrella and the wind caught the umbrella and I went up in the sky and got to float around town in the sky and it was awesome, but then all these cans of beer started falling out of my purse (because I always carry beer around with me) and I got really freaked out and let go of the umbrella and fell to the ground. What do you suppose that means?"

* * *

If I didn't have a rape-related nightmare, I dreamed about alcohol and drugs. I constantly had dreams in which I desperately searched for alcohol with none to be found. In my dreams, I held a full bottle of liquor, trying to pour it into my mouth but no liquid would come out. The panic and desperation and frustration I felt about not being able to get alcohol in my dream paralleled the same feelings I had while awake. The most recurring drug-related dream I had involved one of those stuffed animal claw machines—except instead of stuffed animals, the machine was filled with cocaine. I either put money into the machine to try to grab cocaine with the claw, which never worked, or I scrambled around inside the machine, my whole body surrounded by cocaine but unable to get any into my nose. I knew it was a bad sign that I had stress dreams about drugs and alcohol.

*   *   *

BLOG: OCTOBER 15, 2008—
"Today I had my court date. I got up at 6:30am to get ready and look nice and everything and then I went and had to sit in the court room for 3 hours until they called my name and I went up there for about 30 seconds and said "guilty" and that was it. What a waste of a day… And now this week is War on Sobriety…I don't think I'll have any problem fighting in that war."

*   *   *

War on Sobriety, an annual EIU Homecoming tradition, took over Charleston for a week in October during which hundreds of students would gather at a different location each night during Homecoming week to get drunk. There were War on Sobriety t-shirts, War on Sobriety chants, it was a whole empire. I'm ashamed to admit that I felt like I was fighting for something important with my peers, even after having almost killed my friends in a drunk driving accident.

The unfortunate reality of my trauma and addiction was that it didn't just affect me, but when in the grips of this disaster, I couldn't see how my actions affected those around me. It was like flames completely engulfed my body—I flailed around trying to survive, unable to notice all the other stuff I set on fire.

THE NEXT LEVEL

SOMEHOW, I CONTINUED to carry on with my life. I didn't know what else to do. Three months after getting the DUI, I started graduate school in the same biology department that had just awarded me a bachelor's degree. In my last semester of my undergraduate studies, I took my first neurobiology class and realized that the brain may hold all of the answers—and the questions—I searched for. The brain somehow controlled everything that intrigued me about the human body, and I had to learn more. After receiving my bachelor's degree in 2008, my neurobiology professor offered me a position in his lab to pursue a master's degree, as he thought of me as one of his brightest students with much potential. I didn't know what else to do with my life, and I loved biology, so this was a good opportunity.

The deeper my understanding of the human body became, the closer I felt to God. Even though science could explain how so much of the natural world worked, I knew that there was some more powerful force behind it all of which I had no understanding whatsoever—and to me, that was God. Memories and emotions and what makes a person an individual especially intrigued me—we're all made up of the same basic materials, but every person experiences life differently and is capable of forming strong emotional connections with other people. I don't know if science will ever explain what some people call a soul or how people form intense bonds of love and compassion with one another, but if we ever do find that, I think we will have found God. From the perspective of a scientist, all I can say is that something caused what we call life to come into existence, and whatever that may be, is God to me.

I became interested in how to repair damaged brain cells, so for my thesis research project, I learned to grow mouse neurons in a dish, damage them, and then re-grow them. I found that estrogen helped damaged brain cells re-grow their axons, and data from my research were published in the *Journal of Biomedical Science*.

I also continued to develop my teaching skills during my two-year master's program where I served as a graduate teaching assistant for two classes each semester, including genetics, biology, endocrinology, animal physiology, and human physiology. As with my human anatomy undergraduate teaching experience, I found that my passion for learning hinged on an ability to teach.

But even though my biology studies and becoming a serious scientist genuinely interested me, I had such a difficult time focusing on anything beyond the current day. I never thought I'd live long enough to complete my master's degree, so I only did what I had to do to survive each day, which sadly required alcohol. By implementing alcohol as a reward for completing my school-related responsibilities each day, I usually prevented myself from drinking in the morning and early afternoon.

Throughout the entire day, though, I had alcohol on my mind. I'd think about what I wanted to drink after I got done with school. Would today be a whiskey day? Or a wine day? Or just a regular beer day? Or how about a fuck-it-all-and-drink-whiskey-wine-and-beer kind of day? Should I go out to the bar? Or just stay at home and drink? Would any of my friends be around to drink with me? Or would I end up drinking alone?

Toward the end of the afternoon, I became so anxious about when I'd get to drink that I couldn't take it anymore. If I needed to do research in the evenings or on the weekends, I let myself drink in the lab since nobody else was around. Sometimes I scheduled my research for the evenings or weekends primarily so I could drink in the lab.

And my walk to campus every morning in the rain, sleet, or snow juggling my purse, backpack, twenty-pound laptop, coffee mug, and cigarette became my self-inflicted punishment for losing my driver's license and for wasting my potential by making such bad life choices. I was carrying my own cross to hell.

* * *

BLOG: JANUARY 13, 2009—
"So school has officially started and I'm officially a grad student...so far I like it a lot. It feels good to be back in school. I did a couple things in the lab today, but had a meeting with my alcohol counselor at 11:00. I thought I was going to get in trouble because the meeting was about this one time I went to alcohol class "smelling of booze" apparently (which I don't know how that happened...I went out the night before but it's not like a drank before class). So I was all freaked out thinking I was going to get in trouble and shit, but it all ended up being fine and I just got a little lecture and it's all good now."

* * *

When I couldn't drive, I felt like I had DUI written on my forehead and that my irresponsibility was the only thing anybody noticed about me. But once I got my driver's license back, people seemed to forget all about my DUI and my alcoholism—or maybe I just chose to forget about it.

* * *

BLOG: JANUARY 28, 2009—
"Soooo...I got my license back today! I went home and dug my car out of 9 feet of snow and put on my sunglasses, lit a cigarette, and drove to Mattoon for no reason and listened to Portions for Foxes about 5 times."

* * *

I quickly became an ally of the professors who drank—the ones who I imagined kept expensive bottles of scotch in secret bookshelf compartments in their offices. It started at the plethora of social gatherings the biological sciences department had to welcome incoming grad students, to judge interviewing faculty candidates, and to celebrate successful thesis defenses. Like all college-affiliated social activities, these dinners revolved around alcohol. I'm sure there was a food table or something at these events, but the unlimited free booze was all I cared about.

I literally hung around the water cooler the whole night with the other drinkers, and I wondered if they saw (or smelled) the alcoholism on me just as I sensed it on them. I eventually infiltrated the boys' club in the basement of the biology building.

On Friday afternoons, a few professors and grad students gathered in a basement laboratory to pass around a bottle of Irish whiskey and relish the upcoming weekend. This wasn't the group of glued-to-a-lab-bench molecular and medical biologists of which I was supposed to belong—these were the guys who took canoes out on sewage-infested rivers to collect water samples, who trekked into the woods in inclement weather to capture snakes, and who collected snails from swamps to study their parasites. Of course, I was the only woman in this pact of burly field biologists, and I felt a responsibility to prove that I could hold my liquor in order to earn my place in the group.

I learned to drink a "Johnny Jump Up" like a champ. To make this drink, the guys instructed me to drink only the neck of a Strongbow Cider bottle, and then fill it back up with Powers Irish Whiskey. I tried to sip the concoction slowly, but it tasted so good, I drank three or four in less than an hour. I stood my ground and downed shot after shot of liquor—never slurring my words, never stumbling, and absolutely never passing on a swig from the bottle—until the group fizzled down to me and another graduate student who'd accompany me back to my apartment or the nearest Mexican restaurant to continue drinking.

The approval of the professors that followed these sessions served as the positive reinforcement I needed to know that my plan to be a functional alcoholic worked. One of the professors even offered me a paid adjunct researcher position with one of the teams who went out to collect waters samples. I went to Decatur, known as the smelliest town in Illinois, to help the guys plunge their contraptions into the water, but mostly I just drank whatever liquor they brought along and steered the boat.

All of my accomplishments and responsibilities meant more because of how much I drank the day before. The more I drank, the more impressive it became that I could do everything I did. Only once I got off campus and away from the professors who I tried to impress would all the alcohol catch up with me—one time as I stumbled into my apartment at 6PM, I fell backwards into my coffee table and bashed the back of my skull on the corner of the oak top so hard that all I could do was lay on the floor and watch the cigarette in my hand burn down to the filter, which I likely called "taking a nap."

The only time I could sleep was when I was completely passed out drunk, which was usually either on someone's couch or sitting upright in my computer chair or face down on my living room floor. Otherwise I'd wake up at least once an hour, which was partly due to the nightmares and sleep paralysis and night terrors I often experienced. I could rarely experience any kind of peace, and when I did find a way to relax, the feeling passed so quickly it taunted me.

* * *

BLOG: FEBRUARY 23, 2009—
"Tonight before bed, I took a bath and drank some tea and read for a while and it was one of the most relaxing things I've ever done! I can't believe I've never experienced this. I guess usually before going to bed (aka passing out) I'm crawling up the stairs to my apartment at 3am and when I finally reach the summit, it takes me so long to figure out how to open the door that I end up just passing out on the living room floor right in front of the door. I'm not saying this whole Being-A-Normal-Adult-Non-Alcoholic-And-Winding-Down-Before-Bed thing will become a routine, but it was a nice change of pace. By the way, the acronym for that would be BANANA. Maybe someday I'll try BANANA."

*   *   *

After one of my lab-drinking Fridays, I drove ten miles out of town to a professor's country ranch where another grad student house-sat for the weekend. We drank the professor's liquor, swam in the professor's hot tub, watched the professor's big screen TV, and drove the professor's tractor around the acres of prairieland, chicken coops, and graveyards. It was a grown-up version of playing house that I enjoyed very much until the guy wanted to have sex with me.

He pulled me on top of him in the hot tub, and I entered into a frozen panic as his naked body slid under my naked body. I knew I couldn't get out of this situation, nobody knew where I was in the middle of nowhere, and I was too drunk to even get out of the hot tub, let alone find my phone to try to call somebody to pick me up. I was angry that I couldn't have one drunken evening without having to have sex—I wished I was a man so this would stop happening to me. I knew I shouldn't have gotten in the hot tub.

When the guy went inside to go to the bathroom, I lay paralyzed in the hot tub and wished the water was deep enough that I could drown. I waited for him to return to claim my body, but after what felt like an eternity, he still hadn't come back. I mustered the strength to climb out of the hot tub, my naked body dripping all over the professor's polished wooden floors, and found him passed out naked in the living room. I grew ecstatic as I saw my chance for freedom.

I frantically ran all over the house—upstairs, downstairs, outside—to gather my clothes and purse and phone and keys, always peeking back into the living room to make sure he was still asleep. Once I had all my belongings, I made a quick stop in the kitchen to scrounge for food as I hadn't eaten in two days. I shoved a handful of raisins and a couple Oreo cookies in my mouth as I ran out the back door to make my escape. I was sopping wet in my car and too drunk to drive home, but any alternative beat staying in that house for one more second. Even getting a second DUI.

I thought my performance at school and the respect of my professors depended on alcohol, but at the same time, alcohol caused my personal life to endlessly fall apart. My relationships with my friends began to plateau or even stagnate, as they could never count on me to show up to a gathering or remember any conversations we had. They pleaded to spend time with "sober Apryl," which I didn't understand at all. I hated sober Apryl. My friends planned things for us to do that specifically didn't involve alcohol, but I always had alcohol stashed in my purse and drank on my own. Eventually, they realized that if they wanted to see sober Apryl, they'd have to catch me earlier in the day before I'd already drank too much. I didn't understand at the time why they cared if I was drinking or not, but I now appreciate them sticking by me all those years, as they ended up being my true friends.

INCOGNITO

DURING MY FIRST spring break in grad school, I went to Memphis with Elizabeth. We went to Graceland and Beale Street and unexpectedly bumped into our all-time favorite songwriter, Ryan Adams. We were so excited to see him, but tried to act super cool. This should've been one of the highlights of my life, but as usual, I was wasted. I had to run away from our conversation with Ryan to pee, and when I got back, I realized I hadn't quite made it to the toilet and had urine all over my jeans. I could've had the chance to sing karaoke with one of my musical heroes, and his band The Cardinals, but instead I was just drunk. And with this disappointment, I wrote my very last Myspace blog.

*   *   *

BLOG: MARCH 29, 2009—
"All of us went back to Beale Street then and I finally found my Big Ass Green Beer and we just walked around and drank and then we randomly saw Ryan Adams walking in the street by himself so we went up to him and we were like blah blah blah and he was like "you wanna go sit over here?" So we went over and sat on this big concrete barricade thing and talked to him forever about random shit and then he got a phone call and told the person that he was hanging out with these "cats from middle Illinois" and then the rest of the Cardinals came to where we were and hung out for a bit. After

sitting there drinking for that long I was about ready to pee my pants so I had to get up and go to the bathroom and when I got back Ryan and Co. were gone but Elizabeth said they'd asked if we wanted to go to this karaoke bar. So we went over there and it was $5 to get in and it was really bad karaoke and I pretty much just passed out in the booth."

*   *   *

When I somehow survived to finish my first semester in grad school to see my twenty-third birthday, I commemorated the occasion with another set of ear piercings. It marked a memorial to one more seemingly impossible-to-survive year, and again, what I thought would be one last tally mark of existence.

Shortly after my birthday, I'd started my first summer in grad school, and when I heard incessant banging on my front door in the middle of the night, I directed my anger at whoever interrupted my peaceful slumber. I tried to ignore the knocking and go back to sleep, but the persistent pounding wouldn't stop. I opened my eyes to see what time it was, and realized that I couldn't see anything at all. Thick, grey smoke completely filled my apartment. I stumbled to the front door to find my neighbor, who had traced the cause of his beeping smoke detector to my apartment. When I opened the door, smoke poured out into the hallway.

"Oh my God! Call 911! What the hell is going on? Your apartment is on fire!" screamed my neighbor.

"Nahhh, everything's fine. Don't get the authorities involved. I'll just put it out with my fire extinguisher," I slurred.

My neighbor finally pulled me out of my apartment after I kept trying to go back in to take care of the fire myself. He called 911. I called my mom. Several fire trucks, police cars, my landlord, and my mom arrived, and the fireman busted out my screens to throw parts of my couches out my living room windows. I'd been unconscious, sitting upright on my smoldering couch, for over two hours after I passed out with a cigarette in my hand, my body just inches away from the burning brown velvet.

One of the firemen told me that I was lucky to not have died from smoke inhalation. He said they usually "pulled corpses" out of those kinds of situations. That statement shocked me, but I didn't feel scared or embarrassed—I mostly felt exhausted after having survived yet another disaster. We joked that smoking cigarettes for so many years must've primed my lungs to withstand so much smoke. The fireman informed me of the next time he'd be at the firehouse in case I wanted to stop by to get the fire report. My mom thought he was cute, and with a wink, she told me I should go see him at work.

Flirting with a fireman was the last thing on my mind—I could've just died. This wasn't some kind of fantasy where a heroic fireman saved me from a burning building and we fell in love. I did, however, feel like a damsel in distress, and wondered what it would take to be rescued from the nightmare of my life.

Since my mom didn't seem concerned at all with what'd just happened, even commenting that those couches were getting too old anyway, I tried to convince myself that almost dying in an apartment fire wasn't that big of a deal. I insisted that I didn't pass out drunk with a cigarette in my hand. I wasn't lying, I just thought that drinking a pint of whiskey wasn't "really drinking"—that was just a small amount of liquor that played no part in my apartment fire.

I lived in complete denial that drinking caused any problems in my life. I didn't want to give myself any reason to have to quit drinking. Everything was fine. I tried to make myself think I always had a great time and enjoyed the how-does-she-do-it remarks I got from my friends. Everybody thought it was remarkable how I could get drunk every night and still maintain a 4.0 GPA in graduate school and keep up with the teaching responsibilities I had for my graduate assistantship. This amazed me, too. Somehow, it made me feel better to think that people couldn't see how miserable I was. But miserable I was. Tortured, even—especially in the mornings.

Ever since my senior year in high school, I'd set my alarm to get up three or four hours before I needed to be anywhere in the morning, and I didn't understand what took me so long to get ready. I'd get in the shower, do my makeup and hair, and suddenly several hours had gone by. It made my life absolutely exasperating, to say the least, but I became accustomed to it.

To an outside viewer, this routine looked like me standing in front of the mirror perfectly separating each and every eyelash, maybe taking off my mascara to do it all over again, pulling out the eyelashes I didn't like with tweezers, perfectly drawing on penciled eyebrows, perfectly straightening my strands of curly hair, and pulling out the hairs on top of my head that I didn't like. I absolutely could not leave the house—not if I was running late for class, not even in the case of some emergency—without completing this routine.

But what I thought was just an obsessive grooming habit, I later remembered was accompanied by intense flashbacks of Jared's rape and Adrianne's abandonment. All that time I spent in the mirror, the events of the night Jared raped me replayed in my head over and over. The blank spots in my memory from when I was blacked out or unconscious filled with the same questions I asked myself in the days after the rape. I relived my interactions with my schoolmates and thought of what I could've said or done differently to have avoided the backlash I received from most of my friends. I wished I'd never told anybody anything about what'd happened with Jared.

It was almost six years later now, and I still stared into the same mirror, captive to the vortex of memories of a story with no dénouement in sight. As hard as I tried to drown out my thoughts with loud music or TV or drinking a pot of coffee, I couldn't keep the invasive, poisonous memories from the forefront of my mind. After a couple hours of reliving that nightmare every morning, I reached a point of complete physical and emotional exhaustion that usually allowed me to put it out of my mind for the rest of the day. But if not, I could start drinking and immediately feel better. Gradually, I started drinking earlier in the day and in larger amounts. I often took "naps" at the bar, and I noticed the repercussions of drinking so heavily.

When I locked myself out of my apartment, which happened often, I'd walk over a mile to my mom's house at 3AM, curl up in a ball on the back porch to sleep, and wish my mom could see how desperate I was for help. But I'd just wait until she got up in the morning and act like I'd just stopped by to get my spare key. One time when I walked home, beer-in-hand, from a friend's house in the early hours of the morning, I decided to lie down and sleep under a tree on campus with branches that extended all the way to the ground. When morning came, I heard students walk to class while I lay under a tree with a half-empty bottle of Coors Light. Sometimes I slept in the tube-slide at the park across the street from my apartment, and wondered why I slept in the park like a homeless person when I had my own apartment right across the street.

It just made more sense, felt more comfortable, to haphazardly fall asleep around town instead of going back to my own safe apartment. I never felt safe at home anyway. When I slept in my own bed, and only in my own bed, I awoke paralyzed and terrified, feeling entirely alert and looking around my room, but completely unable to move my body. I tried excruciatingly hard to move, to the point my muscles ached, and my labored breathing and heavy sweating shook the bed. A tremendous pressure weighed me down, like being pushed through my bed straight into the earth. I saw, or at least sensed, some kind of body over me, holding me down. I tried to scream for help and felt my vocal cords contract, but I couldn't make any noise. I seized an awareness of absolute terror and unimaginable fear. I'd rather experience any kind of physical suffering. I sensed an acute sensitivity to the most vulnerable parts of my body—my vagina and my ribcage—and there was nothing I could do to protect these part of me. I tried to reach for my phone to call my mom for help, but I'd be unable to move for close to ten minutes.

I never felt like the successful, pretty, outgoing college girl who everyone else saw because my internal world was a nightmare from hell. When what I felt at the core of my being didn't match the picture of my life that I outwardly displayed, it confused and disconcerted me so much that I needed to find some congruence between my internal and external worlds. I thought that a person with their own apartment, car, job, friends, and family shouldn't be in the excruciating amount of pain I felt every day, and outwardly displaying my drunken mess validated my reality so I knew that what I experienced daily was actually real—that I actually existed. But most people never saw that part of me—the part that I thought was the real me—most people saw a smart and successful girl who liked to have fun and party.

HUNGER

I CONTINUED TO LIVE behind a mask so nobody could see the real me who I hated so much. I felt so ashamed for letting myself get raped twice and then sleeping around with a bunch of guys, and I felt so guilty for wasting my potential on drugs and alcohol. I especially hated myself for not being interested in men—I didn't know if I was gay or lesbian or what the difference was, but anytime I'd notice myself attracted to women, I'd beat myself up about it for days.

What's wrong with you? This isn't normal. Why do you look at her like that?

I had totally lost my sense of self. I'd also lost a lot of weight the previous year living mostly off of alcohol, cocaine, and cigarettes, and I became obsessed with controlling my weight. I tried to eat as little as possible to keep the weight off.

I don't know how it started—I woke up one day and felt the burden of my pathetic, shameful life weighing down on me. I thought if I could just lose five pounds, maybe I'd feel better about myself. I started exercising and dieting with Rebekah, and lost over thirty pounds in a couple of months, probably mostly due to the coke and not the physical activity. A spaceship-looking machine at the gym told me that I'd obtained a "normal" weight and body mass index for my age and height, and for the first time, I realized that I was even overweight to begin with. I wondered how I'd never noticed my chubbiness before.

I wasn't obese but my weight at my first workout approached 180. It intrigued me how I didn't become aware of my body until it

started disappearing—like I'd never looked in a mirror before, I
didn't think anything of my jean size, and I had no idea how many
calories were in that chicken strip basket and Oreo Blizzard from
Dairy Queen that I ate for lunch.

I now know that meal clocked in at over 2000 calories—my brain
may forever be branded with nutrition facts for every food and meal on
the planet. I wish I could forget how many calories are in a chicken
breast or how many grams of fat are in an avocado, but for the next five
years after this initial weight loss, my whole world revolved around
numbers. Calories. Weight. Grams. Pounds. Inches. Servings.

I felt so good in my new clothes and so comfortable in my new
body—I experienced a high like I never had before. I never wanted
to gain another pound. I arbitrarily assigned myself an 800-calorie
daily limit when I decided that 500 calories a day seemed too
anorexic, but consuming 1,000 calories just sounded…huge. Most
days, I adhered to the 800 calories, or if I was really triumphant,
maybe 500 calories or none at all. Of course, the calories from all the
alcohol I drank every day didn't factor into this limit. Alcohol was a
necessity. It was like a medication I had to take, so I didn't think
about how many calories I ingested when I drank. As long as I ate
under 800 calories a day, I allowed myself to drink whatever I
wanted—as long as it was light beer or white wine or whiskey with
diet soda. I learned those were the "cheapest" ways to drink. I
referred to my daily calories as if they were money:

"Pizza is too expensive" (too many calories).

"I think I can afford this sandwich" (350 calories wouldn't put
me over 800).

"Oh no, I spent too much today" (I went over 800 calories).

I was already an alcoholic at this point, and my life quickly
spiraled out of control—knowing that I could still control what I put
into my body and that I could control that number on the scale made
me feel like I was still healthy, or at least functioning. As the
frequency and quantity of my drinking increased, I decided that I
needed to be even stricter about what I ate in order to maintain my
weight. I only ate baked chicken breasts, eggs, green vegetables,
canned tuna, and baked salmon—those were my safe foods.

If I didn't have time to cook, and I felt like I couldn't make it
through the day without eating, I allowed myself to get a Subway

sandwich. The guy on the commercials lost a ton of weight eating Subway, so I couldn't feel guilty about that. If I had to go out to dinner with friends or family, I ate as little as possible the day before, nothing else the day of dinner, and made sure to order a healthy option on the menu (after spending hours beforehand looking over the restaurant's menu and adding up what each item would cost me calorically). If dinner plans came unexpectedly, and I'd already eaten that day, I made up an excuse not to go, or I promised myself I wouldn't eat the following day. All of this felt perfectly normal to me, and I felt successful in life.

I began to develop obsessive thoughts about controlling my food intake and weight. I spent countless hours looking at nutrition facts on the internet, and I knew the caloric content of basically every food on Earth and every item at any restaurant or fast food chain. If I didn't pass out drunk somewhere before putting myself to bed, I lay in bed to count the calories of everything I ate that day. I started at the beginning of the day and added up everything I ate in order, which wasn't too difficult because I usually only ate once a day. But to be sure I didn't forget something, I then started at the end of the day and worked backwards adding everything up I ate back to the beginning of the day. If I couldn't convince myself that the half chicken breast I cooked for dinner was actually under a hundred calories, I hopped out of bed and ran to the kitchen to look at the package of chicken, sometimes digging through the trash for it.

If the whole package weighed 0.93 pounds and I only ate one half of the three breasts, then I ate 0.155 pounds of chicken, or 2.48 ounces. Since there are 110 calories in 4 ounces of chicken breast, or 27.5 calories per ounce, I only ate 68.2 calories of chicken. Okay I can go back to bed now.

As hard as I tried, I couldn't control the calories scrolling through my head as I lay in bed, like an adding machine from hell with a mind of its own. But at least when calories completely consumed my mind, I didn't think about being raped as I tried to fall asleep, so I accepted the compromise. It also minimized the frequency of my nightmares as I often just dreamed about food.

I tried to not eat at night because I was afraid if I went to sleep too soon after eating, all the food would turn to fat by morning.

Every morning I woke up, I ran my fingertips over my ribs and hips to make sure I could at least feel some sort of bone. Then, I proceeded to the bathroom to weigh myself. The number on the scale determined how good about myself I'd feel that day, and it usually disappointed me. I didn't even care how I looked to other people, but I needed the scale to say 145.0 or below. If it said 145.1, my heart dropped into my stomach and then I'd wonder how many calories my heart cost me in that moment.

During my morning assessment of my body or any time I looked in a mirror, my eyes only focused on my stomach—what looked like a disgusting, protruding, flabby stomach. Maybe only this area concerned me because that's where I could feel the burden of my self-hatred, in the deepest part of my gut. I hated myself for probably being gay, I hated myself for being an alcoholic, and I hated myself for getting raped, but if I could just get rid of the gut, maybe I'd approve of myself.

Eventually, the people closest to me noticed that my eating habits weren't normal and made comments that irritated me. When I went out of town with friends who stopped at Burger King for lunch, I ran across the street to buy a can of tuna at the gas station. And then I ran to a grocery store when I realized I didn't have a can opener. They didn't understand why I didn't get some "real food" at the grocery store instead of insisting on finding a can opener for my gas station tuna. It's not like I was underweight or even losing weight anymore, so I didn't understand why there was a problem.

To get my friends to leave me alone about my eating habits, I wanted to make sure that when I did eat, I ate around them. If I wanted to eat an apple at some point during the day, I carried it around in my purse until I was with one of my friends so I could eat it in front of them. Pretty soon, I almost never ate anything alone.

This all got so exhausting after a couple years, and being hungry all the time drained me, but I only felt satisfied when my stomach growled. When my body remained weak and starving, hunger was the only thing I could feel, and hunger drowned out my emotional pain. Like my success in school, my weight and the food I put into my body was one of the only aspects of my life over which I felt like I had any control. I'd survived the complete loss of control over my body twice already, and I desperately grasped any source of control over my life I could find—so as long as I did well in school and didn't gain any weight, I stayed in control.

I kept to my strict eating regimen, but I drank every day now and used a lot of drugs. I hung out with Sam a lot more, and while I didn't usually actively seek out drugs for myself, I took anything anyone offered me. There was an unspoken rule in Sam's crowd that pretty girls got to do drugs for free, and being one of the only girls around, I usually got a lot of free drugs. I didn't care what kind of drug I took—sometimes I didn't even care to ask what I'd taken—because almost any drug intensified the effect of alcohol that I liked so much, to feel absolutely nothing.

The only way I knew how to tolerate the constant anxiety and existential pain that dominated my life was to self-medicate. I thought I had the alcoholic thing under control but drugs scared me—they were so unpredictable, and I feared that if I became addicted to any substance in particular, I wouldn't remain successful in school. But being in control only eased a portion of the unbearable amount of pain I felt, so I self-medicated and tried to remain as in-control of my drug use as I could. If I became too reliant on a certain drug, I switched to something else for a while, but I pretty much always used something at least on a weekly basis.

My affinity for Vicodin didn't surprise me. Like cocaine, Vicodin made me feel numb physically, which complimented the emotional numbness that alcohol provided me. My first experience with Vicodin came after running into an old friend who asked me for a ride to the pharmacy. After obtaining several bottles of pills, he offered me some Vicodin for the favor, and I ended up with a sandwich baggie of thirty pills. The mild effect of the painkiller that I'd heard so much about initially disappointed me, but after taking five pills, I felt light and fuzzy and excited.

Shortly after setting my apartment on fire, I went on a camping trip with six of my friends, including Sam and Elizabeth. I still have a picture of myself from that trip in which I'm lying on the ground vomiting. I was in so much pain, and I remember exactly how I felt that day when I drank an entire thirty-pack of Keystone Light and took a lot of Vicodin. I fell to the ground on my hands and knees and vomited. When I got too weak to hold myself up any longer, I lay down and continued to vomit with my head pressed against the dewy grass. My friends all laughed and took pictures of me. Once I felt a little better, I started drinking again, and we all joked about what a mess I was.

Once I realized that the acetaminophen in all the Vicodin I consumed probably destroyed my liver, I decided to start performing cold-water extractions to separate the hydrocodone from the acetaminophen in the pills. I learned this technique from Sam's roommate, and developed a routine of crushing up four Vicodin into an Erlenmeyer flask and dissolving the powder with warm water. I put the flask in the freezer until the acetaminophen precipitated out of the solution, and then I filtered the solution with a coffee filter. The acetaminophen stayed in the coffee filter, and I drank the terribly bitter liquid that contained the hydrocodone—it tasted like bile mixed with chalk. This process took a little while, so I usually swallowed one or two pills while I waited. The resulting concoction produced a perfect feeling of heaviness and lightness all at the same time.

I wasn't that concerned about my liver, but this routine gave me another distraction from my mind when I was alone. I was a total control freak in so many ways, which may've kept me from overdosing. The relief I got from drugs and alcohol wasn't simply about the effect of the substances themselves, but about the process of searching for, preparing, and consuming these things. I researched the pharmacological mechanisms of actions of whatever I took, and calculated the optimal dose for my body weight so as to get the maximum effect with the least amount of drug. This process, coupled with my food obsession, completely consumed my life.

One afternoon when I opened the freezer door to check on my Vicodin solution, I accidently knocked over the Erlenmeyer flask, and the liquid spilled in the freezer. I immediately panicked. I gasped, and my heart raced. I ran around my apartment frantically looking for something to salvage the spilled hydrocodone, and when I became afraid that the solution would freeze to the bottom of the freezer before I could figure out how to recover it, I grabbed a chair from my kitchen table. I put the chair in front of the refrigerator and stood on it so I could get my entire head in the freezer, and I sucked up the liquid with a straw I'd dug out of my garbage can. Once I'd sucked up all the liquid from the freezer, I became aware of the irrationality of what I'd done.

Climbing into a freezer to try to suck up some dissolved Vicodin wasn't something someone would do unless they had a problem. Those weren't even the last of my supply of pills; I was just so desperate for my hit that I didn't want to wait another hour to do another cold-water extraction. I decided I needed to stop taking Vicodin, so I swallowed the rest of the pills in my supply and drank a little more whiskey for the next few days to get over the craving for painkillers.

Cocaine was still my drug of choice, and I have countless memories of coffee tables. Coffee tables made of solid wood, made of fabricated wood, long rectangular coffee tables, small square ones, coffee tables with glass tops (I liked those the best), with tiled tops, coffee tables made out of old pizza boxes, or a cardboard box that once held the five hundred packages of ramen noodles that fed someone for months. Even now, the coffee table is the first thing I instinctively notice when I visit someone's house for the first time. I always knelt beside a coffee table to meticulously prepare perfectly straight lines of whatever powder I inhaled that night. It was like I knelt at the altar of oblivion, completely focused on the task at hand—the sacrifice of any feeling—rocking back and forth, trying to be patient, while I anxiously awaited my blessing.

But at some point, doing drugs the regular way didn't satisfy me enough, so I came up with some creative ways to get high. One of our friends somehow procured an entire box of Fentanyl patches, which are transdermal patches used for chronic pain that are worn on the skin and release the painkiller over the course of two to three days. Instead of wearing the patch, we broke it open, scraped the gel inside onto a square of aluminum foil, and inhaled the vapors by smoking them through a hot glass pipe. The high came immediately and intensely—like being wrapped in a fuzzy blanket and floating up to the sky.

Fentanyl is a hundred times more potent than morphine, and inhaling a concentrated amount of this drug could've easily produced respiratory depression and death, but I decided to take my chances. One night after smoking Fentanyl, I woke up on the floor of

Sam's apartment with a Fentanyl patch stuck to my forehead. I imagine that my intention must've been to make the painkiller go straight to my brain because it was in my own head, my own thoughts, where I felt the most pain.

Halfway through my master's program, heroin suddenly showed up as the new ghost in town that lurked around me, breathing in my air. The heroin junkies were a mirror of my future from which I couldn't look away. For a while, I avoided it because heroin was the one drug I knew I couldn't control—the one drug I couldn't even lie to myself about using to have to a good time. But as heroin quickly replaced the cocaine on my favorite coffee tables around town, I never refused a line.

After snorting heroin, I couldn't do anything but nod off for the next several hours, sometimes banging my head into a coffee table or wall. It made me so cold and itchy. I hated the itchiness so much, it felt like mosquito bites covered every surface of my skin, and the next day, I woke with scratches all over my face and chest. After a heroin binge, I'd be sick for at least two days.

I'd never felt as sick as I did after I stopped doing heroin. It was like someone simultaneously pulled my intestines out of my mouth, crushed my head in a vise, and drowned me in a pool of vomit. I knew the only thing that would make the sickness go away was to do more heroin, but that's exactly how people got addicted, and I wouldn't let myself become a junkie. I often called my mom to bring me lunch on days like these so she could see how much trouble I was in, hoping she could help. But all I got was a Subway sandwich that I'd immediately throw up after eating.

"I just hate seeing you like this," my mom said as she left to return to work.

Even being so sick, I still forced myself to go to school as long as I felt well enough to stand without falling over. But I couldn't stay awake for any length of time, especially not in class, where my eyelids weighed a thousand pounds and pulled my whole head down to my benchtop. After falling asleep and then vomiting during the endocrinology class for which I served as the graduate assistant, I went back to my office and lay on my stomach across the top of my desk. One of my lab mates asked what was wrong with me.

"Oh I think I'm just sick from the heroin I did yesterday," I said as if this was a perfectly common condition for a graduate student to be in on a Wednesday morning.

The look on my lab mate's face communicated utter shock and disbelief. I realized that my behavior had progressed past my "party girl" image, and I decided I needed to avoid heroin, or at least hide it better. But even though I knew I wouldn't enjoy myself and that it would make me unbearably sick when I stopped, I'd do it anyway. I knew heroin would make my pain go away, and all I could focus on was getting through the current day. I didn't care what happened to me; as far as I could tell, I was already dead and in hell.

My first encounter with an actual heroin dealer took place in the upstairs loft apartment of a shoddy three-story house in Charleston. Up until this point, I'd been getting it from some mysterious friends-of-friends channel, and I felt proud to have earned the drug ring's trust enough to be allowed into the dealer den. I felt special to have gained access to this secret "privileged" part of town.

All the dealers must've used the same interior decorator because the walls and ceilings of the smoke-filled rooms were always covered in Grateful Dead posters and psychedelic fabric wall coverings that glowed under blacklights. I'd stepped into a time machine back to the 1960s, and I pondered why that peace and love movement fell apart—was it because once we realized that we can't make any political or social change, we started doing heroin and never left the house again?

As usual, I kneeled next to the glass coffee table and watched as the dealer pulled apart and emptied capsules of St. John's Wort to fill them with heroin from his supply. The steadiness of his hands amazed me—mine were always shaking. For orders larger than these single-hit "capsules," he carefully weighed out the powder on a scale just like those in my lab, which I knew could've cost close to a thousand dollars, and he neatly folded up the heroin in an aluminum foil pouch. Doing a hit with the dealer was customary—I don't know if it was farce to pretend like we were buddies or an unspoken display of pride in his product—so I inhaled a capsule with him and went on my way back to Sam's apartment where I felt safe nodding off for the next couple days.

But at Sam's apartment, as one of our friends nodded off after snorting heroin, I realized I wasn't truly safe there. He sat upright on the couch, and the back of his head hit the wall behind him over and over, but nobody thought anything of this common occurrence — until his throat started making gurgling noises. He foamed at the mouth, and everybody knew he overdosed, but nobody wanted to call an ambulance because they didn't want the police aware of the location of our drug hub.

I left the apartment scared and found out later that they dragged our overdosing friend outside and called 911, leaving him in the grass by the side of the road. I couldn't believe people would treat a friend like this, but I realized that most of these people weren't real friends, and knew it'd only be a short matter of time before I'd end up in the same situation with nobody to help me.

There were so many nights I spent at home alone or passed out at someone's apartment after having used a dangerous combination of drugs and alcohol that I feared not waking up. I thought every day could be the last day of my life, and not only because of the risk of overdosing. I'd experienced how unpredictable and unsafe the world was, and knew I held a live grenade every day, waiting to detonate.

My second summer in grad school, exactly one year after my first trip to Memphis, I went back for the Beale Street Music Festival with Ashley and a couple other friends, and my experience wasn't much better than the first time. Even if I did run into Ryan Adams again, like I hoped might happen, I doubt I would've remembered it at all this time. After the first night of the festival, I was so drunk that I couldn't even walk straight as I stumbled down the middle of the street. Ashley had already gone back to the hotel because she grew tired of my belligerence. My other friend and I tried to get a cab back to the hotel later, but nobody stopped for us. We chatted with a guy, also trying to get a cab, who asked us if we wanted any cocaine. My friend said no, I said yes. I was so drunk anyway, I didn't see what difference it would make if I did some coke with this guy — maybe it would help. We followed him down a side street to get out of view, and I snorted a couple bumps out of his coke bag.

Then he suggested that we go back to his house to get in the hot tub, and he asked some guys in a pickup truck if they'd give us all a ride back to his place. The scrawny white boys in the truck looked like they were in high school, and they happened to stand beside their truck in a dark parking lot near where we hailed cabs—I thought this must've been planned. We got in the bed of a pickup truck with this stranger who handed these kids a wad of cash. The guy gave the driver directions to his house, and I had no idea where we were headed or who these people were. I wondered what the fuck I was doing going to some stranger's house. Memphis was one of the most dangerous cities in the country, and I was terrified, so I did a couple more bumps of coke in the back of the truck to try to make the fear disappear. I wished I'd gone back to the hotel earlier with Ashley. I wished I could know that I was safe instead of having absolutely no idea what would happen to me in the next five minutes. I wondered if there was any way I'd be able to get out of having sex with this guy.

Fuck it, I thought, and became that person who wasn't me. I pretended I was in Las Vegas, as the wind whooshed through my hair, I stood up through the sunroof of a limo, the city lights blurred by my head, getting smaller and smaller behind us as we drove into the dark, and I let out a primal howl.

My friend passed out in a chair as soon as we got to this guy's house, so he and I took off our clothes and got in the hot tub. He snorted lines of coke off my bare chest, and I was angry that he didn't offer them to me anymore. We had sex in the hot tub, and I pretended I was Elisabeth Shue's prostitute character in *Leaving Las Vegas*. We eventually moved to the bed, but when he saw the sun coming up, he abruptly handed me the rolled-up twenty-dollar bill through which we'd been snorting coke and told me to get a cab back to my hotel. I felt like a whore.

When I got back from that trip, I smoked crack for the first time—or it could've been meth, I never asked what it was. I'd just met these guys at the bar and ended schmoozing around with them for two days, smoking crack and making crack pipes with a blow torch in a dingy trailer. I couldn't believe that a day earlier I'd given a lecture on the menstrual cycle to an undergraduate human physiology class and in two days I'd be taking a final exam in my graduate-level neuropsychology class. My life didn't make sense to me—who the hell was I?

Once I finally made my way home, I became delusional that I'd never be able to sleep again in my life, and that I'd always remain in this constant state of paranoid alertness. I didn't know what to do except call my mom, pleading for help. She came to my apartment, and I told her I'd been up for several days on crack or meth and just wanted to go to sleep.

"I am so sick of living this way, Mom. I don't know what to do," I nearly cried.

"Well, when you were a kid, I accidentally did meth one time, thinking it was coke, and it was just terrible. Your grandma took me to the hospital but they couldn't do anything except just wait for the drugs to wear off. So it'll go away eventually," my mom recounted as I tried to think of where the hell I would've been while she was on meth.

I would've gladly gone to the hospital if I thought somebody there could help me get my life together, but I curled up on my couch and laid my head on my mom's lap, which felt awkward since we hardly ever even hugged each other. It took so much effort to try to keep my eyes closed—my eyes actually felt like they'd pop out of my head. I never could fall asleep in the hour my mom stayed with me, and she eventually told me to think long and hard about where my life was headed, and then she went home. I sat on my couch, angry at the amount of sunlight that shone through my closed blinds—angry that the outside world moved along while I stayed trapped in this internal hell.

That summer, I went on a road trip with Elizabeth, who arranged for us to stay with her family in Tucson and Phoenix. I couldn't believe Elizabeth wanted to go on such a long road trip with me after I'd almost killed her when I got my DUI two years earlier—I knew the reckless endangerment of my friends' safety made me unworthy of their companionship, but I wanted to get out of town for a while and away from heroin. I decided that it would be fun to trip on LSD at the Grand Canyon, so I picked up six hits of acid from Sam right before Elizabeth and I embarked on our journey.

Sam only had liquid LSD in an eyedropper bottle, from which we'd usually take a hit by putting a drop on our tongues or on a sugar cube. Sugar cubes didn't seem like a practical option to transport acid across the country, but we couldn't think of any alternative, so Sam put one hit of acid each on six sugar cubes and wrapped them in an aluminum foil packet for me. I went to the grocery store with my mom to buy a small cooler and some ice with which to keep the acid-laced sugar cubes cold, as I was afraid they'd melt in the heat of the Southwest. To make a cooler appear less conspicuous, I threw some grapes in there too.

Elizabeth drove for the first few hours before we made a pit-stop, and while she filled up the car with gas, I filled up with my own fuel. Under the fluorescent lights of the truck-stop bathroom, I poured out a small pile of cocaine on the back of the toilet. Backward-straddling the toilet seat, I meticulously crushed and scraped two perfectly-parallel lines on the back of my checkbook and inhaled the bleach-laced air through a rather soft dollar bill. I bounced through the parking lot with electric energy and anticipation to start my leg of the drive. I stopped every hour or two to refresh my cocaine buzz in whatever dirty gas station bathroom I could find, thinking Elizabeth didn't know what I was doing (I just have to pee again!). I wondered how, in the past five years, I'd gone from being afraid the cops would catch me playing flashlight tag in the park after 10 PM to being afraid the cops would catch me driving while intoxicated (again) and transporting controlled substances across the country.

As I drove through the great Saint Louis gateway to the Wild West, crossing natural boundaries and temporal lines, the time changed from 9PM to 8PM. Then from 9PM to 8PM again. And I wondered if I continued in this way long enough and fast enough, could I rewind the past seven years and end up back in high school with a second chance at life? As quickly as I raced into the setting sun, I accelerated to escape its reproachful glare behind me as morning came. Thirty-three hours later, we were in Tucson, and all that time I'd escaped caught up with me. I ended back where I started—tired, angry, and out of coke.

FROZEN

I MADE IT BACK to Charleston, hoping something would've changed during the time I was in Arizona. Getting away actually did break my heavy drug-using routine, and I held a generally sober gathering at my apartment with about eight of my close friends. We hung out, drank a few beers, and played cards. It wasn't anything rowdy, and I was glad for a low-key night for a change. By the time people left, it was pretty late, and one of my friends had fallen asleep on my couch. After everyone left, I got ready for bed and went in my bedroom to sleep, leaving Jake still on my couch. But a few minutes after I lay down, he walked into my room.

"Apryl? Apryl? Are you awake?" Jake whispered.

I hadn't fallen asleep yet, and I became so frightened when Jake came into my room. He was one of my trusted friends, but I didn't know what he wanted from me—all I could think about was when Jared pounded on my door nine months after raping me, but that this time he'd made it into my apartment. I didn't want to open my eyes because I didn't want to know if Jared actually was standing in my room. I pretended to be asleep, and wondered if he heard my heart pounding.

"Apryl?" he beckoned again, a little more loudly.

I kept my eyes tightly closed, but I felt his energy at the foot of my bed. It felt like how you can always tell when a muted TV is on in a room. He didn't turn around to exit my room quickly enough for my comfort. I thought maybe he would just ask for a blanket or pillow or glass of water, so I opened my eyes and asked Jake what he wanted.

"Can I eat your pussy?" he requested.

I couldn't believe Jake had asked me that. Was I dreaming? How can a person walk into a girl's bedroom, wake her up, and ask to "eat her pussy?" I hated that word. I saw him tower over me as he stood next to my bed. Jake was gigantic.

"Umm…I don't know? Are you really asking me this?" I thought maybe I'd misheard him.

"Please. It's been so long," he pleaded.

I considered my position: I was alone in my apartment in the middle of the night with this strong man, and I didn't want to find out what would happen if I told him to get the fuck out of my apartment. I didn't want to ever feel as helpless as I'd felt when I was raped before. I figured if I told him no, he'd either accept my answer and leave, or he would overpower me and do what he wanted. That was a fifty-percent chance I'd have to re-live feeling powerless over my own body, and that was a risk I wasn't willing to take. I did feel powerless, though. I felt like I didn't have a choice.

"Umm…okay, I guess," I said with hesitation. As long as I'm saying yes, I'm not getting raped.

I wanted to get this over with as effortlessly as possible. I told myself this would be okay because Jake was a friend who I'd trusted. I told myself that adding one more guy to the list of men I'd slept with wouldn't make any difference to my already depleted amount of dignity. What's one more? I told myself he probably needed sex because he'd just returned from overseas military duty—I told myself I was doing a service to my country. Who was I kidding? I didn't give a fuck about my country.

The next day, I didn't answer Jake's phone calls. He sent me a text message telling me to call him because he wanted to talk. I didn't have anything to say to him, but I finally called him back two days later, and he wanted to make sure I was okay with what'd happened. He also wanted to make sure I was on birth control. I told Jake I was fine with what happened (I wasn't), and I told him I was on birth control (I wasn't). But I felt like I'd been violated. Not so much by Jake, but by Jared and Jason who destroyed my control over my body. And by whomever probably told Jake that I was easy or slutty or that I'd have sex with anyone if I was drunk enough. I thought I was safe in my own apartment with my friends in whom I trusted. But if I was so paralyzed with fear anytime a man came near me, I wasn't safe anywhere.

A couple months later when Jake came to a party at my apartment again, he was asleep on the couch when everybody left, just as before. This time, I shut and locked my bedroom door when I went to sleep. When I awoke to the sound of my doorknob turning and the door opening, I pretended to be asleep and wondered how he got into my room. I deliberately locked my door to avoid this situation. Did the lock on my door not work? Did he pick the lock? I thought if Jake picked the lock of my bedroom door, then he definitely wouldn't accept no for an answer, and there was no chance of me getting out of whatever was going to happen. As I pretended to sleep, Jake laid down next to me in my bed. We had sex, and no words were even exchanged between us. If I couldn't be safe in my own apartment, with my closest friends, alone in my bedroom with the door locked, where could I possibly be safe? Nowhere.

Even years later, I'd become terrified if somebody unexpectedly knocked on my apartment door. Was it Jared pounding on my door again? Or was it some other guy who wanted to sleep with me who didn't care if my door was locked? I immediately froze, my heart pounded. Images of all the horrible things that'd happened to me scrolled through my mind like I was looking into one of those View-Master toys, but with each pull of the plastic lever, a different traumatic image clicked into place.

I stayed petrified and silent for a moment before I slowly tip-toed over to the door. I contemplated whether I should look out the peephole—if the person on the other side of the door was looking into the peephole, they'd know if I moved my head in front of it. I turned my phone on silent in case whoever knocked tried to call me. If I had the television or music on already, I'd be even more frightened because I knew the person probably heard it, but if I turned it off they'd definitely know I was home. I thought if I left the TV or music at the same volume, maybe they'd think I'd stepped out or I was in the shower. But then I became afraid that if the person thought I wasn't home, they'd come into my apartment to wait for my return. I stared at the doorknob fixedly, expecting to see it turn any second. If I wasn't dressed, I'd bolt into my room to throw on some clothes, and then quietly go back to staring at the doorknob, my breathing interrupted and shallow. Once I heard the person leave, I ran to my window to get a glimpse of who walked out the front of my apartment building.

Oh, it was just a kid selling candy bars.

DEATH IS ONLY THE BEGINNING

AFTER THESE INCIDENTS with Jake, my sense of safety and trust went from fragile to non-existent, and I was ready for my life to be over. My pre-occupation with death intensified as I watched my grandmother quickly approach the end of her life. My grandma had been living with Parkinson's disease for about ten years when she became ill enough that she had to be in hospice care. I'd never lost anybody close to me before, and seeing the way my mother suffered over the agony her own mother experienced made it even more unbearable. So naturally, I drank.

Until I was ten-years-old, my grandma lived directly across the street from my mother and me, and I'd go to her house before and after school to get my hair done and watch Oprah. My grandma would pick me up from school, and take me to Dairy Queen to eat ice cream and play rummy. She always beat me at rummy. As I thought about all the good memories I had with my grandma, I grieved for the last five years that I'd drifted away from her because I was too focused on getting drunk. I felt like a selfish asshole.

By the time my grandmother lay on her literal death bed, I was at the height of my drinking, in a different kind of death bed. It'd been four years since I'd gone a day without drinking, and that constant haze I looked for was now an omnipotent force that surrounded my mind and body. When my family left me alone with my grandmother to say my last words, I wanted to tell her how much I appreciated her caring for me all those years, for always feeding me, for letting me park behind her car in college because her apartment was close to my classes—I wanted to tell her that I loved her. But I looked at her and swallowed the lump in my throat with another swig of the wine that my family snuck into the nursing home.

She looked like a dying E.T. laying on her back, all grey and ashy and wrinkly, and in a way, I kind of felt like Elliot in that movie. We were dying together—except I didn't have any desire to break her out of the hospital, I just wanted to die with her.

I drank in the nursing home next to my slowly-dying grandma, and I drank at her funeral. I got so drunk at the funeral dinner, I don't even remember leaving, but I do remember visiting my grandma's gravesite with my mom and Jim after the reception. The three of us stood around the grave, said a few words, and I stumbled and fell face-first on the fresh mound of dirt over my grandma's casket. Even with my parents' help, I struggled to get up, my heels stuck in the mud and my neatly-pressed black pants covered in wet dirt. I wondered what my grandma would think about her little girl with whom she used to eat ice cream and play rummy who now fell down drunk over her dead body. My grandma probably turned over in her grave, and I was ashamed of myself.

My mother told me about her father's graveside service, which took place at the same cemetery thirty-five years earlier, right next to my grandmother's grave where we stood now. She recounted how her uncles, who were also alcoholics, were completely drunk and falling over in that cemetery during their brother's service, exactly as I was. I tried to contemplate how these intergenerational behavior repetitions propagate, but I just passed out in the backseat of the car on the way home.

WE'RE NOT IN KANSAS ANYMORE

A FEW WEEKS after my grandmother's death, I found myself at my twenty-fifth birthday—a whole quarter of a century—and I decided to get another ear piercing to commemorate my survival, another tick mark to scratch into the wall of my prison. I'd finished all my classes for grad school and most of my research, so all I had left was to write and defend my thesis. With my advisor's encouragement, I applied to some PhD programs, and the Michigan State University Neuroscience Program offered me a position with paid tuition and a stipend for the next five years.

I imagined leading a successful life in Michigan while still drinking every day and using drugs occasionally as needed. I didn't have any other choice because that was the only way I knew to escape the pain that radiated to the very core of my being—a pain that was impossible to live with.

I didn't know how to get out of this self-destructive cycle I was in. I told myself I was going through an "experimental drug phase." Marijuana, mushrooms, Vicodin, Valium, LSD, cocaine, heroin, crack, opium, 2-CB, 2-CE, 2-CI, ecstasy, MDMA, chloroform, Adderall, Fentanyl, whip-its, ketamine, and who knows what else I can't remember. I usually only did drugs on the weekends, and not even every weekend. Sometimes I'd go several weeks or even months without using any drugs at all, so I thought I had everything under control.

In June 2011, I received my master's degree with a 4.0 GPA, and during my thesis defense, my advisor announced that I'd been his "best student, to-date" and that the work I did should've earned me a PhD. I published my master's thesis entitled *Estrogen Promotes Neurite Outgrowth in Olfactory Epithelial Explant Cultures through the Estrogen Receptor*. But when I received my student loan statement and realized that I'd spent almost $30,000 on drugs and alcohol over the past three years, I didn't feel like a successful student. I'd dug myself into a huge hole. With a substantial increase in salary at MSU, I thought maybe I wouldn't have to take out any more student loans and I could get my life back under control.

In July, I moved to Lansing, Michigan, six hours away from Charleston, to start work on my PhD in neuroscience at MSU. Shortly after settling into my new apartment, I made friends and developed a busy social life, even before school started that fall. I liked my new friends, and I liked that they didn't know anything about my past. I thought I could get a fresh start and become the person I wanted to be—an ambitious, productive, successful, professional, normal college girl. It was the Michigan State Spartan Apryl vs. the Charleston High Trojan Apryl in a brutal war that I waged against myself.

Since I had this fresh start, I briefly considered being a lesbian in my new habitat, but I still couldn't accept this idea. It couldn't possibly be that, with everything that'd happened to me, I happened to be a lesbian, too. Maybe I just hadn't found the right guy yet, and with a new pool of men available to me, my experience could be different now.

I explored the bar scene, which was much different from the quiet, local dive bars I frequented back home. The bars in this busy college city were always packed with shoulder-to-shoulder people who couldn't even talk to one another over the pounding dance music. I went out dancing with my friends, and I hated guys grinding on my legs and my hips and my butt, but everyone else seemed to enjoy it, so I kept drinking to go along with it. I wished we could instead sit at a small basement establishment and drink enough liquor to glue us to our seats until the last-call lights in the bar came on.

My friends didn't understand why I wasn't interested in the guys they tried to set me up with, and I didn't understand either, except that I wasn't attracted to men. I got so frustrated with myself for not wanting to have a relationship with any of these guys who were so nice and normal, and with whom I actually enjoyed spending time. I didn't have the same attraction and connection with men that I felt toward women, and I was angry that I couldn't make myself feel that way about any guy.

My previous routine of sleeping with any guy who showed interest in me returned in an accelerated form. I'd only been living in my new home for five months and had already slept with seven different guys. Of the guys who I actually liked hanging out with, I thought sleeping with them might make me feel some kind of connection to them that would make it easier to date them. And the other guys I felt threatened by and afraid to refuse their advances for fear of getting raped again. I chose to have awkward, unsatisfying, unprotected, dissociated sex with a complete stranger rather than risk the possibility of not having any choice in with whom I had sex.

I was twenty-five years old; shouldn't I do something more important with my life than get drunk every day? I realized I'd been drunk almost every day for the last five years. I could actually remember each day during that time in which I didn't drink, and I could count them on one hand. My blackouts became more frequent. I blacked out several times a week—sometimes for only small portions of the evening, sometimes for the entire night. Waking in the morning and not remembering the previous night always alarmed me, regardless of whether I'd made it back to my apartment or if I woke up at someone else's house or in my car or in a park.

After making sure I still had my driver's license, phone, and credit cards, I began my post-blackout routine of piecing my night together. I looked through all my text messages and pictures on my camera for clues as to when I lost cognizance. I looked for any crumpled credit card receipts shoved in my pockets or purse to figure out where I'd been. The time printed on the receipts was always helpful. Having to go back to the bars in Lansing the next day because I'd left my tab open or lost my phone or camera or wallet or jacket was so much more of a hassle than it was in Charleston where I knew all the bartenders who recognized my belongings and saved them for me.

But as much as I hated blacking out, it always made me feel like I'd wiped out all my bad memories and feelings about myself, which made my subsequent flashbacks and anxiety and self-loathing more tolerable. Several days in a row of all those horrible thoughts and memories piling up on one another and taking up more and more space in my mind like an expanding balloon in the middle of my brain became unbearable. By drinking to the point of blacking out, I could pop that balloon to make room for the cycle to start all over again.

In August 2012, I began my first semester in the MSU Neuroscience Program. I had two classes to take—Neuroscience Laboratory and Physiology and Pharmacology of Excitable Cells—and I had to complete a lab rotation in which I chose a lab to work in for the semester. I chose a lab group that studied Parkinson's disease at the MSU College of Human Medicine campus in Grand Rapids, an hour-long commute from the main campus in Lansing. I didn't exactly know why I wanted to study Parkinson's disease, but as with many of the other major life decisions I'd made, I didn't know what else to do.

I drove to-and-from Grand Rapids three or four times a week to learn tedious skills like performing live rat brain surgery, harvesting and slicing rat brains into paper-thin sections, and doing computer-aided 3-D reconstructions of individual neurons. Back in Lansing, I learned about the chemical and electrical properties of brain cells in class, which demanded more of my cognitive abilities than college had in the past. For the first time in my life, I struggled to keep up in school. I noticed that when I studied for exams, I couldn't memorize things with one glance of a page like I always could before. I took my exams and left questions blank because my brain couldn't formulate any answers whatsoever.

I was completely exhausted all the time, and I usually left home at least slightly still drunk in the morning to go to work or class. The smell of booze radiated from my pores, and I always dressed like I was either getting ready to go out on the town for the night or like I'd just rolled out of bed. I perpetually got ready to go out and simultaneously passed out in this endless cycle of destruction. I lived in this constant haze that allowed me to tune out everything around me and everything within my own head. I moved through my days with my eyes closed, completing my responsibilities at school in a robotic fashion. Sometimes in a rare moment of clarity, I'd wonder what the fuck I was doing.

Moving away from home didn't provide the positive life change I'd anticipated. I thought moving away from my Charleston, which had constant reminders of being raped and an endless supply of drugs and drinking buddies, would give me the distance I needed to clean up my life. Instead, I started drinking even more. I drank alone more often. I liked drinking alone anyway because I could drink to the point of passing out without having to worry about getting home or embarrassing myself or vomiting in public or spending a ton of money.

On my way home from work, I'd buy two unrefrigerated bottles of chardonnay from the Quality Dairy gas station across from my apartment. I thought if I could wait for the wine to chill before drinking it, I was still in control of my drinking problem. So I put the bottles in my fridge and suited up in my running gear. I ran around the maze of parking lots and curved roads that flowed through my apartment complex until I'd been running long enough that my wine chilled and I could go home to drink straight out of the bottle in the shower.

I also used cocaine and other stimulants to "help me study," and when I found myself crushing up and snorting Adderall in the bathroom stall of a pie shop during a study session with a classmate, I realized my life wasn't changing course at all. I could run away from home, but I couldn't run away from myself. I hated myself, and I hated that I still constantly thought about being raped. So many years had passed, why couldn't I just get over it? I couldn't spend one second alone with myself, and I continued my usual routine of going out almost every night. I knew I jeopardized my future, but I couldn't envision my future at all—I didn't think there was any way I'd be alive for even a few more days, so all I had to do was make it through each day, and drinking was the only way I knew how to survive. But drinking wasn't even remotely fun anymore. I used to be able to control my public drunkenness until I made it home alone where I could drink as much as I wanted, but now I'd get so drunk that I'd fall down in the street, embarrassing myself in front of my new friends and classmates.

One of the first social activities I attended with the other students in my program was a Halloween party. Representing my Illinois homeland, I dressed up as "Baberham Lincoln" with a skirt and heels and a beard and top hat. By the time I got to the party, I'd already drank at least a pint of whiskey and stumbled around extremely drunk. I dropped a whole bowl of Jell-O on the kitchen floor of the host's home shortly after my arrival, so I decided that I needed to avoid talking to anyone if I wanted to keep any shred of dignity in front of my new cohort. I left that party with a couple friends to go to another party that I don't remember.

The next day, my friends told me that I was so drunk at the second party that I couldn't even stand, and I'd passed out while dancing with a guy (I can't even imagine what that would look like). I realized that I'd lost my wallet, so I got the address of the party, and after initially walking into the wrong apartment, I recovered my wallet. The guy who lived in the apartment didn't recognize me without my beard, but when I reminded him that I was "Baberham Lincoln" the night before, he remembered me as the girl who was really drunk. I wondered whether the world would remember me as "the girl who was really drunk" after I died, and I contemplated whether I wanted that to be my legacy. I envisioned the epitaph on my tombstone:

Beloved friend and daughter
Always imbibing, and not of water
Here lies Apryl, everyday drunk
Six feet underground, she has now sunk

When I just couldn't figure out why I lived the way I did, I experienced another twist of Internet fate when I did a search for PTSD, post-traumatic stress disorder. Like my "what is rape?" search six years earlier, I didn't immediately realize the profound impact this search would have on my life. I read over the symptoms and causes of PTSD for hours, and my learn-everything-about-the-brain-in-an-insanely-short-amount-of-time neuroscience classes came in useful for my understanding of what I read—but my own life provided me with the most in-depth comprehension of what PTSD actually was. It surprised me to learn that a person could get PTSD from anything other than military combat, and when I read that rape commonly led to the development of PTSD, I was floored.

With my own life in mind, I read all of the PTSD symptoms again and realized that I'd experienced almost every single one of the twenty symptoms listed, including persistent intrusive memories of the traumatic event, nightmares, emotional numbing, avoiding reminders of the trauma, increased startle, and hypervigilance. I couldn't believe I'd been suffering from PTSD for the past eight years and was completely oblivious to it. I felt comforted by the fact that all of my problems could be explained by a four-letter acronym and that maybe I wasn't just a crazy mess. As with my Internet search for rape, the naming of this thing initiated a profound healing process for me.

But I became completely dejected when I learned that PTSD had no effective treatment, that suicide rates among PTSD patients were among the highest of any demographic group, and that PTSD symptoms can persist and continue to worsen over the course of a lifetime. I was in the middle of a dangerous game of tug-of-war between suffering and death.

With my background in neuroscience, I had all the resources I needed to learn about PTSD, and like a sponge, I soaked up all the information I could get. But when I became more aware of what having PTSD meant, I felt like I'd been diagnosed with some terminal illness that I'd have to fight every day for the rest of my life until it finally killed me. The feeling that something horrible would happen any minute—like I held a live grenade—was PTSD. My jumps and screams at the phone ringing, the door knocking, the postman—that was PTSD. My heart pounding up into my neck for hours at a time, waking every twenty minutes at night to check my surroundings—that was PTSD. What's happening? Where am I? What day is it? What time is it? I was hyper-alert, hyper-aware, on guard, jolted, terrified, and absolutely exhausted.

A few weeks later, I went to the annual Society for Neuroscience Conference in Washington, D.C. This was a huge conference with over 30,000 attendees from around the world who meet to exchange the latest research findings related to the brain. The conference provided a great educational and networking opportunity to get my feet wet in the neuroscience community, and I hoped I could find out more about research on PTSD. The conference started three days before my monthly payday, so I was low on money. I made plenty of money to live on, but I still spent $400-600 a month on alcohol. So by the last week of the month, I'd usually only have a few cents left in my checking account and no food in my refrigerator.

Before the conference, I rationed out what little money I had left so I'd spend as little as possible on food without starving to death, and the rest of the money would go toward alcohol. The other students went out to dinner or to the bars at night, but I knew I couldn't afford to buy drinks at a bar, so I bought the cheapest whiskey I could find at a gas station and brought a flask with me when we went out in the evenings. But flasks don't hold nearly as much liquor as I do, and being out with my friends without being able to drink as much as I wanted tortured me. I didn't care about exploring the city or spending time with my friends, I just wanted to drink. The conference had lectures, poster presentations, and symposia all day long, but I took breaks in the middle of the day to go back to the hotel to drink my cheap gas station whiskey.

One of the times during the conference that I walked to the gas station to get whiskey, a man stood in front of me to buy the cheapest gin in the store. He looked like he'd never showered in his life, he'd lost teeth, his clothes were torn and dirty, and he counted out pennies and nickels and dimes to pay for the $3.99 pint of gin. He was a few cents short and scrambled around looking for change. I felt so saddened for this man who probably had no home and had to spend what little money he could scrounge up on liquor. I wondered if he used to have a normal life and how this man ended up so hopelessly despondent. I wondered how much more it would take for me to be in his condition. I knew the desperation and anxiety that he must've felt, and I wanted to help him, but I didn't have any cash either. I'd completely run out of money by that point, and I'd maxed out my credit card months ago, so I decided to use my debit card one time to buy some whiskey, accepting the $40 overdraft fee.

The man finally got his gin, and when he turned around, I saw the familiar relief on his face that comes when an alcoholic knows he has enough liquor to make it through one more day. But behind the relief, lived so much pain in his eyes, and I felt lucky to not be standing in this man's tattered shoes. Although by overdrawing my checking account to buy liquor, I essentially paid $50 for an $8.99 fifth of whiskey, which I knew was still pretty desperate. I wondered if that man saw the same pain in my eyes, dressed in my business clothes and using my shiny debit card to buy a fifth of Kentucky Gentlemen Bourbon at eleven o'clock on a Monday morning.

I wondered why I wasted my time and money at this neuroscience conference if all I could do was get drunk. I told myself I needed to take my career more seriously, but I knew I had more pressing issues than just furthering my education. I didn't think I'd survive through the end of that year, and part of me felt okay with that notion.

I finished my first semester of my PhD program, and didn't plan on going back for my second semester. I knew I couldn't keep up with school anymore, and I didn't think I would even survive much longer anyway. But somehow, I managed to get a good GPA that semester, and in my lab rotation evaluation, my supervisor praised my success.

"Apryl's substantive contribution was such that when we publish this second study on which she worked, she will be included as co-author. She worked diligently, displaying a high level of skill and curiosity."

I wondered who the fuck she was talking about—certainly that wasn't me. And how the hell did I get a GPA of 3.78 that semester? I felt like I barely survived. I'd have been much more comfortable with a failing GPA and an evaluation letter that recognized I was a serious mess and needed help. But this didn't make sense to me. My life didn't make sense to me.

I went home for Christmas, and stayed at my mom's house for the first time since I'd moved out in high school eight years earlier. My mom and Jim told me that I was the most miserable person they'd ever seen and that my anxiety in the mornings made it impossible for them to be around me until I had some alcohol in my system. Now that made sense to me.

The day before New Year's Eve, I left my mom's home and went to visit a friend in Chicago who hosted a party. It was pretty late by the time I got to the party, and I needed to catch up with everyone else's lack of sobriety. I mentioned how tired I felt, and my friend took me into her room and showed me the largest pile of cocaine I'd ever seen. I had an endless supply of coke for the rest of the night, and didn't deny myself a line anytime I felt like I needed one. I ended up having sex in the entryway with some guy at the party, and three hours later, once it was breakfast time, I left to meet some other friends who'd started drinking for New Year's Eve. I hated my life, but I didn't know what else to do. If I didn't keep drinking and partying and socializing, what else would I do? Sleep? Relax? Not possible.

I hardly remember the rest of that day, but I do remember that, when it was time for everyone to ring in the New Year, I was having sex with a guy who kept biting me. Every time he bit me on the neck or lips, I woke up from my drunken haze and realized I was in the middle of having sex. I didn't remember how I ended up in his bedroom, but sleeping with two different guys in the same day marked a new all-time low for me—I still believed that "promiscuous" girls were sluts, that women shouldn't have casual sex. But maybe that was my way of justifying why I hated sex without acknowledging the effect rape had on me or acknowledging my attraction to women. I couldn't imagine how my life could get any worse—2012 wasn't off to a good start.

A week later, I started the second semester of my PhD program. I hadn't planned on going back to school, but something in me kept going on with my life. And I didn't know what else to do. I only had one class to take that semester, Systems Neuroscience, and I decided to do my second lab rotation on the main campus in Lansing, so I didn't have that hour-long commute to Grand Rapids anymore.

On January 18, 2012—just one week after the semester started—I went to my first in a series of "Responsible Conduct of Research" workshops that I was required to complete before receiving my PhD. I didn't have class that day, so I worked in my new lab, and after I went home for "lunch," which consisted of two beers, I brought a Subway cup full of whiskey back to work with me. The Subway cup also doubled as a decoy to make people think I'd actually eaten lunch. I drank and worked until my workshop that evening, but I'd run out of whiskey, so I stopped at a liquor store on the corner of campus to get a pint of Jim Beam with which to re-fill my Subway cup.

I sat in a small, wobbly desk in the overcrowded seminar kiva and wondered if any of the other three hundred students attending were also drinking. I felt so alone and invisible surrounded by my fellow graduate students who had no idea how tortured I was, and the irony of being drunk at this workshop entitled "Misconduct in Research and Creative Activities" was completely lost on me. I never considered drinking in the lab to be "misconduct" of any kind—that was just my life. And nowhere in the ninety-four slide presentation did anybody discuss the issues I faced. They talked about plagiarism, manipulating data, and breaching confidentiality, things I didn't worry about, as I'd already been trained as a diligent and honest scientist in my time at EIU.

After the workshop, I decided I was too drunk to drive home, so I drove to the bar to sober up (I had terrible rationalization skills when I drank). I thought drinking a couple beers would help me come down from the whiskey buzz more gently. I occupied myself during my first beer by sending my friends a text message summoning them to get an after-work drink with me. During my second beer, I called my mom so I didn't have to look so pitiful sitting at the bar alone staring off into space. I told her I waited for a couple friends to meet me for a drink, but I knew no one would come. During my third beer, I decided to call my father who I hadn't spoken to in a month, but he didn't answer the phone. So there I was, alone and drunk at the bar on a Wednesday night—what a worthless, unwanted, miserable existence I was. I even felt proud of myself for not eating that day, but now there was nobody around to enjoy my accomplishment with me. So I decided I might as well get a frozen pizza.

I hopped in my car and headed toward the closest Meijer to my apartment, about a fifteen-minute drive. While I didn't care if I got another DUI or killed myself in a car accident—I would've even welcomed that at this point—I felt horrible for driving around drunk, endangering other people's lives so I could get my self-pity pizza. This made me feel like even more of a worthless asshole who didn't deserve to live. I especially didn't deserve my friends and

family who'd put up with me all these years, or the free opportunity
to work on my PhD. What I did deserve, however, was this fucking
pizza and I would eat the shit out of it.

I spent what felt like an eternity in the frozen pizza aisle at
Meijer, carefully examining the nutrition labels on all the thin crust
veggie pizzas, trying to find the one that would cause the least
amount of damage to my diminishing self-worth. When I couldn't
find a satisfactory pizza, I decided I'd go home and go to bed
without eating. On my way home, however, I remembered there was
a Kroger about ten miles away. Maybe Kroger had some healthier
pizzas. It took me about thirty minutes to get to Kroger because I
kept getting lost, but as soon as I walked in, I grabbed a package of
pink, heart-shaped marshmallow Peeps. I didn't even like Peeps. I
needed to get this pizza and get the fuck out of there before I
grabbed any more ridiculous food items. Blankly staring at the
frozen pizzas, I couldn't concentrate on the nutrition labels because I
had to pee so badly. I hobbled around the store with my Peeps,
looking for the restroom, and made it to the toilet with only a
minimal amount of urine on my jeans. I returned to the pizza aisle
and began my routine of trying to find the lowest calorie frozen
pizza, but decided that was too much work. Maybe if I didn't buy
the Peeps, I could allow myself to get whatever kind of pizza I
wanted. I put down the Peeps, grabbed some kind of supreme pizza,
and got out of the store as quickly as possible.

I managed to not pass out while waiting for the pizza to cook,
which often happened. When I fell asleep while cooking a pizza, I
always felt relieved when I woke up that my apartment building
hadn't caught on fire—and even more relieved that I hadn't undone
all my hard work by eating that stupid pizza. But I ate this entire
pizza and didn't feel satisfied at all. I decided that since I'd probably
either kill myself or ruin my life one way or another soon, I might as
well have another pizza delivered to me. Hell, since I acted
responsibly this time and didn't get in my car, I let myself have some
breadsticks, too. I did pass out waiting for this pizza to come, and
when I awoke to the delivery guy knocking on my door, I wished I'd
slept through it.

I started eating and finally felt satisfied when only two pieces of pizza and four breadsticks remained. I put the leftovers in the fridge and initially felt impressed with myself for not eating all of the food. But getting ready for bed, I realized what I'd done. I ingested more food in one hour than I usually ate in a week, and I felt the shame and guilt and hatred for myself settle on my stomach with every passing second. I had to get this out of me—I had to regain control of my body.

I curled myself around the toilet shoving my fingers down my throat, then my toothbrush when that didn't work. How could I possibly not vomit after all that poison I put in my body? I eventually gave up, feeling like even more of a failure for not being able to get rid of the food I'd just eaten than I did for eating it in the first place.

When I woke the next day, I decided something needed to happen. I'd lived in hell for so many years, and it only kept getting worse. I was tired of hating and destroying myself and trying so hard to make everyone around me think I was perfectly normal and happy. I saw only two options: either kill myself or try to get healthy.

Since I didn't understand how I became this way in the first place or how to go about getting help, death seemed like the best option. I didn't think anybody could help me. I wasn't even underweight, so nobody would believe me if I told them I needed help with an eating disorder. That thought made me feel even more hopeless—all these years of hard work trying to obsessively control my weight and I didn't have anything to show for it. I thought nobody would believe me if told them I needed help with substance abuse because outwardly, I had my life together. And there didn't appear to be anything that could be done about PTSD. I was a fucking mess.

And when I looked back on my twenty-five-year-old life, it was like only two days had passed—the day surrounding Jared's rape, and the day surrounding Jason's rape. And that was it. I had no concrete feelings of accomplishment or of love, although I knew they were in there somewhere. It was just two long, horrible days that stretched out over twenty-five years.

Yet when, in a dark December,
The frosty woods are grey,
By whiles we shall still remember
What years steal ne'er away, -
This golden hour undying
When the hound and the horn are crying,
And the echoes loud replying
At the dawning of the day.

–Cicely Fox Smith "At the Dawning of the Day"

THE DAWNING OF THE DAY

THE REVELATION

I THOUGHT IF I could wait out the pain, it would eventually go away. Time heals all wounds, right? Wrong. Time marched on—sometimes painfully slowly, sometimes frighteningly fast—and dug its sharp serpentine hands into my festering wounds with each oscillation of the pendulum. After eight years of each day being worse than the day before, I finally realized that my life wouldn't get any better. I thought about my father who'd been involved in a fatal car accident over thirty years prior, and he still had daily nightmares and flashbacks and panic attacks. I realized that he had PTSD, and felt a connection with him that I never had before.

I understood why, instead of bedtime stories, my dad told me about the car accident that spared only him, detailing the screaming and the blood and the limp children's bodies. I understood why my dad never drove again after that accident, he never slept soundly, his body fell apart, and he became a recluse, completely shut off from the world outside his living room. I didn't want to live that like for the rest of my life, but my life looked more and more like my father's life each day.

In my personal research, I learned that PTSD isn't only something that veterans experience after a war. Several studies showed that while most people experienced at least one traumatic event in their lifetime, PTSD develops in seven percent of the general population, which includes twice as many women than men—as many as one-in-ten women. While any traumatic event can lead to PTSD, experiences involving rape and military combat have the highest risk, and PTSD symptoms can persist in a person for a lifetime without intervention. These symptoms include re-experiencing the traumatic event, avoiding reminders of the event, negative alterations in cognition and mood, and hyperarousal. Research hadn't been able to explain why some people easily recover from trauma while others can't, but what was for certain was that people who develop PTSD incur very real damage to areas of the brain involved in memory, mood regulation, and fear. I knew my brain was damaged.

I decided to go home for the weekend to see my friends and family for what I thought would either be my farewell visit on my journey to death, or what I hoped would be the support I needed to give me the will to live. Since I thought this might be one of my last times around other people, I decided to explore my attraction to women. I thought it might be the last chance I got to figure out one more piece of the puzzle of what was wrong with me. For the first time in my life, I opened my mind to what it would be like to be with a woman. Before I left on my journey home, I watched music videos of my favorite female singers—Jenny Lewis, Emily Haines, Neko Case, Regina Spektor, Karen O, Gillian Welch—and acknowledged an additional layer of my love for them. I was attracted to them. I didn't want to be like them, like I thought I had, I wanted to be *with* them.

When I got back to Illinois, I attended a bachelorette party with my old college friends. At the bar, I made note of my attraction to women but not men, and at the end of the night when we all found sleeping places on the furniture and floor of my friend's apartment, I shared a sleeping bag with one of my favorite girlfriends. As we fell asleep, I curled up a little closer to her and wished I could full-on spoon her. I'd never experienced a feeling like this before—I'd spooned plenty with Lance, but I'd never felt this kind of yearning and comfort and, frankly, arousal. It just felt so natural. But upon waking—and sobering up—the next morning, I knew I'd never have that kind of connection with a woman again. It was too late, I was too far gone, too sad and angry about all the time I'd already wasted on men and on alcohol.

So after a debaucherous weekend of partying with my friends, I met my mom and Jim for a booze-filled Sunday brunch, after which my mom waved me off as I drove back to Michigan drunk. That my mother let me embark on a six-hour drive after watching me drink two Bloody Marys, a martini, and a shot of whiskey within an hour-and-a-half infuriated me, but I realized that nobody but myself could help me. I'd been waiting to hit some unidentified rock-bottom that I thought would suddenly alert everyone to the fact that I needed help, but I'd already busted through so many rock-bottoms on my downward spiral and another one always waited for me.

I'd like to say that I had this moment of revelation where I gathered an enormous amount of inner strength and decided once-and-for-all that I'd get my life together and get sober, but instead, I decided once-and-for-all that I'd finally give up. I knew I would die if I kept up with my current lifestyle, but I also knew that I couldn't live without alcohol, so I just gave up. If I couldn't tolerate being in my own skin without drinking, then my life wasn't worth living. I made it back to Michigan, and instead of stopping at the liquor store on my way home, I gave up on drinking, and I gave up on living.

Having not had anything to drink since noon that Sunday, the alcohol withdrawals were in full-swing when I woke up Monday morning. I didn't realize what'd happened to me, but I'd never felt so physically or emotionally agitated. I always had a generally placid demeanor, but I turned into a short-tempered monster overnight. Another creature clawed its way out of me through every pore on my skin. The blood pulsed through my veins, and it felt like poison. Every cell in my body vibrated. What I'd done that day and what I was supposed to do confused me. Time stopped. I don't know if I slept that night or not, but the next three days were a blur. I aimlessly wandered around campus and wondered what to do and where to go. I couldn't tell if anything that happened was actually real or if I dreamed it. I thought I would die any minute, but then again, I couldn't be sure that I hadn't already died. I was nauseous and sweating and afraid—and completely alone.

Alcohol withdrawals never occurred to me. I thought alcohol withdrawals involved "the shakes" and were a physical craving for alcohol that probably felt like needing a cigarette really badly. The five days following my last drink at brunch that Sunday were some of the most confusing, disorienting, emotionally disturbing days of my life. I felt physically tortured, but I could handle that. It was the emotional turmoil that distressed me so much about the alcohol withdrawals. I fell backward into a black hole, and nothing could possibly rescue me, not even alcohol. Eight years of desperately trying to not feel any pain left me absolutely, completely numb all the time, but now I felt every possible emotion all at once in a terrifying way.

When I finally felt like I wouldn't survive another second, I stumbled into the counseling center on campus as soon as they opened that morning, and all I could say was, "I need help." I spent the next thirty minutes in a cubicle filling out computerized surveys about how I felt, but I could hardly focus on the screen that whooshed back and forth in front of my face. The only part of the survey I remember was the question about my sexual orientation in which I checked the box next to "questioning."

The receptionist finally called me from the empty waiting room to see a counselor, to whom I told everything. I told her I'd been raped twice. I told her I dreaded eating because I didn't want to gain weight. I told her I drank and used drugs all the time. I told her I thought I might be a lesbian and I didn't know what to do about it. I told her about my suicide attempts and that the last few days I thought I'd die any minute because I stopped drinking. For the first time in my entire life, I spilled my guts to something other than a toilet. When I finally stopped talking, she looked at me and I could tell she didn't know what to say. She told me I should go to the hospital and gave me a four-page list of phone numbers of local agencies I could call in the meantime. She made sure I wasn't suicidal, not by asking me how I felt, but more by coercing me into saying I wouldn't kill myself—"now, you're not going to hurt yourself, right?" in a patronizing tone that reminded me of a mother dropping her kid off at the babysitter. She told me they'd review my case the following week, and I left disheartened.

I called one of the organizations on the list, but they didn't get back to me for several days. I didn't think anybody would ever help me. But I made one last-ditch effort for help: I went to the university health center and asked for a physical exam. I didn't expect much out of a physical exam, but I did want to know what kind of state my body was in since I felt like I was dying. The doctor, concerned, told me that there was a 35% chance I could've died from alcohol withdrawals. I guess I should've gone to the hospital. She warned me that if I ever started drinking and suddenly stopped again, the withdrawals would be even worse and more dangerous because of a process called kindling.

"So we need to get you healthy. Let's run some tests and get some appointments set up for you. You'll be okay."

Her statement rattled me. I didn't expect to hear this hopeful and helpful outlook. I thought she'd tell me to think long and hard about the direction my life headed before she sent me away. I didn't plan to also tell the doctor about being raped twice, developing an extensive eating disorder, increasing use of cocaine and heroin, getting arrested, losing my driver's license, and realizing that I'm probably gay—everything I was ashamed of—but it poured out of me. Telling the counselor all those things the day before made it so much easier to speak it out loud again.

"Wow, you have fortitude," the doctor said as she shook her tilted head a little bit and smiled.

Fortitude! That was all it took for someone to say to me, and I had the motivation to get my shit together. She didn't say, "Wow, you really didn't handle being raped very well," and she didn't say, "Wow, you really should stop telling people about all this, it's embarrassing," and she didn't say, "Wow, you've been acting very selfishly." These are things people have actually said to me, but this doctor didn't tell me I was weak or fucked up or selfish or that I'd wasted all of my potential, she told me I was strong. She told me she was glad I'd survived long enough to get help and that I'd be okay.

Now I knew I could never go back to drinking, so I needed to find somebody to help me live my life sober. The doctor called upstairs to set up a meeting with a substance abuse counselor. She didn't want me to leave the building until I at least met this person, and within the first five minutes of our meeting, I felt hope. Here was someone who'd been through a lot of what I'd been through and made it out okay on the other side. I still didn't know what the hell I needed to do to get better, but I at least knew that it was possible. She noticed that I was "edgy and shaky" as I squirmed around in the leather armchair in her office, but she told me it would get easier. I scheduled another appointment with her for the following week.

The next day, I remembered that I still went to school. *Oh yeah, I'm getting my Ph.D. in neuroscience*. It was the end of the third week of the semester, and when I looked at my syllabus, I saw that I had an exam at 8AM the next morning. I couldn't remember if I'd even been to that class more than once, so I looked through the lecture slides that night and still disoriented from withdrawals but a little more stable, I went to take the exam and got the highest grade in the class. Maybe my brain wasn't totally broken.

The next week, I went to my first AA meeting and saw a counselor through MSU's employee assistance program. I saw a psychiatrist who officially diagnosed me with PTSD, and the laundry list of other diagnoses on my medical record shocked me—generalized anxiety disorder, alcohol dependency, substance abuse (multiple), eating disorder (NOS), amenorrhea (secondary), possible exposure to sexually transmitted disease, suicide history, high blood pressure, hyperlipidemia, and I thought *Wow, I'm a mess*. But, to my surprise, being gay wasn't on the list of things that were wrong with me.

My doctor and substance abuse counselor continued to check in with me for many months. This is exactly how the healthcare system should work, and I got so lucky to have gotten in touch with all the right people. I'd found myself in front of so many healthcare professionals who didn't listen to me, who thought I exaggerated my problems for attention, who thought I just wanted drugs, who thought I was just going through a phase, or who thought I looked completely healthy, and with every visit like that, I left a little piece of my hope and self-respect behind me in the waiting room. But this time, my doctor saved my life because she took my issues seriously, she believed that I could get help, and she made me feel that I was worth helping.

I didn't think talking to anybody would make any difference in my behavior, and I knew that talking about it wouldn't undo anything that'd already been done. I didn't think I needed somebody to tell me what was wrong with me—I thought I knew what was wrong with me, and I thought it was a permanent injury that I just had to endure. But it turned out that what I needed was to share my story with someone who could listen and empathize. It wasn't in a moment of absolute strength that I finally started talking—it was in a moment of absolute brokenness. It was the strength of whom I told that carried me.

AWAKENING

AFTER GETTING THROUGH the alcohol withdrawals, I felt like I'd survived a hurricane, and realized that there was a whole world outside I'd never noticed. When I thought about the last thing I remembered before I stopped drinking—my time at home sleeping next to my friend—my first revelation was, oh my God, I'm a lesbian.

I'd been aware of my attraction to women since I was about eleven-years-old, but when I was raped in high school, I got completely lost and had no chance to explore my sexuality in a healthy way. Over the years, I slowly began to realize that an intimate relationship with a man, physically or emotionally, didn't feel natural to me. I thought about all of the close relationships I'd ever had in my life, all of the people to whom I'd ever been physically attracted, with whom I wanted to be intimate, for whom I yearned, for whom I'd do anything—and they were all women. I could name every person I'd ever had a crush on since fifth grade— and they were all women. I became cognizant of the people I noticed in a bar or at the gym or walking down the street—and they were all women. I thought about with whom I wanted to live, build a life, raise children, cook dinner, argue, watch movies, grocery shop, vacation, miss—and it was a woman. Oh, my God, I'm a lesbian.

When I realized I'd either have to spend my life alone or accept my sexuality, I wondered why I'd been so against being gay in the first place. When so much of my life had been completely broken, I had this one part of myself that survived the storm because it'd been buried underground from the beginning, and I realized there was nothing wrong with me—whom I love is a fundamental part of who I am. And who I am is someone who's going to be okay.

Suddenly, my whole future opened up. I became hopeful that I might be happy someday, that I wouldn't be alone forever. Thereafter, when I found myself attracted to a woman, I wouldn't hate myself and tell myself there was something wrong with me and try to force myself to be attracted to some guy. Instead, I felt so elated because I finally let myself feel what I naturally felt.

I developed a huge crush on the phlebotomist who drew my blood and offered me apple juice in my first year of recovery while my doctor kept an eye on my liver enzymes and cholesterol. I did my hair and put on my favorite shirt, and if she wasn't in the office when I went to get my monthly blood samples taken, I waited to come back on a day she worked. After the third time of seeing her, I finally worked up enough courage to actually speak to her. My heart fluttered and so did my stomach. I finally grasped a sense of my true self that I'd lost so many years ago—I started to love myself.

When I no longer felt ashamed of my inner-self, I suddenly became comfortable with my natural outward appearance. Hiding behind my straightened hair, blackened eyes, and penciled-in eyebrows, I used to sleep with my makeup on if there was a chance anyone would see me in the morning before I had time to get ready. If I ever stayed with friends or shared a hotel room with somebody, I slept in my makeup and woke up several hours before everyone else so I could shower and put on a fresh face before anyone else saw me. Sometimes I slept with my makeup on because I didn't want to see myself without it. Whenever I saw myself in the mirror au naturale, I didn't recognize the reflection. I wondered who that person was staring at me in my bathroom.

But after I accepted my lesbian-self, the face I hid behind slowly began to fall away. I stopped wearing twenty pounds of makeup, I stopped straightening my hair, and I'd even go to the store or work without any makeup on whatsoever if I didn't feel the need to get ready that day.

I'd finally accepted my natural sexual orientation, and I went through this process alone. I initially planned to wait to come out until I had a girlfriend. I thought it would be much easier to bring up the topic once I started dating someone, rather than say, "Hey everyone, I'm a lesbian!" completely out of the blue. Hey everyone, you've known me for years, but that was all a lie! I also worried that people wouldn't believe me or would think I was just going through some phase, especially because I didn't look gay at all. In a culture that assumed everybody's heterosexuality, not looking like a "typical lesbian" presented challenges in not only attracting other women but also keeping men from pursuing me.

I felt like I needed some external validation of who I was, so since I was sans girlfriend, I thought about chopping all my hair off and wearing cargo shorts and t-shirts to say hey everyone, I'm a lesbian! but that just wasn't me, so I didn't know what to do. I decided to slowly start telling people I was gay. I didn't want to live one more second of my life knowing that everybody saw some version of me that was a lie.

First, I told Elizabeth, who responded in such an accepting and loving manner. She told me she was so happy for me, and I thought *This isn't so hard at all*! A few days later, I called my mom, and told her I was gay.

"I've been expecting that," she said with the same tone she used when she responded to my DUI call from the police station.

My mom told me that she didn't know if being gay was a sin or not, but she didn't think God would send me to hell for it. What? I didn't ask my mom's theological opinion on homosexuality. My mom told me that she'd love me unconditionally anyway, which I appreciated, but I still thought she believed something was wrong with me.

I turned to books to learn more about myself. I stayed home for two weeks and read memoir after memoir about rape, addiction, lesbians, eating disorders, and alcoholism. The first book I read was *Lucky* by Alice Sebold, and the opening line changed my life.

"In the tunnel where I was raped..."

For some reason, I didn't expect to see that R-word so soon and written with such conviction. It took me so many years to figure out that I was raped, even longer to speak about it, and I couldn't imagine ever sitting at my computer and typing "I was raped." Part of me still hoped maybe that's not what'd happened to me, but after I read *Lucky*, I knew I was raped and that I didn't have to be ashamed of it. Addressed to Ms. Alice Sebold, I sent the first and only "fan letter" I'd ever written.

"Your bold and honest language gave me the courage to find my voice and tell my story." I confessed to Ms. Sebold that it was the language in her book, the words, that helped me find my own words, without which, all I had were images and feelings that I couldn't describe.

Oranges Are Not the Only Fruit by Jeanette Winterson and *Unbearable Lightness* by Portia de Rossi helped me find my voice as a lesbian. Toward the end of *Unbearable Lightness*, I felt an eerie sense of déjà vu, like I'd heard this story before, and it all came back to me.

I stood in my mom's living room on November 2, 2010, a year-and-a-half earlier, when the TV caught me. Oprah interviewed Portia de Rossi about her book, recovery from her eating disorder, about being gay, and it completely captivated me. I stood there for the whole hour of the show, inches away from the TV screen, and then I went to the EIU library to check out the book.

I read it sometime in the middle of my second year in my master's program, and saw vague flashes of memories of laying on my couch in my apartment in Charleston reading *Unbearable Lightness* while pouring wine down my throat. The book must've shaken me to the core of my truths about my own eating disorder and attraction to women that I completely blocked the whole thing out of my memory.

I was nearly three-hundred pages into the book this time before I realized I'd read this book before. I wondered how many other books I'd read that I didn't remember, how many other moments of healing I'd missed. I guess I wasn't ready to face myself until now.

SILENCE SHATTERED

MY FIRST APPOINTMENT with my therapist, Lois, was on February 21, 2012. I'd been seeing a counselor through MSU's employee assistance program, but I used up my limit of sessions with her, so she recommended this off-campus therapist to me. I knew my health insurance covered twenty-five visits per year, which I thought was more than enough for me. I couldn't imagine talking to the same person twenty-five times about a couple of bad experiences I'd had.

As soon as I walked into Lois' office, a cozy den attached to her home, I felt at peace. Lois reminded me of Aunt Meg from the movie *Twister* with her long gray hair, youthful face, and flowy, old-hippie kind of style. She was kind and smart and so wise. Until I met Lois, nobody had ever asked me how anything I'd been through made me feel. When faced head-on with having to answer how I felt about being raped, I realized that I'd never consciously thought about it. I didn't know that I felt so ashamed and guilty and blamed myself for everything that'd happened to me. From the moment I was first raped, I thought nobody would ever love or respect me again. I thought I was broken beyond repair.

When Lois asked how being drunk every day made me feel, my surprising answer was nothing. Being drunk made me feel nothing and that's why I drank. That little light bulb floating above me finally knocked me upside the head—of course! I didn't drink and use drugs because I wanted to have fun or forget what had happened to me—I knew I'd never forget that. I just couldn't tolerate the way I felt about myself and how I thought everyone else also felt about me. Everything I did, I did to avoid the pain of being raped — to avoid feeling the pain from the past and to avoid ever re-experiencing that pain again. While self-medication didn't excuse my destructive, careless, illegal, and dangerous behavior, it did explain it.

Why I lived so recklessly had always confused me, and I felt so guilty, especially now, about putting other people's lives in danger, but I didn't know how else to tolerate the constant intensity within myself. I needed help with this overarching shame and guilt and pain, not simply some kind of treatment for an eating disorder or a drug addiction or alcoholism. Getting sober and eating healthy wouldn't end the constant fear, intrusive memories, and negative beliefs I had about myself. I was in complete hell, tortured every day. My life was a war zone.

I thought that getting raped shouldn't have been that big of a deal for me. People have sex all the time, why should a couple bad experiences ruin my life? But Lois taught me that rape isn't about having "bad sex." Rape isn't sex. Rape is the loss of control over one's own life and body. The loss of free will. The loss of integrity. The loss of dignity. A physical and psychological violation of one's very existence. When something that should've been so innately mine and mine alone became public domain for anyone to use however they pleased, it did devastate my life. My life was no longer my own. I had no respect for my body, and wanted to stay as far away from my mind as possible.

I never felt like I could talk to anybody about what'd happened to me. I didn't want to make anybody feel uncomfortable or awkward or embarrassed, and I didn't think anybody would understand anyway. But I underestimated the power of vocalizing my pain to another human being, and after meeting Lois, I believed that giving a voice to rape victims was critical to ending the torment and suffering people endured every day. I knew the subject of rape made people uncomfortable—as it should—but I knew the more openly rape was discussed, the more people would understand the trauma and burden rape could etch into a person's soul. The more people who comprehended the gravity of this horrific act, the more comfortable rape victims would feel about talking to someone. I learned that it was crucial to talk to someone. Some people may be too uncomfortable to listen, but I found people who could help. Rape wasn't something that I could "just get over." It didn't just go away.

A NEW CHAPTER

WHILE I RECOGNIZED the importance of vocalizing my pain, after a handful of sessions with Lois, we both realized that talking about the things that'd happened to me wasn't actually helping me recover. Talking just overwhelmed me, and when I'd come to my next session and repeat everything I'd talked about two days ago, not remembering what I'd already told her, Lois knew that I dissociated during therapy—much like I'd done the first time I read *Unbearable Lightness*.

I learned that dissociation described a range of experiences involving a detachment of one's conscious awareness from their immediate surroundings. This could be a coping mechanism to tolerate extreme stress or trauma. In the case-studies I read of molestation, children often spoke of the "place" they went during the abuse or described a feeling like they were floating above their body—they were dissociating, a way for the brain to protect itself from feeling the pain of, and from being damaged by, its own reality. In my PTSD research, I learned that survivors of other trauma also experience dissociative states when confronted with reminders of their trauma, and these states often go unnoticed to the untrained eye.

So instead of talking, I tried writing. I wrote my first journal entry since I'd written my last blog almost exactly three years prior, and it started out much more honestly than my blogs ever were.

* * *

JOURNAL: MARCH 1, 2012—

"I'm angry. I'm angry that I have to deal with all this shit from the past and that I have to deal with not drinking. Other people don't have to struggle with making a daily conscious decision to avoid alcohol, they just don't drink if they don't feel like it and that pisses me off. I have to be cognizant of my thought processes and feelings at any given time or I may just find myself face down in a pool of vomit at the bar."

*   *   *

I went to therapy twice a week, so every few days I read to my therapist what I'd written since the last session. Yes, I paid Lois to sit there and listen to me read. But by consciously giving narrative context to what I saw and felt, those memories began to be stored differently in my brain—my nightmares became dreams, and those dreams weren't scary anymore. My memories became stories, and I knew those stories were no longer happening to me. I reprocessed the events of the past with a completely different perspective that didn't overwhelm me like it did when I talked, or even thought, about it. Writing gave me the words that gave me the strength to speak without having a complete breakdown.

After weeks of hiding my face behind what felt like the steel-coated protective sheets of paper that I read out loud to my therapist, I could finally speak to Lois face-to-face, and I realized that I no longer blamed myself for what'd happened, and the guilt and shame for how I reacted lessened. I realized that I do deserve to be happy and healthy and that I could help other people too.

Once I started writing again, I didn't stop. I wrote for twelve, sometimes sixteen hours a day, and after a couple weeks, I realized that I wasn't just journaling, I was writing a book. I thought to myself, if I'd have read something like this eight years ago, it would've saved me a lot of suffering. And that's when I knew I had to finish, and eventually publish, this book. If I could prevent someone else from feeling so confused and alone, then everything I'd been through would've been worth it. Within a month I had a 40,000 word draft of this book written.

I still went to class, at least on the exam days, and worked in my lab a few days a week, but I prioritized my writing and therapy over everything. I talked to my mom on the phone nearly every day, as I had since moving out of her house eight years earlier. My mom was so angry and upset the first time I told her I'd been raped that I didn't discuss it with her again until now that I'd finally received professional help. When I told my mom I was in therapy, she couldn't understand what was so horrible about my life that I was such a mess—my mom kept asking me what she did wrong.

"I'm sorry I was such a bad parent that I couldn't keep you from getting raped. I'm sorry I couldn't keep you from destroying yourself when you were drinking and using drugs. I'm sorry I couldn't make you go to rehab," my mom said in a self-pitying tone.

I never blamed my mother for any of the things that'd happened to me—I only wanted her to hold me and tell me everything would be okay. I thought I needed my mother's support to get through my recovery, and since she clearly didn't understand what I was dealing with, I sent her the first draft of my book. When I told her that I needed her to understand what I'd gone through and asked her to read my words, my mom told me that she wasn't going to read it right away because she didn't want to get too depressed during the weekend. And I wrote another angry journal entry.

*   *   *

JOURNAL: APRIL 7, 2012—
"Yesterday, I sent my mom my memoir. I told her that I knew it would be hard to read, but I needed her to read it because I needed her to understand what I've been going through. She emailed back to tell me that she wasn't going to read it yet because she didn't want to get too depressed on her monthiversary. I can understand that, but what I really wanted to say was, "I'm sorry that the hell I've been in for the last eight-and-a-half years might make you too sad for one of your anniversaries that you celebrate every month." I just told her to spend some time processing what I wrote and to think about what she really wants to say to me before saying anything."

* * *

When she finally read what I'd written, my mom sent me an email telling me she knew I could "move positively forward in freedom, love, and forgiveness" and she apologized for the "wrongs" she'd done and hoped I forgave her. It was such a generic response. Freedom, love, and forgiveness? What the fuck was that supposed to mean? I wondered if she even knew to what "wrongs" she vaguely referred because I certainly didn't. I wanted my mom to understand how much pain I'd been in and for her to offer some affection and nurturing, but I realized I'd never receive that comfort or warmth from my mother. She also warned me not to ever let anyone else read what I'd written. I thought I was doing something good for society by sharing my story, so my mother's response confused me terribly and staying sober got more and more difficult.

* * *

JOURNAL: APRIL 15, 2012—
"As of today, I've been sober for 12 weeks. This isn't as exciting to me as I thought it would be. I'm in so much pain right now. I'm feeling all of these emotions that I've tried so hard not to feel the last eight-and-a-half years. It doesn't matter how long ago these things happened, it feels like it was just yesterday… if I was just raped yesterday, would I really feel like going into the lab today to count cells? No. I just want to be held. And to exercise. And to sleep. School is the least important thing to me right now. I just feel so alone."

* * *

Facing my past for the first time in my life brought up so many unexpected emotions that I didn't initially understand. Being sober didn't suddenly solve all of my problems, but it made me more and more aware of how the trauma I experienced affected every aspect of my life. While drugs and alcohol contributed to so many of the problems in my life, being sober for the first time actually made my life more difficult than it had ever been. For years, I somewhat effectively self-medicated my anxiety, nightmares, flashbacks, and hyperarousal, but all of those things emerged in full force as soon as I got sober.

With my new, sober skin came all of the emotions I hadn't felt in the past eight years. I felt like a burn victim who'd just had her bandages taken off, and all my healing tissue was exposed for the first time. Along with feeling hopeful for the first time in years, I felt a muddled combination of sadness, anger, nervousness, fear, anxiety, and some other unidentifiable emotions running through my veins. It was like everything that happened to me had just happened the day before—like the last eight years was just two long, horrible days. Without being able to drink, I felt like I'd just had my pacifier taken away, and I had no idea how to soothe myself. After more than eight years of not feeling any of these emotions, I was tempted to drink to return to the numbness with which I was so familiar.

THE DOG RETURNS

ON MY TWENTY-SIXTH birthday, I got another ear piercing, my birthstone emerald in the cartilage of my right ear. Sitting in the Lansing parlor, I realized that I'd eventually run out of room on my ears if I kept getting piercings on my birthday—a thought I'd never had before. It was my first adult birthday that I didn't think would be my last.

When I finished reading Stephen Chbosky's *The Perks of Being a Wallflower*, I thought, and journaled, about my own childhood.

* * *

JOURNAL: MAY 16, 2012—
"I spent nearly every day at the McCormick's house between the ages of 2 and 6, and still spent a lot of time there hanging out with Colin for many years after that. A few years ago, the McCormick's got divorced, and my mom found out Randy had been molesting his daughter since she was a little girl. My mom asked me if Randy had ever done anything to me, and he hadn't as far as I could remember. But I've always remembered feeling incredibly uncomfortable with Randy in the swimming pool, especially one occasion that I vividly remember."

* * *

More than twenty years later, I became aware of the fact that my babysitter's husband, Randy, molested me when I was a child. I'd always had these memories of Randy touching me, but could never acknowledge or understand what actually happened until I started talking about it in therapy. I was possibly too young to remember some of what happened to me, but I always felt incredibly uncomfortable around Randy, especially in the swimming pool. Randy rarely swam with us, but when he did, he touched me in a way that confused and terrified me. He held me in the water and repeatedly grabbed my crotch, and it seemed like it would never stop. As a toddler, I didn't know what'd happened, but I knew it was wrong. Randy wore teal swim trunks that I hated, and I always wanted to stay as far away from them as possible.

It was the McCormicks who suggested my mom and I go to Charleston Community Church, and I saw Randy twice a week at church for the eight years I went there. Even after I stopped going to that church, I saw Randy at the gym on campus because he worked at EIU, and I hid behind exercise equipment, stared at the floor, or simply left the gym when he was there. My heart pounded, and I immediately went on guard. I didn't understand why Randy, who was a father-figure to me, made me so scared and uncomfortable. One time, my own father actually told him, "Thanks for doing such a good job raising Apryl." I always thought that was a strange comment for my dad to have made, and it's even more disturbing to think about in retrospect.

I couldn't stop thinking about Randy, I paced around my apartment, weighed the pros and cons of going to the liquor store, as alcohol was the only thing I knew that could possibly save me. Then, I noticed a few empty glass airplane-sized bottles of bourbon in my kitchen that I'd saved. I got this bourbon gift pack at a white elephant gift exchange in my first semester at MSU, when I did my lab rotation in Grand Rapids. Another student there, David, brought that gift, and he happened to get the gift I brought, a chia pet. I, of course, drank that bourbon right away, but I saved the bottles because they were so damn cute.

But now, I was furious at Randy, and at alcohol. I'd been sober for over three months and I didn't want to ruin that streak. I had an impulse to throw those mini bourbon bottles at the wall, but the thought of that made me so sad, as I associated them with happy memories of David and my other friends and coworkers in Grand Rapids. So I thought, what if I filled them with paint and smashed them onto a canvas? And that's exactly what I did.

I felt a surge of empowerment and anticipation to create this piece of art, so I drove over to the craft store, bought two canvases and some paint, and smashed the hell out of the bottles with a hammer. It released all of my frustration and the end product was actually stunning. I immediately made another painting by smashing some old shot glasses, and I went to bed sober and calm that night.

But I had nightmares about Randy, and kept thinking about him the next day. I became fully aware of the fact that my babysitter's husband—my closest childhood friend's dad, an authority figure in whom I trusted—molested me and his own daughter and probably others. I couldn't get the memories and feelings of fear and confusion and shame out of my head. I didn't want to think about Randy molesting me or the other girls who were around at that time. I didn't want to think about what went through his head all those years that I stayed at his house as a child, at church as an adolescent, and when he saw me at the gym as an adult.

So after three months of sobriety—my longest sober stint thus far—I got drunk that night. It was a Friday, and I called up an old drinking buddy and asked if he wanted to go out because I knew I couldn't survive without some time away from my thoughts. So I had a few hours of relief, but then I felt like shit on Saturday and thought about Randy again. So I got drunk on Saturday night, too, and felt like shit on Sunday and thought about Randy again. So I got drunk on Sunday night and felt like shit on Monday. The pounding headaches weren't even the worst of this, it was the fact that the issues I'd tried to run away from still stared me straight in the face when I sobered up, and I hadn't made any progress toward making them go away. It was then that I understood why it was so hard to stop drinking in the first place—as soon as I sobered up, I felt an unbearable pain that I could immediately relieve with alcohol.

As my memories of Randy became more and more prominent and invasive, I had to tell my mom. I had to know if she knew something I didn't. My mom told me that Randy had been accused of molesting at least two other girls, including his own daughter, but she hoped I'd been spared. Still, I doubted that what I remembered had actually happened—maybe these were "false memories"—but Randy actually admitted to having molested me.

After I told my mother what I remembered, she felt increasingly guilty for not being able to protect me from that abuse when I was a child. She couldn't have prevented what had happened to me at the McCormick's house then, but she was determined to do something about it now—she met with Randy and confronted him directly about what he did to me all those years ago. They both still went to Charleston Community Church, and she set up a meeting with Randy, his new wife, and their new pastor (Rebekah's dad had recently retired). Randy confirmed that the memories I had actually did happen. I learned that admissions like this are rare in cases of child abuse. Victims often go their whole lives only wanting their abuser to admit they were wrong and apologize, but that rarely happens, instead the victim just feels crazy for thinking they were abused. Randy's confession helped me move past my own fears of "false memories," but it didn't provide the closure for which my mother hoped.

The pastor told my mom not to tell anyone else about this because he didn't want Randy to feel embarrassed in front of the congregation. My mom told me that another girl in church had recently come forward about her father molesting her. Her father was the previous pastor's son-in-law, Rebekah's brother-in-law, and one of my former youth group leaders. My mom said the church helped the girl and her father-the-molester forgive each other as God would have them do. As if the girl—the child—had something to be forgiven for. I wanted to vomit when my mom told me this, and I wondered how many other girls, or boys, this had happened to.

I felt so betrayed by this church, even though it'd been nine years since I'd gone there. I spent my whole adolescence there, thinking this was a progressive church full of reasonable people. The fact that members of the church turned out to be child molesters didn't bother me as much as the fact that the entire church swept it under the rug and acted like it was no big deal.

I had more frequent and more intense intrusive memories of being at the McCormick's as a toddler. I remembered getting spanked there—I hated having to go into their tiny bathroom to pull my own pants down like I was asking for it. I remembered a time when the babysitter's oldest son held my entire body underwater in the swimming pool for so long that I thought he'd kill me. I heard his muffled, echoed laughs above the water as I tried to struggle and scream, but he was a teenager and four times bigger than me. I didn't know what I'd done wrong then to deserve that, but I figured I'd done plenty wrong since then to make up for it. The more I talked about my childhood in therapy, the more frequent and intense the terrifying flashbacks and nightmares of this time became—to the point where I was afraid to even attempt to go to sleep.

The thing that upset me the most about experiencing the nightmares was that I had absolutely no control over it. I'd fall asleep, it would happen, and there was nothing I could do about it. Before I started therapy, these things happened, and I'd be terrified because I had no idea what was going on, but I just got drunk or high and forgot about it. I blamed my oblivious ignorance of my condition on why it took me so long to start my recovery in the first place, but to what could I attribute this resurfacing of severe PTSD symptoms now? I did everything I thought I could do to help myself—I went to therapy every week, wrote regularly, talked about my issues, lived a healthy lifestyle—but I couldn't keep my brain from presenting these horrible memories and the fear associated with them. It was then that I realized PTSD is a real disease of the brain, like a brain tumor or Parkinson's disease, where brain regions are damaged, cells died, and circuits were re-wired incorrectly.

I realized that drinking doesn't help me cope with my issues at all. When I got drunk after my three months of sobriety, I was unable to process thoughts and emotions the way I could when I was sober. The same memories and feelings and ideas kept circling around in my mind, and drinking diminished the innate ability of my brain to integrate memories and emotions and interactions with people into my psyche in a cohesive way. When I was drunk, I couldn't make progress toward healing from any kind of painful experience, partly because alcohol made any kind of clarified mental processing impossible. When I was sober, my mind constantly absorbed information from whatever experiences I had and the people I interacted with, and even though it was sometimes painful, I gradually gained insight into what makes me do the things I do, what makes me feel good or bad, why events might've happened in the past, why I reacted the way I did to any given event, and how I might react the same or differently if that situation arises again. So I re-committed myself to sobriety.

DISILLUSIONMENT

THE NEXT WEEKEND, I went back to Charleston to visit my mom, hoping to talk about her meeting with Randy. She offered to get me a hotel room, maybe because the last time I stayed there, at Christmas, my mom and Jim realized that I was the most miserable person they'd ever seen. As soon as I walked in the door, Jim clearly avoided me, so I asked my mom what was wrong. She said he was upset with me, so we had a "family meeting." With the three of us sitting around the kitchen table, I asked Jim what was going on.

"You made a huge mistake by sharing all of that stuff with your mom," he scowled at me. "You just made her feel all your pain. You have no idea how much you hurt her."

"Umm…" I pondered in disbelief.

"You're just selfish for bringing us into your trauma."

"What?" I said.

"You're ruining my first year of retirement. I just wanted to relax and play golf, but now I have to deal with all this shit!"

I didn't even know what to say as my mouth gaped wide open and my heart pounded.

"You're ruining my sex life with your mom!"

"Oh, please, she has nothing to do with that," my mom finally chimed in.

"I was raped. Twice. And molested as a child. You think this isn't hard for me too?" I finally found my words.

"Well you didn't handle getting raped very well. You just got drunk instead of talking about it with anyone."

And my words were gone again. I wanted to tell him to let me know the next time he got pinned down and fucked in the ass, so I could see how well he handled himself, but I just sat there in disbelief.

"I can't bear this alone anymore," I finally blurted out, on the verge of tears.

"Well that's what therapists are for," Jim professed.

I thought if anybody could help me carry this pain, it would be my family. This was the second time in my adult life in which I cried. I sobbed, not only because I was angry and hurt, but because I realized that if my own family wouldn't help me bear my pain, nobody would—unless I paid them.

My mom set a box of tissues in front of me, and her Jim sat there and watched me cry. I felt humiliated.

"Geez, give her a hug or something," Jim barked at my mom.

We awkwardly embraced, and I decided to stop sharing my personal life with them. I knew that being open with the important people in my life was crucial to my healing, but times like this reminded me why it always felt so much safer to keep everything hidden within myself.

I went back to Michigan, confused about all the anger and sadness I felt about my life, especially when I knew I had so much for which to be grateful. Everything in my life was going well. I finished my second semester of my PhD program with a 4.0. I liked my new friends. I should've been feeling great, but I felt anxious, angry, and selfish all the time.

I wanted to blame Jared's rape on my problems and on my alcoholism, but I always wondered if I would've had those problems anyway. After all, I did drink alone for the first time before I was raped, but I didn't know what I would've been self-medicating then. The week before the rape, I sat at home alone while my mom and Jim went out to do something, and I drank from a bottle of baking amaretto until I felt woozy enough to fall asleep on the living room floor while watching the 2003 National League Championship Series that my beloved Chicago Cubs played in. I loved the calmness of it, and felt at peace with a bit of liquor in my veins.

For over eight years, I wanted so badly for my story to be simpler. I wanted to say that I was this perfect Christian girl, and I'd never drank or kissed a boy or done anything wrong until this evil asshole came along and turned me into a self-destructive monster. If that was the case, maybe I could've more easily told someone what happened, but something was clearly wrong with me before Jared came along, and whatever it was, I thought meant I deserved to get raped. I thought I was just born a bad person, and I knew that's what people would tell me once they found out I wasn't the perfect victim.

I now know it could've been many things that led my strong response to alcohol as a teenager. Maybe my anxiety and anger stemmed from feelings of emotional abandonment from my continuously-stoned and narcissistic mother, maybe my feelings of worthlessness and shame came from teachings in church and my father-figure molesting me as a toddler, maybe my self-loathing came from my internalized homophobia, and these feelings of never being quite who I was supposed to be all disappeared when I drank. And once Jared raped me, I had a lot more feelings that I wanted to go away.

* * *

JOURNAL: JUNE 10, 2012—
"I want to attribute these feelings to my rape/molestation, but I just keep telling myself what happened to me wasn't that big of a deal. Maybe if something worse would've happened, I wouldn't feel so ostentatious. What could've happened to make this worse? I could've been penetrated as a child. And remembered it. Repeatedly. For my entire childhood. By multiple people. Adults that I trusted. I could've been gang-raped in high school. By the football team. Left behind the school to bleed to death. And it was videotaped. And the whole school saw it. I could've been beaten and raped in college. In a dark alley. Walking home from the library. Black eyes. Bloody nose. Skinned knees. Bruised neck. And got pregnant. Had an abortion. That would make these feelings justifiable."

* * *

I read the works of psychologists Alice Miller, Mary Ainsworth, and Donald Winnicott about mother-child attachment theory, childhood trauma, and the child's sense of being. I realized that I'd been living with this idealized version of what I thought my life was. I always thought that I had the perfect childhood, and coming to terms with a lifetime of delusion led to a painful mountain of disillusionment. I'd missed out on being able to experience so much of the most important years of my life, and with that realization, came great sadness.

It was like when somebody dies—the loved ones they leave behind might grieve for a long time after the death. You think about the role that person played in your life and wonder what you're supposed to do with yourself now that they're gone—that's exactly how I felt, except I felt that way about myself. What am I supposed to do now that the person who I thought I was has died?

I benefited from approaching my healing as if going through the stages of grief. For the first time, I grieved the loss of my innocence and idealized childhood, the loss of my sense of safety and control over my body. I went through the stages of grief—denial, anger, bargaining, depression, and acceptance—as most people do at the loss of a loved one, and thinking about my emotional states in terms of this culturally accepted model made me realize it was okay to feel the way I did.

At first, I felt so guilty for directing so much anger toward my mother and toward the people who'd violated me, but when I accepted that I was moving through the stages of grief, I let myself feel that anger, knowing that I'd eventually accept the reality of what happened to me. But I was anxious to finally reach the acceptance stage of grief because even though I moved through my healing process, I still felt so much pain and struggled every day.

MOVING ON

I FINISHED THE first year of my PhD program, at which point I had to choose a permanent lab to start my four years of dissertation research. I decided to move to Grand Rapids to go back to the lab I did my first rotation in to research Parkinson's disease. Therapy with Lois had been going well, and I couldn't imagine trusting anyone as much as I trusted her, so I decided that I'd drive back to Lansing once or twice a week for my therapy sessions.

Shortly before I moved, I went to the Chicago Pride parade with my cousin Heather and her girlfriend. I'd never been in an atmosphere where I identified as lesbian and nobody questioned it or looked at me funny, and I felt so free. I was grateful to have Heather's support and to have someone to talk with about being gay. But I saw people with signs that read "I'm proud of my gay son/daughter," and felt both happiness and sadness because I knew I'd never receive that kind of support from my mother. I'd worked with Lois to tolerate feeling two seemingly-opposing emotions at the same time, but it was more difficult than I could even grasp, so I drank that entire weekend to take the edge off.

The next day after getting back from Chicago, my mom and Jim came to Lansing to help me move to Grand Rapids.

* * *

JOURNAL: JUNE 25, 2012 —
"My mom and Jim just got here this evening to help me move to Grand Rapids tomorrow. I think they liked me better when I used to

pretend to be happy all the time. When I used to drink all the time...
Jim said he thinks an hour is a pretty long way to drive every week
for therapy. They don't think therapy is helping. I guess they think I
should be ecstatically happy all the time."

*   *   *

Moving from Charleston to Lansing didn't fix any of my problems,
but for some reason I thought moving might help this time. I thought
I was strong enough now to get that "fresh start" I'd been wanting,
and when I walked into the lab in Grand Rapids, nobody recognized
me. I walked right past all of the people I'd worked with a few
months earlier, and they had no idea who I was. This was actually a
huge relief, as it confirmed that I wasn't the same person I used to
be—that person I hated.

Instead of hiding behind my makeup and my booze, I
completely opened up with my coworkers about everything that'd
been going on with me and why I looked so different. I told my
advisor that I had PTSD and needed to go back to Lansing once or
twice a week to see my therapist. I was scared that the people I
worked with would think I was incompetent because I was mentally
ill and a recovering alcoholic, but they treated me like a human
being should be treated—with respect and compassion.

All I wanted was for people to accept me for who I was, and for
the most part, they did. I'd never before felt so loved for being
myself—but that was because I never was truly myself. I developed
deeper relationships and felt so much more love than I'd ever felt
once I allowed myself to be open with the people I saw every day at
work. Feeling vulnerable terrified me, especially when I'd been hurt
so much by being honest with my mother, but I knew it was the only
way I could make a truly fulfilling life for myself. I couldn't hide my
true self any longer.

I voiced my frustration to Heather about not knowing how to be
gay or how to date women, and she suggested that I make a profile
on an online dating site. My heart pounded as I selected the "I am a
gay woman" option on OKCupid and searched through my matches.

I had no idea there were so many lesbians in Grand Rapids, which was dominated by Calvinist right-wing conservatives. I exchanged messages with potential matches, and when I went on my first in-person date with a woman, I knew I was exactly where I wanted to be. I'd never before experienced anticipation for a date or for a kiss—with men, it was always dread and boredom—but with women, it felt natural.

But I kept meeting the same heavy-drinking, self-destructive people that I tried to avoid, which included many of my neighbors. There were always parties going on near my apartment, and I started drinking regularly again.

*   *   *

JOURNAL: JULY 22, 2012—
"I don't know why I'm drinking again. I think part of it is because hanging out with these kids makes me feel like I'm 20 again, and I feel like this is an opportunity to re-live my early 20s the way I wished I could have before. Unfortunately, I seem to be making all the same mistakes—staying out way too late when I have to get up early in the morning, smoking cigarettes, drinking too much, etc."

*   *   *

I realized that moving to Grand Rapids hadn't helped me at all—in fact, things were worse than ever, and I even started smoking cigarettes again. After smoking a pack of cigarettes every day or two for the past five or six years, I quit cold turkey when I got sober. The first few days were rough, but when I wasn't drinking, I could control my impulse to smoke. I'd always considered cigarettes to be the least of my problems, and when overcoming everything else I overcame, cigarettes were just another drop in the bucket.

I realized that I mostly went out to smoke when I was anxious and needed to get out of my office or away from whomever I was with, so Lois suggested that any time I felt a craving for a cigarette, I go outside for five minutes and inhale and exhale as if I were smoking a cigarette. It actually worked and relaxed me. But once I started drinking, my fuck-it attitude returned, and I bought cigarettes again.

Even though I made new friends, I got so sad because I thought I'd never get to see them again. I always felt like I was back in high school, finally belonging to a group, only to have it all fall apart in one night. I consciously recognized that it was "the trauma speaking" and my new friends weren't going to disown me, but I couldn't stop the physical feeling that I just got punched in the stomach.

I'd get so scared when I was alone in my apartment with one of my guy friends. I knew in my mind that there would be no problems, but I couldn't control the tension in every muscle in my body, my racing heart, and the knots in my stomach because I was afraid he wouldn't leave my apartment when we finished our movie or board game. I hated feeling that way about my friends. My awareness of the reality of the situation was completely separate from my emotional response.

One of my new friends had a red Jeep, and every time I saw her car in the driveway, I'd think about Jason. I remembered getting in Jason's red Jeep and deciding that I didn't want to go home with him, and then getting raped. I remembered my cousin driving over to Jason's house to yell at him afterwards and seeing him storm out of his house to get in his red Jeep, and even nine years later, I felt afraid that he'd come after me. I knew in my mind that the fear I felt was a residue of past trauma and not an actual immediate threat, but I couldn't control the visceral reaction in my body to want to scream and run. Sometimes I'd feel extremely anxious for reasons I couldn't explain.

If I didn't understand why I felt anxious or upset, I self-destructed. If I could pin down a reason for my anxiety, it was much easier to deal with the emotions by talking about them or writing about them, but when I couldn't figure out what gnawed at me, the only way I knew to immediately make the feelings go away was to drink. But when I tried to stay sober, I found that cutting myself had a similar effect as alcohol.

When everything was going well in my life outwardly, but I felt so much internal despair, the conflict tormented me so much that I needed to validate my pain. I dragged a razor blade across my wrist, and when I looked at the long, straight, red line dripping with blood, I thought, "Yeah, that looks about right." I'd expressed the pain and fear I felt inside that I didn't know how to grasp any other way. I kept trying to tell myself that everything was fine and I had no reason to be upset, but when I looked at my cut-up wrists, it validated my internal feelings of despair—obviously everything was not okay if my wrists were bleeding.

I realized that I always tried to find some congruence between my internal hell and my external life. I felt so much emotional pain and fear and distress that my "successful" life never made sense to me. I didn't understand how I could have independently achieved so much in my education, world travels, friendships, and jobs, but still be in such utter despair. When I'd walk home from the bar at 2AM and choose to sleep in the park instead of my apartment across the street, it made me feel more aligned with my true inner self. I didn't think a person with their own apartment and a warm bed should be so broken, but a person passed out drunk in a park was clearly in trouble.

Some people would call these kinds of behaviors cries for help—and they were to an extent—but it was really a way for me to make sense of my pain that I couldn't grasp. Every time I slept under a tree, cut myself, got detentions in high school, drove around drunk, jumped off of balconies, put out cigarettes on my arms, got into cars with strangers, went to the bar in my pajamas, stayed in unhealthy relationships, and wallowed in complicated situations, I felt like myself—that life made sense to me because it matched what I felt internally. Every time I gave lectures, won awards, mastered a skill, wrote perfect essays, aced exams, had travel adventures, graduated with honors, or went the extra mile, I wondered who the fuck I was—that wasn't me because a person in so much anguish wouldn't engage in all these healthy activities.

It troubled me so much when my internal life didn't match my external life—when what I felt to be true about myself wasn't mirrored back to me by the people around me or by the lifestyle in which I engaged. This sentiment continued to echo for me in regard to my sexual orientation—when I dated men and had sex with men and everybody around me viewed me as heterosexual, it completely clashed with my internal feelings of attraction toward women, and I totally lost my sense of self. When my reality wasn't validated by the people around me—when they marginalized or dismissed it—I validated my reality for myself.

But after one of my friends saw the bandages on my arm and knew what I'd done said, "Eww, you don't want to become a cutter," I knew why drinking had worked so well for me—it was socially acceptable.

CONTROL FREAK

EVEN WITH THE AWARENESS that my brain needed to completely abstain from alcohol in order to heal, I still wanted to drink, especially because I knew I didn't want to keep cutting myself. After moving to Grand Rapids, I drank a couple times a week, sometimes only having one or two beers, sometimes having enough to get drunk, but I never felt like I over-did it. When I first quit drinking, I thought that if a drop of alcohol ever touched my lips again, I'd immediately burst into flames and die. Realizing that it was possible to drink socially initially reassured me—I could have one or two beers and not go off the deep end for another eight years, which meant I had my life under control.

The feeling of having power over alcohol intoxicated me more than the liquor itself, and all I wanted was to be in control. One of the biggest problems I had with AA was admitting that I was powerless over alcohol, which was step one, so I obviously didn't get far with that program. I couldn't tolerate thinking that I was powerless over anything. I'd had my power taken from me, and I wouldn't allow myself to lose whatever power I had left to anything again, not even alcohol. I hadn't gone to an AA meeting since moving to Grand Rapids.

I hated that AA kept me in constant fear of a relapse. AA convinced me that my addiction always waited to sneak up on me at any moment, and I had to remain hypervigilant about my internal and external environment because any mistake, even one drink, could lead to a full-scale relapse. I hated that AA encouraged me to define myself as an alcoholic/addict for the rest of my life, and by revisiting my alcohol-related memories and hearing others talk about their alcohol disasters, I constantly re-lived my memories of addiction and all the emotions that came with it—just like my other PTSD symptoms. I lived with constant anxiety and fear and avoided any people or places that reminded me of my addiction. For some people, this may be the only way to stay clean and sober, but for me, living with fear and constant reminders of past horrors was exactly what I tried to remedy in my recovery.

So I thought by being in control of my drinking, I could avoid living in fear of a relapse, but the amount of energy and focus it took for me to only have one or two drinks exhausted me physically and emotionally. I had no idea how to "drink normally" since I used to never take more than ten minutes to finish any drink and rarely stopped drinking until I passed out. I carefully watched everyone I was with to try to match their pace, which felt excruciatingly slow, so I often finished my drink before everyone else even halfway finished theirs. Then, I refused the offer of another drink until everyone else caught up to me, which was torturous. Once my company decided to call it a night, I went home to spend every ounce of my remaining energy trying to convince myself to not go to the liquor store to continue drinking alone. Eventually I got worn down, and gave into drinking as much as I wanted.

I had so many "relapses" that, even though I was "in recovery," I knew I still drank more than most people. So I decided to let myself drink in what I determined were "normal amounts in normal situations" (e.g. happy hour with coworkers) and by not fighting it and not hiding it, I escaped some of the feelings of defeat and frustration of drinking. It was kind of like when parents tell their teenagers that if they're going to drink, they can only drink at home when an adult is there—it works for a while to provide a false sense of safety and control, but when something goes wrong the guilt is unbearable because you allowed it to happen.

My first major relapse consisted of nine days in a row of being drunk after I went out for a couple drinks with some of my new friends from work. It was a warm fall night, and we stood out in the light drizzling rain barefoot and smoked cigarettes. I felt like I was

back at my mom's house with my friends in high school on
Columbus Day of my senior year—we got out of school early that
day and stood outside my house in the light drizzling rain barefoot
and smoked cigarettes. I started to make friends and be independent,
and I was excited about what the future held. This is exactly how I
felt that day after work, but with those parallel feelings came the
memories of being raped just a couple weeks after that day in high
school, when my life suddenly fell apart. I felt like it was only a short
matter of time before something horrible would happen, and my
anxiety increased to an unbearable level, so I kept drinking.

*   *   *

JOURNAL: SEPTEMBER 24, 2012—
"So I went to the gas station to get a 6 pack of beer, and when the
cashier asked for my "adult party card," I shook my head in disgust
because it's not a party when you're going to the gas station at 11PM
on Monday night in your pajamas to buy a few beers."

JOURNAL: SEPTEMBER 25, 2012—
"I'm not going to say much, but I'm drinking for the fifth day in a
row, and I'm wondering why I quit drinking in the first place. I feel
great; relaxed, not thinking about yesterday or tomorrow; telling the
people I love that I love them; what's wrong with this?"

JOURNAL: SEPTEMBER 29, 2012—
"I bought a pack of cigarettes—smoking cigarettes really makes me
feel like I'm in control, especially when everyone I'm around
disapproves of smoking. Having a cigarette is something I'm
choosing to do because I want to have one, not because anybody else
is putting it in front of my face or making me feel pressured to have
one."

*   *   *

After drinking about twenty drinks in one night, I experienced some
withdrawal symptoms in the morning and I dreaded re-experiencing

my first withdrawal nightmare so much that I just kept drinking. I thought I'd completely lost control of my life during those nine days and that I'd re-experience the fiasco of the last nine years all over again. I thought I wouldn't survive much longer. I knew I couldn't deal with this alone again, so I confided in some of my new Grand Rapids friends about what was going on. Being able to talk to my friends about my issues was instrumental in my healing. Just knowing that people could see me for who I was and still want me to be healthy and happy gave me hope, and I continued to fight for my sobriety.

But at this point, I'd hit another roadblock with my therapist. After every session, I'd turn all my anger and fear and shame inward on myself like I always had, just with an acute awareness of it now. I had more flashbacks and nightmares than ever, I drank often, and I startled so much at work that people stopped approaching me at all. I wondered why I even went to therapy if it caused me more problems.

ANNIVERSARY

EVERY DAY I WOKE up during the first year of my therapy, I made a conscious decision whether or not I wanted to put up the fight to live. I'd left behind many of my unhealthy and self-destructive coping mechanisms, but that left me vulnerable and unable to cope with anything at all. Even a magnet falling off my refrigerator reduced me to a pile of tears. And then knowing that I couldn't (or at least shouldn't) drink to numb the pain of said broken magnet summoned an upwelling of fear and anger and sometimes rage (I know, I know—it wasn't really about the magnet. It's never about the magnet). I'd tell myself, "You don't have to do this if you don't want to." Knowing that I could end the struggle at any time gave me the strength to at least make an attempt at getting through the day.

Once I decided to live, I'd decide whether or not I'd drink that day. It used to be that I had to drink in order to endure the pain of living, but now drinking made me feel like I'd given up on life. I knew I'd die if I returned to drinking again, so by making the choice to live each day, I also made the choice *not* to drink. I didn't want to die, but I didn't know how to live either. I thought it was too late for me to get my life back, I'd already wasted so many years, and the things that should've been making me happy now were making me sadder.

There were so many books I didn't read, so many movies I didn't see, so much music I didn't write and play, and so many connections I missed having with my friends. I mourned the loss of those years I'd never get back, and I desperately tried to hang onto them. When I went to my first few concerts sober, along with pure bliss, I felt deep remorse about the hundreds of concerts I'd been to that I didn't remember or pay attention to because I was too drunk. When I started making friends who'd only known me sober, I experienced a closeness and authenticity that I couldn't attain when I was constantly drunk and not remembering half of what I did with my friends anyway. Again, I felt two opposing feelings at once—relief for being sober, but also sadness for all the years I wasn't sober.

* * *

JOURNAL: OCTOBER 14, 2012—
"It's been two weeks today since I've had any alcohol whatsoever—I think that's probably the longest I've gone without drinking since I moved to Grand Rapids. James went with me to see one of my favorite bands, Murder By Death, downtown last night, and I'm so glad I didn't drink."

JOURNAL: OCTOBER 15, 2012—
"The more and more I do things sober, the more I grieve over what I missed out on all those years. Dione came to Grand Rapids tonight to go to a concert with me. We went to dinner first, and it was great to catch up—her and I used to drink quite a bit together, but it felt very natural and comfortable to hang out tonight with neither of us drinking, so that felt good. We saw one of our favorite singers, Regina Spektor, and the show was excellent. I felt sad because I thought of all the hundreds of concerts I've seen that I don't remember or wasn't paying attention because I was too drunk."

JOURNAL: OCTOBER 16, 2012—
"This time next year, it will be 10 years since this all started, and that's long enough to live with this."

* * *

The Sunday morning before Jared's nine-year rape anniversary, I awoke and immediately started writing. Within seconds, I went from sleeping in my bedroom to typing furiously in my living room. I didn't know what I wrote until I stopped and read my computer screen.

* * *

JOURNAL: OCTOBER 21, 2012 —
"Please don't tell people that I was always such a happy girl, that I was always so carefree. I suffered an unbearable amount of pain for much of my life. I know my death will cause many people grief, but I'm not being selfish or weak. I have always been unable to communicate my suffering to those who love me. I didn't think my mother could live with herself if she knew of my anguish. Nobody could see my pain, and thus, nobody could see me. Suicide is the only way to express such indescribable pain—the only possible way to express my true self, without whom I'm merely a shell of a falsely-constructed being, and that is not a life. In death, I will find my life. I loved you all very much."

* * *

I'd written a suicide letter, admittedly one with a dramatic flair. I felt an enormous amount of pain for reasons I couldn't explain, but then I realized that the nine-year anniversary of Jared's rape was coming in three days. This would be the first year I faced this time sober, and I was completely unprepared for what I'd experience. Over the course of the next week, my dreams, emotions, and physical sensations chronologically paralleled what I'd gone through in high school in a real, terrifying re-experiencing of the past. Anniversaries of traumatic events often trigger intense "anniversary reactions" in people with PTSD, which can range from mild distress to more extreme re-experiencing, panic attacks, or suicidality.

In the days surrounding this rape anniversary, I felt the pain in my vagina and even bled heavily for a couple hours even though it wasn't my period, I felt Jared's hands on my ribcage, I woke up paralyzed, I had dreams and nightmares about the time surrounding the rape, I desperately tried to get help from psychiatrists for my severely increasing anxiety but experienced the same frustrating lack of support that I received in high school. The doctors I made appointments with looked at me and saw an attractive, clean, young woman who was probably under too much pressure like all the other PhD students out there—even though this time I was completely open about my history of rape, substance abuse, suicide attempts, etc. I refused to take benzodiazepines because, according to AA, this would be considered an "alcoholic relapse" and I didn't want that kind of failure on my conscience. But I knew the antidepressants they prescribed me wouldn't help my acute state of crisis. I saved my suicide letter and told myself I'd get my affairs in order at work so I wouldn't leave my coworkers in a bind, and then I'd end my life.

But during this time I stayed with my coworker friend, Kristi, with whom I could talk about the whole range of experiences I'd been having all week. I realized for the first time, that even if something horrible did happen to me again, I wouldn't be alone this time. Unlike this time nine years earlier when I had no support from my friends at school, I at least had Kristi and my therapist who listened to me and made me feel safe.

The following week at work, I physically and emotionally felt like I'd just been raped the week before. I was so lethargic and indifferent to anything that went on around me. I feared I'd never be myself again. I fell asleep at work and in class, and felt like none of my friends at work wanted to be around me in my depressed state. I felt exactly as I'd felt in high school after I was raped—sleeping through all my classes and avoiding my friends. I experienced so many intense, raw emotions, pains, dreams, and memories—it was like I was processing what'd happened to me nine years ago for the first time.

But my experience that week wasn't like I re-lived the rape over and over as I'd done in my nightmares and flashbacks for so many years, it was like I re-experienced the rape in a whole new context. The dreams I had and the events that triggered flashbacks were all slightly different than what'd happened to me the first time, and this time, I had a therapist and doctors and supportive friends. I wasn't alone this time. Staying at Kristi's house probably saved my life—I got a second chance to re-process that traumatic experience with the help I needed.

*   *   *

JOURNAL: OCTOBER 28, 2012—

"I told my therapist I was afraid that I was broken beyond repair, and she told me I'm fundamentally *unbroken*. Something about that terminology made me so hopeful for one of the first times."

*   *   *

Kristi's three-year-old son, Gus, gave me an entirely new perspective on life. I watched him experience life and discover what he liked and didn't like and what was important to him. His pure innocence made me realize that life itself wasn't such a terrible thing that I'd have to endure until I died. I didn't know I could love someone else's child so much—I didn't want or need anything in return from Gus, and there was nothing he could've done to make me love him less. I never thought I'd want children of my own because I couldn't bear to imagine the possibility of them having a traumatic life like mine, but I realized that life—or at least love—is a beautiful thing worth experiencing. The ability to love and be loved makes life worth living, and makes living in a way to allow everyone to love and be loved worth fighting for. I survived that week, but tragically, one of my friends did not.

One week after I wrote my own suicide letter, my coworker, David, killed himself. This was the friend who'd given me those mini bottles of bourbon that I used to create my first smashed-glass art piece. This heartbreaking news hit me hard, not only because David was a friend, but because I'd also been seriously suicidal over that past week. The first thing I felt when I heard about David's suicide was envy—envy that David could end his suffering while I still lived with an unbearable amount of pain every day.

I felt like I was floating around in space, and I'd drifted so far that I was surrounded by nothingness—no light, no planets, no sound, just a complete void. I had no frame of reference to time or space. There was no way anybody could find me, and I couldn't move myself in any direction—I was completely helpless, slowly starving to death and running out of oxygen. I knew I'd die a painful death in the near future, so of course I wanted to end my life quickly and painlessly. I held onto hope that somebody would rescue me, but when I was surrounded by people who didn't notice how lost I was, I felt completely helpless and hopeless.

In watching how people reacted to David's death, I learned that suicide is generally seen as an impulsive, rash decision, but I knew there were many years of pain leading up to his decision to end his life. People said that David had no reason to kill himself—he had plenty of opportunities and he was smart and nice and cute—but I understood why a person who had a lot going for them could still want to die. Even when you have a lot of things to live for, there can still be a lot of things you don't think you can live with.

When I attended David's funeral, I couldn't help but think this could've been my funeral. I saw the grief everyone experienced, and couldn't believe that two weeks earlier, I'd written a suicide letter. I couldn't believe that I'd felt like I needed to end my life any second, and I couldn't believe that I'd felt *envious* of David for ending his pain. Now, I wished that he could've held on a little longer so he could've found some hope.

People said that David's suicide was a selfish act, but I saw it as an act of pain, not an act of selfishness—someone who wanted to remove themselves from existence wasn't being selfish. When people said that David was selfish for not thinking about his loved ones, or that there was no reason he should've killed himself, they refused to acknowledge the amount of pain that he must've been in. Having no validation or form of expression for such extreme pain was precisely what led to my own suicidal ideation. When people said David was weak, I wondered if they'd walk up to a person who was on fire—their entire body consumed in flames—and tell them that they just need to be stronger to get through the pain.

But I understood that many of these reactions were expressions of grief, and being at David's funeral made me realize how people could see suicide as a selfish act when it seemed that he didn't think about the pain his death would cause others. I always knew a lot of people would be devastated if I died, but I thought that once I killed myself, they'd know the excruciating pain I felt, and they'd be relieved that I ended my suffering. During David's funeral, I recognized that my suicide wouldn't have helped anybody to understand my pain or made anyone feel relieved. This realization shattered my impression of what suicide actually was—I'd revered suicide as this powerful thing that held my life in balance, but now I finally believed that suicide was the ultimate end to any hope of things getting better.

I felt immensely sad for David and haunted by the fact that it took another person's suicide to give me the perspective and motivation to figure out how to live a happy, healthy life. I felt a responsibility to give other people hope so David's death wouldn't be in vain. I wished David could've had some assurance that things could get better—it's the hopelessness that is unbearable—but I was in no position to give him that while he was alive. I didn't know things could get better either. I, too, thought death was the only way out. And it was too late for David. I learned that the pain could end, things could get better—there was hope to heal a broken life, and there was more to life than simply surviving each day.

I thought that I could go through my life not feeling anything whatsoever. I was willing to sacrifice any happiness or pleasure in order to not feel the pain, and it worked for a while. But after so many years of complete numbness, I wasn't even sure that I was alive anymore, and I didn't know why I kept putting up the fight to live every day if I was already dead. When I finally allowed myself to feel my anger and pain, I thought the power of those emotions would surely kill me—I couldn't live with those intense forces weighing down on me, and I didn't know how I could ever make them go away without returning to the numbness.

But Lois helped me learn to tolerate and experience my pain and anger, instead of trying to make them go away. She suggested that I find a way to physically act on these emotions instead of turning them inward. So I started letting myself scream in my car or pound on a punching bag at the gym, and the frequency and intensity of those seemingly intolerable emotions subsided—they came and went in waves, and in between the suffering was great joy. The more I worked to acknowledge and accept my past and to express my true emotions, instead of ignoring them and numbing them, the more I experienced all of the beautiful things that makes life worth living.

* * *

JOURNAL: NOVEMBER 1, 2012—
"My mom just emailed me telling me that she believes God can help tremendously and that God loves me and that I should 'tell God exactly how I feel.' I thought that sounded like bullshit, but I am going to tell God exactly how I feel:

> *God, I don't even know if you exist, which is fine with me. I don't think there needs to be some supreme omnipotent being with the power to condemn a person to an eternity of suffering in order for people to be good. I don't think there needs to be some supreme omnipotent being with the power to grant a person an eternity of bliss in order for people to have a reason to live. But what I think is irrelevant because one way or another, a truth exists—I just don't know what that truth is. If there's no threat of hell or promise of heaven, then what is the point of life? Regardless of how life was created or how it ends, life is a beautiful thing in and of itself—or maybe, love is a beautiful thing. The ability to love and be loved makes life worth living, and makes living in such a way to allow everyone to love and be loved worth fighting for.*

Oh, my God, I just cried for the third time in the last 10 years. I feel like I'm alive. It's so easy to want to kill yourself when you feel so dead inside, but I am alive!"

THE BODY OF A TIGER

AFTER MY NEAR-SUICIDE and David's death, I knew I had to do something different with my treatment. Almost a year into recovery, I still "white-knuckled" my survival every day. I'd heard about eye movement desensitization and reprocessing (EMDR) from both my therapist and from friends who'd done it, but I hesitated to try it because it didn't seem "scientific" to me and I didn't understand how it worked.

So I did some research on it and found out that Francine Shapiro developed the technique in the late 1980s. EMDR mimics REM sleep, but while awake. In the case-studies I read, the patient followed a stimulus back and forth with their eyes to simulate the rapid eye movement that occurs during REM sleep, which put the brain into a kind of dream-like state, much like when sleeping. When the patient thought about a specific traumatic moment, the brain automatically made many abstract connections and consolidated memories in the way that they should be stored in the brain. In a groundbreaking study, EMDR completely cured 60% of PTSD patients compared to 10% who only took Prozac. Additionally, patients who had done eight EMDR sessions continued to show improvement indefinitely without further treatment, while those on Prozac relapsed almost immediately after they went off the drug (the same results were found when compared with Celexa, Paxil, and Zoloft). So I started EMDR with my therapist, who was certified in the technique and had decades of experience with it. The best way to illustrate how this process worked for me is to read the journal entries that I wrote after each EMDR session:

EMDR DAY 1: NOVEMBER 4, 2012 —

I realized that I *did* tell Jared no. I told him I wanted to go home; he told me I was too fucked up to go home. If I was too fucked up to go home, then I was definitely too fucked up to fuck. I told Jared not to take my clothes off; he told me it was his bed, and he wanted my clothes off. I realized then that saying no wasn't getting me anywhere, and Jared was going to do whatever he wanted. I thought about all of the guys I'd slept with since then and almost all of them at some point during the encounter asked if what was happening was okay. Jared never asked me if it was okay for us to have sex. He didn't ask me if I was okay when I was bleeding profusely. He didn't ask me if I was okay when my head was bashing against his headboard. Jared didn't ask me if it was okay because he knew it wasn't okay. I realized that I couldn't have got myself out of that situation even if I tried to run out the door—I could hardly even walk.

EMDR DAY 2: NOVEMBER 5, 2012 —

I didn't really feel like I was "permanently damaged" anymore, but I did know that I'd never be the same after that. I thought about how I could use tampons after that, and when my mom noticed I was using them, she suspiciously asked how I was able to use tampons all of a sudden when I'd had no luck getting them to work previously. I wondered what she was thinking—if she thought I'd started having sex? Could she have possibly thought about rape? My thoughts started to drift toward being back in school, and I felt like maybe all my friends at school really didn't dislike me anymore, but I just felt like they did. I knew Adrianne hated me, so maybe I just assumed that everyone else did, too. I thought that maybe since I was so depressed and sleeping through class and leaving school during lunch, people just didn't want to be around me anymore. Still, I wondered why none of my classmates or teachers asked if I was okay. Or maybe people did ask if I was okay, and I just assured them that I was.

EMDR DAY 3: NOVEMBER 12 2012 —

I no longer felt like I was permanently damaged when Jared raped me. I was definitely damaged in that experience, but I realized that I can recover. I wish I could've known that when I was seventeen. I still feel like I'll never be the same, but that's not necessarily a bad thing—I might not be the same person I would've been had I not been raped, but I can still be a healthy, whole person.

EMDR DAY 4: DECEMBER 17, 2012—
I started thinking about the moment when Jared lifted me on top of him, but my thoughts quickly went to the moment when I woke up paralyzed in his bed. I felt scared, but when I saw Jared next to me and realized where I was, I felt safe again. I thought he was somebody I could trust, and I wished I'd have known what was about to happen to me when I awoke. But I realized that even if I *had* known what was going to happen to me at Jared's, I still wouldn't have been able to do anything to prevent him raping me—I couldn't even move. I thought about the night I met Jason and how I'd initially trusted him also, and I wished I would've known what was about to happen to me when I kissed him goodbye. I felt like I could've gotten myself out of that situation if I'd known what Jason was going to do or if I'd taken my increasing irritation and suspicion of his behavior more seriously that night.

EMDR DAY 5: MARCH 8, 2013—
I started thinking about the moment Jared lifted me on top of him. I think the sudden jolt of going from lying down for over sixteen hours to suddenly being upright made me realize that something was happening—wait, what's going on? What am I supposed to do? I remember thinking that I wanted to try to enjoy the experience and try to make it good for Jared so it would be over more quickly, but I had no idea what to do. I didn't know how to have sex. He kept trying to get me to give him an erection, but I didn't know what to do. He kept trying to put his penis in me and telling me to help him, but I didn't know what to do. I think this is the source of my constant, daily feelings of not knowing what to do with myself and always thinking I need to be doing something. I remembered when Jared told me to meet him at the health clinic to get the morning-after pill, I was willing and eager to go. I dreaded having to see him again, but I was relieved that somebody was finally telling me

something to do. I just needed somebody to tell me what to do because I felt completely helpless. I remembered looking at Jared from across the waiting room, and momentarily hating him, but I felt guilty for feeling that way about anyone so I tried to bury that hatred. Then, my thoughts suddenly went to the two times Jake came into my room after I'd gone to bed. I felt the same hatred toward him, but today I felt even more guilty and confused for feeling that way toward him.

EMDR DAY 6: MARCH 15, 2013—
Today, I started with the image of me on top of Jared, but I really couldn't feel anything about that moment at all. I could see it, but I didn't have any emotional response to it.

EMDR DAY 7: MARCH 17, 2013—
I started with the image of me on top of Jared, but it seemed very distant to me. It actually looked like a smaller version of itself, like I was looking at it through at through a concave lens. I started to think about the moment when I first woke up paralyzed and then the moment when it was finally over and I got up to put my clothes on and I was looking at Jared sitting on the edge of his bed putting his shoes on. I felt like I was trying to make sense of what'd just happened, and I didn't know what a person was supposed to do after having sex—should we go get a cup of coffee? I remembered wondering what my mom was going to say or what I was going to tell her. I remembered how my car became my safe place after I was raped—I would sleep in it at school during lunch, I would just go sit in it in my mom's driveway and fall asleep or listen to music, I would go for long drives in the country.

EMDR DAY 8: APRIL 29, 2013—
I had a pretty significant EMDR session. I started thinking about the moment when Jared lifted me on top of him, but when I imagined it, it was just a still picture. I felt like I was in the room just looking at my 17-year-old self on top of him and time had stopped. I told her that everything was going to be okay, that what just happened was horrible, but she can recover. I then picked her up off of Jared and

carried her out of the room back to my mom's house and put her in her bed. I sat with her and told her that I know what she's going through because I've been through the same thing, and I know how hard it is and how much it hurts and how you feel like you're permanently damaged, but I assured her that she would be okay—that I would be there with her every step of the way. She fell asleep for a long time, and when she woke, I was still there. I took her to get the morning-after pill, and to the gynecologist—the things I had to do without someone I trust with me. At the end of the session, I tried to imagine that moment again, but I didn't even see myself in it—I just saw Jared lying in his bed alone. I realized that this is how this process works; this is what is supposed to happen.

* * *

Was I completely cured after only eight sessions of EMDR? No, but I do believe that, had I stopped my treatment there, my life would've been forever improved. EMDR helped me consolidate the narratives I'd written about my trauma with the images of the trauma, and then imagine how things could've been different—not only imagine it, but feel what it would've felt like had someone I trusted been with me. This was how my healthy recovery from bad experiences was supposed to happen from the beginning.

I learned in my studies that children who'd had a bad experience often acted it out through playing—they used their play scene and characters to make sense of what'd happened and learn what could've been done differently. But I didn't have the resources as a child or teenager to do this kind of thing. I wasn't able to make these kinds of associations and I continually re-lived, rather than reprocessed, the memories, until I did EMDR.

Being the neuroscientist I happened to be, I decided to look to the scientific literature for answers about how I could further my recovery. I thought maybe I could participate in some new experimental treatment, but what I learned disappointed me. I found hundreds of studies using various drugs, but more than half of PTSD patients failed to respond to the current standard treatments. The most striking thing I noticed was that ninety-eight percent of these studies used only human men or male rats. Nobody looked at how these treatments worked in women or if PTSD itself was even the same in women. Maybe I looked for something specific to women because I couldn't grasp how what'd happened to me when I was raped as a teenager could be the same as what happened to men in Vietnam. Most studies agreed that women were twice as likely as men to develop PTSD after experiencing a traumatic event, and PTSD persisted four times longer in women than in men. Women were also thought to be more likely to re-experience trauma through intrusive memories like I'd been experiencing for so many years. As many as one-in-ten women suffer from PTSD, but this population is often overlooked.

I found that almost all standard trauma treatments address the brain directly through drugs or psychological talk and behavioral therapies, but so many treatments ignore the contribution of the body to trauma reactions. The theories of trauma healing developed by Bessel van der Kolk and Peter A. Levine served as my practical bible for my own healing.

Both Drs. Levine and van der Kolk focused on healing trauma by targeting and managing the physiological responses of the body. This approach stems from observations of wild animal behavior, which—when applied to humans—involves completing the unresolved stress and survival responses that were frozen at the time of trauma.

In Dr. Levine's observations, when an animal heard a noise or saw an approaching figure, it froze to assess the threat—its muscles tensed, pupils dilated, and heart rate increased—ready to fight or flee. And sometimes staying frozen is the best response for survival (think: "playing dead"). Thus, this response is often also called the fight-flee-freeze response. But if no threat was found, the animal returned to its normal activity. So what happened to all that energy that was mobilized in preparation for an attack? Many animals physically twitched and trembled, starting with the ears and neck, all the way down to their legs—they literally shook the fear right out of themselves. Even humans have been observed doing this.

In one of the Internet's more educational viral videos, a nine-year-old girl, after having just shot her first buck, trembled for close to five minutes. She stood upright, while her arms shook out in front her, her legs twitched beneath her, and her teeth chattered when she said, "Dad, is this normal? I'm not cold, I'm just shaking." From the moment the deer came into her sight, she undoubtedly went into "fight-or-flight" mode, ready to take on this creature, but because she didn't have to physically fight or flee from the deer, all of that energy was released through her shaking. And to answer the little girl's question: that is, in fact, normal.

In many of the types of trauma most likely to lead to PTSD (rape, combat, serious accidents), the victims were often unable to fight or flee. They were "activated"—energy mobilized in preparation to take life-preserving action—but they couldn't escape or fight back because they were overpowered by a stronger person, because they were drugged, because they were physically trapped, or because the trauma happened too fast to react. But they had to release all of that energy somehow—energy, that within seconds to minutes, was transformed and created by converting fat into sugar, moving the sugar to the muscles, releasing endorphins to block pain signals, dumping adrenaline into the bloodstream to increase heart rate and breathing, halting digestive and reproductive systems, and inhibiting unnecessary emotional responses to favor more instinctual ones.

Those are a lot of powerful and fast-acting changes that occur in the brain and body in response to a threat, and the body's natural way to discharge that energy and return to homeostasis—or normal brain and body functioning—is to shake or scream or cry. The fight-or-flight system also has a reciprocal response, sometimes called rest-and-digest, which is activated by another part of the nervous system when the fight-or-flight response begins to dampen.

But so many people with PTSD fight against their visceral reactions so they don't appear weak in the face of trauma, so they can be strong for those around them, or so they can convince themselves that nothing horrible actually happened. The shame, guilt, betrayal of trust, and overwhelming emotional damage that often accompany trauma motivated them to suppress this normal return to homeostasis, but inside, their bodies seethe with unresolved energy.

Humans can't prevent the primitive part of the brain from automatically responding to threats in this powerful way, but we can consciously control how we outwardly express those reactions. Humans are particularly good at this because our neocortex, or "rational brain," is much more developed than it is in other animals. The neocortex, particularly the frontal lobe of the brain, controls our complex social structure, distinguishes between "good" and "bad," and recognizes consequences of actions that either are or are not socially acceptable. The frontal lobe can modify emotions and memories to fit into social norms, but it may do so at a great cost to the body.

When one of my caretakers molested me, my frontal lobe overrode my body's instinct to run away, to scream, and to tell my mom because, as a child, my brain knew that I needed those caretakers for my survival. After Jared raped me, I tried to return to my normal life—to pretend like nothing bad had happened—because it was "socially unacceptable" for me to get raped, to not be a virgin anymore, and to hurt my best friend by telling her what the man she loved did to me. When I told Lance that I'd been raped a second time, his response implied that it was somehow my fault or that I wanted it, and my frontal lobe kicked into overdrive to suppress my need to scream and cry and punch the wall because it wasn't socially acceptable for me to do so.

For years, I never cried, I never screamed, and I certainly didn't shake like a leaf. But what happened to my body? I was left with unbearable anxiety, an inability to sleep, an inability to cope with stress, complete stoppage of my menstrual cycle, and an absolute shut-down of my emotional system.

Had I lived with that much longer, I certainly could've developed chronic pain syndromes like fibromyalgia, auto-immune problems like arthritis, irritable bowel syndrome, asthma, and a slew of other physical problems that are highly correlated with trauma. Is it really this "unreleased energy" in the body causing all these problems? As a scientist, I wanted to see more evidence, mechanisms of action, and the chemical and structural makeup of what this "energy" is and how it causes damage. Could I release some kind of energy that'd been frozen in my body for more than twenty years?

As skeptical as I tried to be of these theories by constantly focusing on my brain and how to influence my brain chemistry and circuits involved in memory and emotion, nothing worked until I paid attention to my body.

I knew that my brain controls almost all functions of my mind and body—but it doesn't control everything. I thought about how reflexes like pulling my hand away from a hot stove aren't controlled by my brain, but rather, the pain signal is received by my spinal cord and immediately turned back around to the muscles of my arm and hand. My brain later receives sensory input that helps it make sense of why the reflex occurred and learn which things are hot for future safety, but it's not involved in the actual reflex movement. If those spinal reflexes were damaged, the problem would've originated in—and could be corrected within—my body.

I could teach a person with damaged spinal reflexes about things that are hot or give them drugs to affect their pain sensitivity, but if they unknowingly rested their hand on something hot, they wouldn't be able to pull their hand away before getting burned. Could there be a "trauma reflex" that doesn't function properly because of some problem in the body, in addition to problems in the brain? Maybe the body and the brain have separate reactions to trauma, and both need to be addressed for complete recovery.

I used to jump out of my chair every time I heard a knock on the door, even after months in therapy of making associations between benign situations and actual threatening situations. But all the talking and all the "anti-arousal" medication wouldn't touch this response—it was a reflex to trauma that may have predominately existed in my body or peripheral nervous system (i.e. the nerves that lie outside your brain).

I realized that I might've been one of the few neuroscientists who was truly skeptical of the "chemical model of mental illness." With the discovery of psychiatric drugs in the late 1970s, scientists put all their eggs in one basket and never looked back—more than forty years later, mental illness was still defined as an almost entirely chemical problem in the brain that should be fixed with other chemicals (i.e. drugs). Had scientists forgotten that the brain is also controlled by electricity and intricate circuitry that can easily get disrupted by social and other environmental experiences?

After I agreed to consider the theories of "body healing," Lois and I experimented with helping me physically know what it felt like to take control of my body. I did breathing exercises—breathing is one of the few actions that the body can control both consciously and automatically—to deactivate that fight-or-flight response and promote its reciprocal rest-and-digest. When Jared raped me, I couldn't scream or fight back—so whenever something reminded me of Jared (which was often back then), I got in my car and screamed as loud as I could. And if I was at home, I went down to the basement and pounded on the punching bag until I completely exhausted my anger. When I could be consciously aware that I was reminded of Jared, and I wasn't completely crippled with fear, I could scream and punch and do the things I couldn't do ten years earlier.

Shortly after I began this regimen, I started crying regularly for the first time in my life—and it felt good! I slept for several hours at a time. I stopped feeling helpless and paralyzed in stressful situations, and I stopped seeing Jared everywhere, and that extended to my memories of Jason and of Randy, too. I became more attuned to my emotions and how to express them instead of trying to bottle them up inside me. I became more attuned to my body and mindful that when my hands were balled up into fists or when my heart pounded, I needed to physically get that energy out of me. I began to learn, physically, that I *do* have the power to escape threatening and unpleasant situations—I began to take control over my body again.

Trauma is a centrifugal force so powerful that it can be nearly impossible to escape. Not only are traumatized people compelled to repeat aspects of their trauma, but after the trauma response develops, they're often helplessly unable to escape it even when there's a way out. I constantly tried to take control of my body by having sex with the men who showed interest in me, which I thought would somehow erase what'd happened with Jared and Jason—as long as it was a positive experience that I enjoyed. But the problem was that I never enjoyed it, and once I realized that I didn't want to have sex with whoever was in my bed, I had no idea that I could simply tell them to stop.

This "learned helplessness" was first demonstrated in the early 1970s in groundbreaking research by Martin Seligman and Steve

Maier. When a dog was placed in a cage with an open door and electrically shocked, it immediately ran out of the cage. But when dogs were repeatedly shocked in a cage with no exit, they eventually stopped even trying to escape, instead just lying there limp and hopeless while they got shocked. After reaching this state of helplessness, the dogs still didn't try to escape even if the door was left open. The only way to get the previously inescapably-shocked dogs to learn that they could, in fact, escape the shocks was to mimic their exit path by pulling them out of the cage several times. They needed help to physically experience their escape in order to learn to do it themselves.

When I was in bed with men, I felt helpless just like those dogs being painfully injured over and over. I didn't know I could escape—I didn't know I could say no. But when I let my body react how it wanted to react, without considering whether it was "socially acceptable" for me to cry or scream at that time, my brain began to follow. I could tell men that I wasn't interested in them, I could ask my close friends for a hug if I needed it, and I could get myself out of any situation that made me uncomfortable. Did I change my brain from the bottom-up, by first managing my bodily reactions?

I learned that these kinds of treatments are considered "alternative" by some scientists and clinicians because they aren't pharmaceutical treatments with known drug targets. But I speculated that the kind of body-learning exercises in which I participated caused physical and functional changes in my brain as powerfully—or maybe even more so—as drug treatments.

In my research, I found that people who received healthy social support after experiencing trauma had a profoundly better chance at recovering without developing PTSD—lack of social support was actually the greatest risk factor in developing PTSD, more than any contributions made by one's genes, other biological characteristics, or aspects of the trauma itself. Socially supported people, who are allowed to talk about what happened to them, to experience and express their emotions without ridicule or judgment, to cry and scream and do whatever their body needs to do to discharge all that energy frozen by a threat to which they couldn't respond, can recover without developing long-term PTSD at all. And, as I found out, that kind of social support was as effective at helping me recover from trauma, even though it didn't come for many years after the fact.

With all that being said, I was always reluctant to give credit to the role medication played in my recovery. I liked to think that I "did it on my own" through the "natural" mechanisms of writing and physically taking control of my body and seeking social support, but the truth is that these things didn't work for me until I was on a stable medication regime. I always resisted taking medication, partially because it obviously didn't work for me the first time I tried Paxil—I ended up trying to kill myself—and because I didn't want to turn into a product of some billion-dollar corporation selling bottled happiness.

But even after I began my EMDR treatment, I struggled to survive with my near-constant anxiety and I couldn't employ any of the body-learning techniques I described here. So I finally conceded to take a new psychiatric medication that increased the effects of serotonin in my brain. Within a month of starting this medication, I could talk to my therapist without getting overwhelmed, and I could actually implement the healthy coping mechanisms I'd been learning about.

We could talk all day about plans for breathing exercises, going to a mental "safe place," and calling supportive friends to intervene in a crisis, but it was nearly impossible to do any of those things when I was crippled by a flashback or felt like I wanted to crawl out of my skin. But with medication, my physical and emotional responses to stress dampened enough that I could take the important intervention measures I needed.

As I learned when I took Paxil almost ten years earlier, medication alone wouldn't help me, but in conjunction with therapy, it was a lifesaver. I don't think any kind of pharmaceutical intervention could've treated my biggest obstacles—the shame, guilt, blame, and self-loathing—but I do know that taking medication wasn't the dehumanizing cop-out treatment I thought it was. PTSD completely compromised my ability to love, communicate, create, and be honest—all the things that make me, me—and that was the real dehumanizer.

Even though I might've been born with a genetic predisposition to maladaptive types of behaviors and illnesses, they aren't part of who I am as a person. As long as I'm able to be me, I know that my medication is doing its job—it's not changing who I am, it's allowing me to *be* who I am. I hope someday there will be treatments for mental illnesses that don't involve having to take a medication for the rest of one's life, but rather that can help permanently re-wire the damaged areas of the brain and re-set the circuit to a healthy state of functioning that will last long after the medication is no longer in the system. But for now, using all the tools available to help people return to a healthy life is nothing to be ashamed of.

TRUE LOVE CANNOT WAIT

AFTER STARTING MY EMDR therapy and medication, my life became more manageable. I still made art, and I entered a few of my pieces into a Take Back the Night exhibit at MSU for survivors of sexual violence. One of the paintings I displayed was the first one I made that used those mini bourbon bottles David had given me before he died. I titled it "Rest in Pieces," and it will forever hang in my house as a memorial to him. In writing my artist statement for that show, I realized the significance of my art.

> *"As a rape survivor, my art is the product of taking back my life after years of pain and can be regarded as a platform with which to shatter the silence and stigma associated with rape and addiction. Inspired by the unpredictability of a shattered life, I employ the volatility of smashing alcohol-based glassware to transform a destructive pattern into constructive works of art. By destroying something that was once itself destructive, I aim to release the grip of trauma and addiction and reveal the beauty underneath the grime of distress."*

I continued making art any time I felt inspired to do so, and it was always a cathartic and meaningful experience.

JOURNAL: DECEMBER 15, 2012
"When Illinois banned smoking in all establishments, I got one of the heavy glass ashtrays from Roc's since they didn't have any use for

them anymore. I was a regular at Roc's when I lived in Charleston; it was my bar home that I probably spent more time at than my actual home for many years. I smashed that ashtray into my painting on Tuesday, and it felt very liberating, like I was closing a door that never needs to be opened again."

* * *

My mom came to Grand Rapids to visit me for Christmas, and when I unwrapped one of her gifts, a Chia Pet, I was stunned.

JOURNAL: DECEMBER 23, 2012
"My mom gave me a Chia Pet, and it made me kind of emotional because I gave David a Chia Pet last year for Christmas, and the last time I saw him before he killed himself, he told me it was still alive. I told my mom that, but she didn't have anything to say."

* * *

I still did the online dating thing on OKCupid, but after a month-long relationship with a woman that ended horribly, I decided to take a break from meeting any new potential matches. I always scoffed when people said things like "you'll find someone the minute you stop looking," but that's exactly what happened to me. And the fact that my life became one of those stupid clichés kind of irritated me.

JOURNAL: JANUARY 25, 2013
"I met this girl online Monday, and it was so completely unexpected, but I felt like I'd just met myself for the first time. I don't know how we started talking about all of the most intimate details of our lives because our conversation started out talking about building couch cushion forts and bouncy balls, but when we were talking about college and she said "life happened" to her and she ended up on a completely different path than she ever expected, I sensed some kind of connection between us. I told her that life happened to me too and

some traumatic experiences completely derailed me for many years, but I'm back on track now. That's when we started slowly sharing little snippets of what we'd each been through, and then we realized how similar our lives had been. She said she completely lost herself under this mask she created, and she worked so hard at making everyone around her think that she was happy that she never actually got to be happy herself. It was a year ago that she got clean and sober and started therapy, just like me. And she's written a few books. She said writing was what saved her, and it's her most effective way of coping and understanding herself and true feelings. Anyway, I could go on and on about the similarities between us, I even considered the possibility that I just created this person as a figment of my imagination and that I've just been talking to myself this whole week."

*   *   *

This "girl online" was Mandy, and a few days after we exchanged dozens of messages a day, we decided to meet in real life.

JOURNAL: DECEMBER 27, 2013
"We met at a bar last night, and as soon as I walked in and saw Mandy across the room, my whole body started tingling — I was instantly attracted to her."

*   *   *

I never believed in "love at first sight," but that was exactly what happened, and that my life had become a cliché love story baffled me. I saw her from across the room and every person and every sound faded away until only a single spotlight shone on the most beautiful woman I'd ever seen. We stayed out all night, sang karaoke, played pool, and flirted. Every time my arm grazed hers or our hands just fell into one another's, I wanted to stay there forever and never let go.

Mandy came over to my apartment the next day for a "Netflix double feature pajama party," and I was so excited when she actually showed up in her pajamas. I thought she may have been joking when she asked if I wanted to have a pajama party. Who goes on their second date in pajamas? We shared our first electrifying kiss, and it was the best day of my life.

JOURNAL: JANUARY 28, 2013

"I think something really significant between us is happening. I couldn't stop staring at Mandy, learning every line and freckle on her face. Learning every curve of her body, every scar, every blemish. Learning the array of her facial expressions. Just when I thought I'd learned every part of Mandy's face, she would make an expression I hadn't seen yet or I would notice another freckle or another pigment in her dark brown eyes, and it was like seeing a newborn enter the world. We described our favorite areas of each other's bodies, and it was what I imagine a blind person would feel like when someone describes to them the colors of the changing leaves in the fall. Hearing Mandy describe my own body to me made me feel more present in my own skin than I've ever felt before. Our bodies fit together like puzzle pieces or cogs in a wheel. On the rare occasion that I took my eyes off of her for a second, I would be amazed at her beauty every time my eyes returned to her. Mandy has such complex scents all over her body—her hair has its own scent, her neck has its own scent, her stomach has its own scent, and there are certain regions where these different scents combine to make a new scent. It felt like we'd known each other a lifetime. I'm still considering the possibility that this woman is a figment of my imagination. As much as I see myself in Mandy, I also see her unique vulnerabilities and strengths. When Mandy has her eyes closed, and I look at her, I don't understand how anybody could possibly want to hurt her. I feel this anger and mourning and need to protect and comfort her that I never felt for myself. I feel like by seeing her for who she is, and giving her the care I never received, I'm simultaneously receiving that for myself. I don't think I'll ever be the same again after meeting Mandy. If last night was the last night of my life, I would've died happy."

* * *

I never knew what love was until I met Mandy, and I loved every part of her. This was how it was always supposed to be. I didn't believe that it could be possible that I'd just met the person I'd spend the rest of my life with. It just couldn't be true. With a relationship that started this intensely, this quickly, I thought it must be a sign of something unhealthy.

JOURNAL: JANUARY 29, 2013

"This can't be the rest of forever, can it? I don't know what the future will hold for Mandy and I—this could all be over next week or it could last a lifetime—but I do know that if we were on the Titanic right now, I would get off the boat with Mandy and leave behind whatever intents I originally had. This has completely shaken me to my core. Nothing in my life has ever positively affected me as much as the last three days I spent with her. I almost want to say that the degree to which this has positively affected me is the same as the degree to which rape negatively affected me—this is like the polar opposite of rape."

*   *   *

After our Netflix pajama date, Mandy and I never spent another night apart, and we both realized that we were miserable in our jobs. Mandy worked in a prison, and I had no passion for my Parkinson's research. I spent most of my time at work reading about PTSD anyway, and I kept thinking, if only the right research—research on women, research on the actual brain mechanisms of PTSD—had been done, there'd be a cure for this. Mandy pointed out that this was what I should research, and that's when that little lightbulb when off over my head—I could do that research.

Mandy quit her horrible prison director job, and with the encouragement of my advisor and approval of the Neuroscience Program director, I made a difficult decision to leave the Parkinson's lab to pursue my true passion—PTSD research. I continued to read all the PTSD research articles I could find, developed detailed project ideas, and wrote literature reviews and summaries of my ideas to send to various labs at MSU, hoping to spark someone's interest. I was willing to do anything—even start over in a new program or school—to find somewhere to conduct my research.

My mom thought I was crazy for switching research directions halfway through my PhD.

"Just stick it out. You've got to make these sacrifices now and then you can do whatever you want later," my mom preached, as she'd been saying her whole life. But I knew there was no "later," at least not for my mom who'd been saying for twenty years that she wanted to get back into making art.

Luckily, I found a lab group at MSU who believed in me and my ideas and gave me the opportunity to do my work. I was so grateful to finally put all my experiences and knowledge to use. My new lab was housed back on MSU's main campus, so Mandy and I moved to Lansing together, and I began researching how trauma affects the brains of males and females differently.

I made the new discovery that exposure to the exact same traumatic stress has divergent effects in males and females in measures of behavior, physiology, and neuronal circuitry. Mine was the first study to systematically examine the sex-specific effects of traumatic stress in adult rats, and my data indicated the same brain regions that are overactive in males following trauma are underactive in females (and vice versa). These findings could have important implications in new diagnostic and treatment approaches for mental disorders that target the mechanism of dysfunction rather than a generalized diagnosis based on symptoms. My life finally started to hold some meaning.

THE SOBERING TRUTH

I SWALLOWED MY last drink three days after moving back to Lansing when Mandy went out of town for the evening to visit friends. We'd just moved into a new house together, and I stayed home to clean and get some boxes unpacked. It took about five minutes of cleaning before I walked down the street to the corner store to get beer. I didn't even have to think about it—drinking and cleaning (I called it D&C), that's what I always did.

I knew a six-pack of beer wouldn't be enough, but I thought twelve might be over-doing it a bit. Should I get twelve and only plan to drink ten? I knew that would be impossible. Then, I saw a six-pack of 16oz. cans and I got my phone out to calculate 16 x 6 = 96oz. divided by 12oz. = 8. Eight! Perfect, that's like eight regular cans of beer. More than six but less than twelve. I knew how to set my limits now. I did my D&C, listened to music, and had a great time. Until the beer was gone. Then, I had a massive inner-struggle to decide if I should walk back down to the store or try to go to sleep so I could stop thinking about wanting to drink more.

I paced around the house, back and forth and back and forth. And then Mandy got home, and I looked at her and didn't feel my usual excitement of seeing her eyes light up, I didn't feel the pull to wrap my arms around her, I didn't care to ask her if she had fun with her friends, and I didn't want to talk about my evening. I wanted to be left alone. I *wanted* to feel her love, but I just couldn't. I couldn't feel anything. I was completely empty.

The next morning, I realized that drinking had killed all of the good things within me. My ten years of drinking before served its purpose because it killed—or at least dampened—all of the horrible and traumatic things within me, but now I had more good than bad to live with.

Thereafter, every time I wanted to stop at the bar for a shot or two before heading home from work, I asked myself if I'd rather have a drink or feel the excitement and comfort I always felt when I walked in the door to see Mandy after a long day. Every morning that I woke up and wanted to have a beer just to be able to face the day, I asked myself if I'd rather have a drink or have breakfast with Mandy. Every night that I wanted to sneak out of bed to grab a case of beer and sit in the basement to drink until morning, I asked myself if I'd rather drink or feel Mandy's arms around me in bed. I was genuinely surprised that I never answered one of my questions with, "I'd rather have a drink," but now, it's been many moons since I've even had the urge to drink. I have too much else to live for.

Ending my addiction wasn't simply about "not doing it anymore," it was about completely re-defining who I was, identifying the reasons I drank and used, learning new ways to cope with stress and pain, and ultimately, making human connections. Humans need social support.

My journey to sobriety began the moment I first talked (sober) about what I went through to a supportive person, after which I started to believe that I deserved to get sober, that I was worth being helped. I realized how important my relationships with other people were in how I defined and saw myself.

Finding my identity was one of the hardest parts about getting sober. When I spent my entire adult life in an altered state, trying to survive each day, I never got to figure out who I was. When I hung around my new friends who'd only known me sober, I had no problem being sober around them because I knew that they liked me that way. But when I hung around my old friends who'd only known me drunk, I worried they'd compare me to my old self. *Apryl isn't as energetic as she used to be. Apryl isn't as spontaneous or talkative as she used to be.*

I had such a hard time being sober around my old friends, even when they weren't drinking. It wasn't about being around alcohol that awakened some uncontrollable urge to drink for me. It was about not having an identity amongst a group of people who'd never known me sober. I didn't know if my old friends liked me sober, so when I was around them, regardless of whether or not alcohol was involved, I felt the urge to drink because I didn't know what else to do around them. Jim even told me that I was a lot more fun to be around when I was drunk. Statements like that confused me because I didn't like myself drunk, so how could I be around people who liked that version of myself that I hated so much?

I felt like I didn't know my friends from all those years anymore, and they didn't know me. When I realized everyone I'd ever known had only known the drunken, heterosexual version of me, I had a major identity crisis. When I stopped drinking, I didn't know who I was or what I liked and I spent several months figuring out what kinds of activities and foods and people I enjoyed. But when I tried to hang out with my friends sober, I didn't know what to do with myself. I was the person in the group who people counted on for a good time, for entertainment, who always did something crazy, and I wasn't that person when I was sober. I used to always have stories of outrageous things that'd happened when I was drunk and of all the guys I'd been going out with, but now I had nothing to talk about. When the conversation lulled, I'd think that if I was fucked up like I used to be, I could at least entertain my friends. I was frustrated that I had no idea who I was because when everybody else developed their personalities as young adults, I remained frozen as a traumatized teenager.

I realized I needed to build a completely new life for myself with people who liked me sober, and thought I'd have to leave behind everyone involved in my "past life." While I did move on from a lot of people, many of my old friends remained in my life in an increasingly fulfilling way. Even though we lived far away from each other, I developed deeper relationships with those people than I ever had with them when we were living in the same town and I was a drunken mess.

AT LAST

EVEN THOUGH MANDY and I met at a bar and drank occasionally in our first few months of dating, we were both committed to getting sober. We really weren't a good team drunk. And once I stopped drinking, so did Mandy. We also both stopped smoking cigarettes. We both smoked a pack of cigarettes a day, but once we weren't drinking anymore, quitting was relatively easy. We found other things to fill our time, and our hands, with.

Mandy encouraged me to immerse myself in the things I loved—art and music. She'd constantly ask me to play her something on the piano or guitar, which irritated me at first because I hadn't played in years, but once I realized how happy it made me, I knew why she kept asking me to do it. I played and wrote music on the piano and guitar more. I took percussion lessons because I'd always wanted to be a drummer. I wrote books and short stories. I made more art, and submitted my art to exhibitions. Doing all of these things emotionally challenged me, and I realized why I'd avoided those activities for so many years, but I always felt so content when I engaged in the things I loved—there was nothing else I'd rather be doing in those moments.

I fell in love with science all over again, and the further out I got from my last drink, the more accessible the creative and intuitive brain I once possessed became. I researched the fundamental elements of biology that underlie PTSD. I studied what specific brain circuits are affected by traumatic stress, what proteins and hormones are involved, and while findings from my research could be the foundation of future diagnostic and treatment measures, I knew more work needed to be done outside of science. The more I got into my research, the farther I got away from it when I realized that nobody would recover from PTSD by me sitting in front of a microscope for ten hours a day. I wanted to believe that if I found the biological reason for why my life fell apart, I'd find a cure. But I realized that life isn't a textbook—I was in a lifelong process of becoming a healthier person, not an experiment with a beginning and an end.

When I truly followed—and shared—my passions and integrated all parts of my life into a cohesive self, I felt peace. Sharing my art, writing, and science gave my life a purpose and made me feel like everything that happened to me wasn't for nothing. I couldn't have done any of that without Mandy's support, who saw how happy I felt when I played music and made art and pointed out that I enjoyed reading and discussing scientific literature on PTSD, not on Parkinson's disease. She encouraged me to do what makes me happy, even though it might not have been the most convenient option for either of us.

A year and a half into therapy with Lois (and way more than twenty-five visits), I could truly say that I found relief from most of the intrusive memories and nightmares and constant hypervigilance that plagued me for the first eight years of my adult life. Some of those symptoms gradually lessened in intensity over that time, others disappeared overnight, and some still resurfaced acutely. I initially tried to approach therapy in a scientific and systematic manner with plans and deadlines for the memories I wanted to process, but my true healing occurred once I trusted my therapist and the process itself and acknowledged that I had no idea what I was doing. I wanted to actively be doing something to ease all my suffering once and for all, but relief truly came to me once I realized that I was in a lifelong process of becoming a healthier person. I knew I'd continue to make progress as long as I had the support I needed and lived a healthy lifestyle, even though I knew there would always be difficult times.

I couldn't fathom how there could've been any purpose to the horrible things that happened to me or that happen to other people.

Do I wish I'd never been raped or endured all of the other painful experiences in my life? Of course. Would I go back and change the course of my life if I could? Probably not. I gained a unique perspective on life that I never would've had if I hadn't been through everything I experienced. I truly appreciate the resilience of the human mind and body, but I also know of the fragility of the delicate balance between being psychologically and physiologically functional and being completely dysfunctional or merely surviving. I'm so glad I fought to survive until I found people who could help me. It took many painful years of searching for help, telling my story to people who didn't understand, self-destruction, loneliness, helplessness, and hopelessness, but I can honestly say that I found peace and am glad to be alive. My life was full of pain, but it was worth facing that to see the immeasurable beauty on the other side of it all.

I wasn't permanently damaged the moment I was raped in high school, and that was one of the most important things I learned in therapy. The first therapy session in which I revisited that night, I consciously connected to my memories and emotions for the first time, and my therapist asked me to pick from a list the phrase that felt most true to me at the time. I chose the phrase, "I'm permanently damaged," and rated that phrase a ten on a scale of one to ten, with one being completely false and ten being completely true.

Over the next several months, whenever I revisited that rape in a session, Lois asked me how true that phrase felt to me at the time, and for a long time, I assigned a rank of seven to ten. But one day, it clicked within me—I wasn't permanently damaged the moment I was raped. I certainly was damaged physically and emotionally, but for the first time, I knew that I could recover my self-worth, my control over my body, my security. I don't know what happened over those few months that suddenly made me comprehend that I wasn't permanently damaged, but I know I never would've come to that realization had I not gone back to that night and talked about, in painstaking detail, what'd happened and how I felt.

The more research on PTSD that I did, the more I began to understand what I'd experienced for so many years—in turmoil and in therapy. When I began writing, I strengthened areas of my brain that'd been shut down during my trauma. Brain imaging studies have shown that while visual imagery systems in the brain are highly activated during a flashback, the speech and language areas of the brain are deactivated—rendering the patient unable to describe what they're feeling or seeing but instead re-experiencing it all over again as images and emotions. When I went to therapy and attempted to talk about what'd happened to me, it triggered emotional distress and terror, but when I slowly wrote my memories down whenever I was emotionally-grounded enough to do so, I gave narrative context to the memories that were previously only images and emotions.

Traumatic memories can get stored improperly in the brain in a way that they lack narrative context, so when reminded of those memories, a person may feel them as a flood of emotions or flashes of visualizations that are completely overwhelming as if the trauma was happening all over again. But when I consciously gave narrative context to what I saw and felt by writing about it in detail and talking about it in detail, those memories were eventually stored with that narrative context. Then, when I was reminded of a traumatic event, I remembered it as I did most other memories, as a chronicle of what happened without the overwhelming emotions and fear.

The goal in my recovery from PTSD wasn't to forget the trauma, but to be able to remember it without being flooded with fear, guilt, pain, horror, and helplessness. Even if there was some way to completely erase traumatic memories, I don't know if that would be beneficial. As long as the memories weren't causing debilitating fear like they did with PTSD, I learned a lot from my past experiences, especially the traumatic ones. I learned how to protect myself and became aware of my own strengths and weaknesses, and for that reason, painful memories can be beneficial. I accepted that while horrible things happened to me that I'll never forget, I can move on from the past and be a healthy, functional person.

LEGAL LIMBO

TWO WEEKS BEFORE our one-year anniversary of meeting each other, Mandy and I played our favorite board game, Scrabble, for the millionth time. I set up the game while Mandy made chili in the kitchen, and I knew that now was the time—I didn't want to live one more second without being engaged to this woman. I ran into my office and shoved a ring in my pocket, along with a few scrabble letters that I picked out from the bag.

Mandy and I'd talked about marriage for the past several months, but same-sex marriage was illegal in Michigan, so we didn't know when we'd be able to get married without going out-of-state. The day after Thanksgiving, I did some Black Friday shopping and bought Mandy an engagement ring that I'd been hanging onto for the last two months.

Mandy brought our bowls of chili over to the game board and I told her to go first. The letters on my rack said MARRYME, I played the word MAR first, and let the game continue for a few rounds before putting the rest of my letters on the board. She said yes! Actually she said "yeah" because she couldn't find an S tile quickly enough, so Mandy put the –EAH underneath the Y of my proposal. The next day Mandy and I bought a ring for me at a pawn shop called Dicker and Deal, and I was so excited to be engaged—I couldn't stop staring at the ring on my finger—but we still didn't know when we'd be able to legally get married.

Two months later, on Friday, March 24, 2014, Judge Bernard Friedman struck down Michigan's same-sex marriage ban, making it legal for county clerks to issue marriage licenses to same-sex couples. As expected, the state's attorney general immediately issued a request to suspend Judge Friedman's ruling until federal appeals proceedings concluded. However, there was a 24-hour window between when the marriage ban was overturned and when the federal appeals court granted the suspension.

When we heard the announcement that the gay marriage ban had been overturned, Mandy and I knew we had to celebrate with sushi. We'd always planned to get married legally first—just the two of us—and have a celebration later on with our family and friends. As soon as Mandy and I made the commitment to each other to be partners in building our life together, we were ready to have our marriage legally recognized. It was the next logical step in securing our partnership financially, guaranteeing our rights to each other's assets, hospital visits, picking up prescriptions, joint insurance policies, all the logistic ins-and-outs of sharing every aspect of your life with another person.

The morning after the sushi celebration, I got up early to make Mandy coffee and breakfast before she had to go to work. I checked my email as I always do in the morning, and read a breaking news message that four Michigan counties, including our own Ingham County, would open their offices that day to issue marriage licenses, as the appeals suspension hadn't yet been processed. As calmly and quietly as I could without screaming, I snuck back into the bedroom and asked Mandy if she would take the day off work to get married. Excitement ensued, followed by oatmeal. I'd never felt as excited as I did when we drove to the courthouse.

I expected to see a huge gathering around the courthouse full of God Hates Fags protesters, countered by Love is Love demonstrators, but everything was silent. I thought maybe we'd missed our chance, and my heart sunk. But before we even got inside the courthouse, people we'd never met before congratulated us underneath the flagpole outside. Go America! Inside, was the most unified celebratory environment I'd seen since I rode the It's a Small World musical boat ride at Disney World ten years ago. People cheered, people clapped, people cried—it was magical.

This environment genuinely surprised me. I expected the courthouse to resemble a Las Vegas wedding chapel full of half-naked, half-drunk people who stumbled over from dancing all night at the local gay club—people who impulsively got married just because they could and just because they were drunk enough. I immediately felt shame for my own stereotypic mindset. Maybe it was internalized homophobia I'd garnered from years of growing up thinking something was wrong with being gay, or maybe I'd spent too many years in the bar scene to have an accurate grasp on what the real world is like.

But what I found was a building full of loving partners and families who were so joyful to be one step closer to equality. Many of the couples were professors who'd been together for decades, many of them had their children with them, and everybody was genuinely happy for everybody else there. I looked around and thought to myself, "If I didn't know what was going on here, I would have no idea I was in a building full of gay people." Stereotypes are dangerous things, and as I'd learned about myself, a person can have ignorant stereotypes of the very demographic to which they belong. I knew the only way to abolish this uninformed thinking was to find common ground with people, embrace our differences, and start viewing people as the individuals they are instead of defining them by a group or label.

There were several friendly clergy members there offering to perform ceremonies, but we decided to have the county clerk, Barb Byrum, marry us because she made this possible in our county. When we told her we didn't have any witnesses with us, she offered a state senator who said, "I'm technically a Republican, I hope that's okay…" and a young woman who graciously took the only picture we captured of our marriage day. As soon as we walked into the courthouse, I realized my camera was broken—if rain on your wedding day is good luck, a broken camera must be guaranteed wedded bliss for life. The clerk recited the most poignant marriage vows and pronouncement I could've imagined, and when she pronounced us married, the room exploded in cheers and applause. I'd totally forgotten that we were in a room full of people.

Some people asked us if we regretted not having our loved ones there, but I thought we were in the best company we could've asked for. Something about getting married with a group of other people who understood how important this opportunity was—not just understood it but lived it—made it the most meaningful legal marriage ceremony. At the courthouse, everybody asked each other how long they'd been waiting to get married, and my answer to that was my whole life. Even before I met Mandy, before I came out as gay, and before I accepted my own sexual orientation, I grew up thinking that I couldn't be with the person I really wanted to be with, and that I couldn't be the person who I really was. I hope the next generation of children will not know what that feels like.

FORGIVENESS

OCTOBER-NOVEMBER 2014

AFTER OUR LEGAL marriage, Mandy and I planned a wedding ceremony to celebrate with our loved ones. Only one person from high school remained close friends with both me and Adrianne, even after Adrianne told her what happened with me and Jared. Maybe Marlene remained friends with both of us because she didn't go to the same school we did, but probably because she was the most non-judgmental, kind, and empathetic person I'd ever known. After receiving our wedding invitation, Marlene told me that she couldn't make it because she'd be officiating Adrianne's wedding the same day.

I couldn't believe that out of all the days in the past eleven years, Adrianne planned to get married on the exact same day as me, and that by taking Marlene, she'd officially won at claiming all of my childhood friends. I thought about how when we were in high school, I used to envision a life with Adrianne like the one I'd been building with Mandy, and the thought of us getting married, separately, on the same day, sent chills down my spine.

I envisioned us all floating in some body of water where each of our movements brought those around us on a lifelong journey through the same ripples. As I thought about how happy I was to marry Mandy instead of Adrianne, I hoped that Adrianne was as happy as me, and I knew that I'd truly forgiven her.

I realized that forgiveness doesn't mean restoring trust in someone after they've wronged me. It doesn't mean excusing what someone did or repairing a relationship. Forgiveness isn't about absolving someone of responsibility for their actions or forgetting and going on like nothing happened. Forgiveness doesn't mean I can't still be angry. Forgiveness is about letting go of needing an admission of guilt, of needing an apology, of needing the person who hurt me to understand and feel what they did to me. It's about accepting that people do horrible things to other people, and it's probably because other people did horrible things to them.

Forgiveness, for me, is making a decision to try to be kind to other people, to understand where they're coming from, to try to contribute more good to the world than bad. I know that people who hurt other people need help, not to be eradicated from society. I hope that people who do bad things can change to do more good.

I'll never forget how Jared and Jason and Randy destroyed my life, and I hate what they did to me, but I don't hate them as people anymore. I hated them for many years, and while I don't regret the time I spent hating them, I can honestly say that finally moving on and "forgiving" them brought me the most peace and freedom I've ever experienced.

When I had so much hate for these men—I wished bad things for them, I wished they were dead, I visualized myself stabbing them in the face, and I vowed to never let go of that hate because that was the only thing that would protect me from going through that again—it, along with my hatred for myself, completely consumed my life in a way that killed every good thing within me. I didn't make a conscious decision to forgive Jared and Jason and Adrianne and Randy, but I did make a decision to accept the fact that, while someone else destroyed my life through no fault of my own, it's still my responsibility to clean up the mess. And somehow over several years, I realized that instead of wishing they were dead, I hoped they could somehow redeem themselves to live a peaceful life so they can stop hurting other people and start making the world a better place. And, for me, that's forgiveness.

The will to survive is an innate human driving force, but the will to help other people and make the world a better place is precisely what makes us human. And that's what we should all be striving for.

WHOEVER HAS EARS, LET THEM HEAR

AFTER EMBARKING ON my PTSD research project, I felt compelled to connect with other people who, like me, had no idea that the reason they couldn't "just get over" their trauma is because they have PTSD. I had to tell them. I thought I had this big secret that if all these traumatized people knew they had PTSD, they'd be okay. But sharing my scientific knowledge of PTSD didn't help people nearly as much as sharing my personal story. Of rape. Of abuse. Of addiction. All of the darkness within me of which I was so ashamed. So I got involved in helping victims of sexual assault on campus, I shared my story at survivor gatherings and art shows, I started a new blog, I got involved with non-profit organizations and activist groups. And once my "darkness" was out there, along with everybody else's, it didn't seem so dark after all. And that's when the shame and the guilt went away.

Shame and guilt were two of the most insidious forces that took over my life after trauma and destroyed my self-worth, my ability to form relationships with other people, my will to live. I don't think any amount of science could've given me a cure or a pill for shame and guilt that didn't involve sharing my story—my human experience—with another human being.

In December of 2014, I joined other survivors of rape and sexual assault to support one another on MSU's campus and work to dispel the myths about sexual violence through media outlets, protests, and public meetings. Through this work, I realized that there are so many survivors who can't find support for their recovery and that I wanted to do something to make sure resources are available for all students in crisis.

Thus, with a handful of other MSU students and alumni, I helped form an advocacy and activist group, Community Leaders in Transformation, to support and advocate for survivors of sexual violence. I spoke on behalf of this group at MSU Board of Trustees meetings, town hall meetings, and roundtable discussions, and our work was the catalyst for MSU hiring an additional, much-needed, counselor for the MSU Sexual Assault Program. We regularly held free workshops on sexual consent for both off-campus and on-campus groups, and hung large banners with resources and definitions of consent at local bars and campus housing. The core members of our group frequently met with MSU administrators to discuss ways in which our campus could be safer and more supportive of our survivors, ways in which our campus could prevent sexual violence through education, and respond to reports of these crimes, and I promised to continue facilitating these discussions and share my story as long as there was still one person left who wanted to listen.

I whole-heartedly believed that speaking openly about my experiences could facilitate the conversations necessary to help survivors of sexual violence recover and incentivize education programs to prevent this from happening in the future. I integrated my research on trauma and the brain with my advocacy work and personal experiences to connect with the larger community of survivors, and vowed to do whatever it took to help my fellow human beings recover from trauma, whether through science, activism, education or writing.

I'd already spent the last year-and-a-half sending query letters to literary agents and publishers regarding my memoir manuscript, but after forty-one rejections, I decided to publish the book myself. Only two of the people I queried even attempted to read my manuscript, and I wondered why, without even reading my writing, nobody wanted to help me tell my story. I thought self-publishing was a failure option for people who weren't good enough writers to get a "real" book out there, but I was determined to tell my story, and self-publishing became an incredibly empowering experience. I asked friends to help me edit, I learned how to format the interior layout for printing, I designed my own book cover, wrote my own blurbs, created official author pages on Amazon and Goodreads, began marketing through local media outlets, held book signings, and secured a book review from a respected Michigan literary journalist, Bill Castanier. Self-publishing wasn't a failure, it was me taking control of my story and not accepting no for an answer—and it was completely liberating.

When my book finally went live online and I started to get reviews from readers, I knew I'd made the right choice. My story was helping people. But the first couple weeks were emotionally straining. Having my entire story out there for anybody to read made me feel more vulnerable than I ever had before. I developed a fear that once the people in my life read my book, they'd abandon me. Whenever I'd bump into a colleague or friend on campus, I'd wonder if they'd read my book and thought I was a disgusting, selfish, horrible person, which was probably due to my mother's reaction.

Before I released the book, I told my mother that I wanted to publish my book because sharing my story had already helped so many people, and I wanted her to know that I included some of our interactions but that I'd left out her story, which isn't mine to tell. She told me that she was glad I was helping others, but when a review of my book appeared in the Charleston newspaper, my mother sent me an email that simply read, "I won't be reading your book and would appreciate if you don't contact me." I asked my aunt and uncle to talk to her and learned that she thought I wrote this book to ruin her life. Maybe the shame and guilt stemming from her trauma, compounded by mine, was just too much to face. This abandonment deeply saddened me, especially because my mother missed out on so many important things in my life during this time—my TED talk, radio interviews, newspaper articles, the play I was in to raise money for a local domestic violence response team, my speech at a mental health awareness week event, my two-year sober anniversary. Even at twenty-nine years old, I still just wanted my mother to be proud of me. My mother had always told me to never tell my father about what'd happened to me because it would surely kill him, so he had no idea of anything I'd experienced. But I didn't want him to read about all of this in the newspaper, so I called him two days before my Charleston book review was to be published.

I told my father I'd been raped twice, that I'd been molested by Randy, that I'd been recovering from PTSD, and that all of my drug and alcohol problems (which he knew about) stemmed from this trauma. My dad reacted in a more genuine way than anybody else ever had. It was like he'd been to one of my panel discussions on how to respond to disclosures of sexual assault, but it just came naturally to him. He told me that he was so sorry I'd experienced all of those things, that I didn't deserve any of it, he thanked me for trusting him with this information, and he said he'd like to know more about my experiences if I was willing to share. I told him more about what'd happened, and answered all the questions he had. The next day, he purchased two copies of my book, and he and my step-mother both read it. I was nervous as my dad read my book, thinking that once he knew the whole story he'd disown me like my mother or would be so upset by it that it really would give him a heart attack. I feared he would think I was a selfish whore and never want to look at me again. I'll never forget the first conversation I had with my dad after he read my book.

"How could anybody think any of that was your fault? None of it was your fault, none of it. How could anybody push you away? I just want to hug you."

I know my dad had a hard time reading the book, but he never once mentioned that to me. He only asked if I was okay and told me that all he wanted was for me to be happy and healthy. My dad shared with me how my story helped him understand his own trauma, and told me the backstory of the "thanks for doing such a good job raising Apryl" comment he'd made to Randy so many years ago.

Whenever my dad saw Randy around town, Randy clearly avoided him, refused to look at him or talk to him, and my dad thought it was because Randy was such a good Christian man that he saw my dad as a terrible sinner for divorcing my mom. And to an extent, my dad believed this to be true. My dad thought that I was an alcoholic because he'd given me the alcoholism gene. But after learning my story, my dad knew that he wasn't the bad man, Randy was, and that he wasn't the one who caused me to be an alcoholic. My dad reclaimed a little of his self-respect after reading my story, and I wish that it could've help my mother in the same way.

I knew I was only in the beginning of a lifelong process of healing, and so many people I love were on this journey with me—there wasn't anywhere else I'd rather be. So, if given the opportunity, would I go back and change anything about my life? Absolutely not. While I wish I hadn't endured so much suffering, and even though I still live with the memories and sadness, I'm now fulfilled and content and loved—that's all I ever wanted.

"Who first beholds the light of day
In spring's sweet flowery month of May
And wears an emerald all her life
Shall be a loved and happy wife."

—Gregorian Birthstone poem

WHERE THE SIDEWALK ENDS

APRIL 2015

WHEN I GRADUATED high school eleven years ago, I vowed to never step into a high school again. Especially not one with the same mascot as mine. And definitely not to talk about how I was raped in high school. But I did just that at the East Lansing High School board meeting on Monday, April 27, 2015.

Alice Dreger highlighted the larger problem of abstinence-based sex education in Michigan when she attended her son's sex-ed class two weeks earlier. Dr. Dreger, a bioethicist of human sexuality, live-tweeted her poignant and witty observations of the abhorrent ELHS "reproductive education" class, which got national attention.

In response, the student-run club, ELHS Students for Gender Equality, decided to speak out about reforming the sex education curriculum at the next school board meeting. Students and faculty from MSU decided to support this initiative by attending the meeting. I knew that if I attended this board meeting, I had to speak. I had to muster so much strength to walk into a high school, I figured I might as well go big or go home.

Walking up to the doors of ELHS, my eyes darted around everywhere, and I made mental notes of how this was different from my alma mater. "It's not the same place, these aren't the same kids," I kept telling myself. And when I walked inside, I was transported into the Hogwarts School of Witchcraft and Wizardry. Well, not literally, but within my brain, yes. I actually went into a dissociative state, which usually wouldn't be a good thing, but in this instance I was grateful for the protection from my own memories, as I suddenly felt like I was in a mystical world of magic.

"Of course this is happening inside your head, Harry, but
why on Earth should that mean it isn't real?"
—J.K. Rowling, *Harry Potter and the Deathly Hallows*

But after three hours of board deliberation, all of the TROJANS banners eventually got to me, and I acknowledged that, yes, I was sitting in a high school cafeteria and these adorable teenagers are the same age as me when I was raped. The go home option of go-big-or-go-home sounded pretty good.

But finally, public comment time came. The first speaker was a representative of the SMART (Sexually Mature Aware Responsible Teen) Program that'd been delivering abstinence education at ELHS for eighteen years. This group, affiliated with an anti-abortion organization, passed out cards during their program for the students to sign that read, "I have chosen to make a responsible decision to protect my future and my heart. I am going to remain sexually abstinent until I get married."

After she spoke about abstinence being the only way to prevent pregnancy and STIs and the only way to achieve "healthy relationships, increased self-worth, and self-control," I hoped that I'd be called to speak next. I was, and this is what I said:

"Hello, my name is Apryl Pooley and I'm a Ph.D. Candidate in the MSU Neuroscience Program where I research the effects of trauma on the brain. I'm here as a representative of Community Leaders in Transformation and to support the ELHS Students for Gender Equality Club in removing the SMART program from teaching the abstinence portion of the reproductive health curriculum.

I can give you all kinds of data on how abstinence-focused education doesn't promote abstinence or sexual health or healthy relationships and data from the World Health Organization that shows comprehensive sex-education programs don't encourage sexual activity at younger ages and can reduce the prevalence of sexual assault and relationship violence. But I'll give you just one piece of data:

1-in-5 women are raped in their lifetime, and 40% of those occur before the age of 18. That comes out to be about 45 girls at this high school who will have been raped before they graduate. And I'm going to tell you how my abstinence education affected me and my classmates.

My senior year of high school, 2003, I was in the National Honors Society, the French National Honor Society, I was a classically trained pianist, and I'd just been accepted into the University of Illinois Physics Program for college. And then I was raped by my best friend's boyfriend. But I didn't know it was rape. I was confused. When I told my friends what'd happened, that I had sex for the first time but I didn't want to because I didn't like this guy and because I was covered in vomit and blood, nobody ever said it could've been rape. Instead it was "just what happens," and I was ostracized by my peers. I didn't take my AP exams and I didn't go to the University of Illinois. I remembered those abstinence pledges so many of us took, and I thought that it didn't matter whether I wanted that or not, I was no longer a virgin and I was no longer worthy of anyone's love or respect. And for the next nine years, I struggled with alcoholism, drug addiction, and PTSD until I finally found a counselor at Michigan State University who told me that it wasn't my fault. I was 25-years-old before I realized that what'd happened to me in high school wasn't my fault. And I was lucky to have survived that long.

If we would've had some education on what sex really looks like instead of just what virginity and abstinence looks like, maybe somebody would've been able to help me. And better yet, if we would've had some education on how to respect each other's' boundaries, how to give and receive consent for sex, how to give and accept a no to sex, how to have a healthy view of relationships, maybe this wouldn't have happened at all.

I know many of the curriculum regulations are state-mandated, but if we care about the health and safety of our kids, we must teach them about consent and physical/emotional boundaries, about gender identity and sexual orientation—and about what sex is and what it isn't. We have to."

I leaned on the podium so heavily that it scooted farther and farther away from me as I spoke. My voice shook, and I swallowed a lump in my throat that I hadn't felt in ages. I told my story all the time, but doing so in a high school cafeteria, in front of and on behalf of high school students, was so powerful because this was where it started for me—and this was where it had to end. And three months later, when I read in the *Lansing State Journal* that East Lansing schools terminated the contract of the SMART program that'd been teaching abstinence education at ELHS for eighteen years, I just smiled and knew I still have a lot of work left to do.

ACKNOWLEDGMENTS

To all those who read early versions of these pages and loved me more, not less, because of it—Amanda, Jenna, Dione. Allie, when you told me, "You should quit this grad school thing and become a writer," it changed my life (although I'm glad I didn't quit grad school).

Jessie, for speaking to me in song lyrics, for taking care of my drunken ass all those years, and for being the best concert buddy and friend a girl could ask for. It's all happening. I heartchu.

Christina, for loving the sober-me when I didn't even know who the sober-me was yet. And for always being up for a thrifty adventure (accompanied by only the best 90s music). XOXO.

Christine, for always keeping me with you no matter how far away from each other we are, for always getting my jokes, and for sharing a love of quirky things like squirrels and antique chairs. I love you.

Aubrey, for being so compassionate, honest, and huggable. Thank you for sticking by my side from the very beginning of this journey.

Lily, I'm so happy your dad happens to be my mom's brother. If you weren't my biological cousin, I hope I would've met you somewhere along the line anyway. You're a true ally and the other half to so many of my favorite stories. My heart will go on.

Jenny and Aaron, for putting me up (and putting up *with* me) in my most emotionally unstable state. I don't know how you did it. Thank you.

Cindy and Marc, for giving me a home in your lab family. The opportunity to do my research with the freedom you allow is worth everything to me.

Dr. Ann Ryan, Becky Allen, and Lisa Laughman at Olin Health Center for being the first healthcare allies to give me hope and help.

Jerilyn, for your unwavering patience, honesty, and wisdom.

To my mother, for teaching me the importance of honesty, independence, and asking questions. And for letting me play with all the boys' toys I wanted and encouraging me to follow all of my dreams.

To my father, for teaching me to laugh and to never be afraid to be a little strange. And to Dad, Kelsey, Ben, and Maddie, words cannot thank you enough for the love and support you gave me when I published the first version of this book. It took me a while to see the family that was always there for me, but nothing can separate us now. I love you all.

Gary and Ava, and Megan, your support on this journey got me through so many of the hard times and gave me strength to keep going. Thank you, I love you.

To my social justice comrades and other world-changers—Elle, Zoe, Mara, Jennay, Noah, Sylvia, Cassie, Tashmica, Silvana, Tricia, Grace, Kintla, Becca, Laurie, Daniel, and so many more—thank you for your unwavering commitment to tackle the most difficult challenges in making the world a better place.

To the publishing team who helped make this possible—Jesse James, Rachel Thompson, Melissa Flickinger, and Wendy Garfinkle. The support you provide is astounding, I've never felt so at home in a place I've never been and with people I've never met in "real life." To my editor, Justin Bogdanovitch, your invaluable input helped shape what I thought was a finished manuscript into an entirely different animal. Thank you for your careful reading, your questions, your suggestions, and allowing my voice to get even stronger.

And finally, to my soulmate, my partner, my love: Mandy. For once, I am at a loss of words to describe what you mean to me. You are my balance, my common sense, and my best friend ever. Your crazy matches my crazy.

Also, to the music that gave me solace and inspiration, that allowed me to be angry, to decompress, to dance. These artists provided the soundtrack to this writing:

K. Flay
Regina Spektor
Neko Case
Laura Marling
Fiona Apple
Emily Haines
Jenny Lewis
Cloud Nothings
Plants and Animals
Beach House
Bon Iver
Conor Oberst
Deer Tick
Grizzly Bear
Menomena
Stars
Jason Isbell
Ryan Adams

ABOUT THE AUTHOR

Apryl E. Pooley is a neuroscientist who believes that everybody has the right to survive, the right to be who they are, and the right to speak their truths without judgment and ridicule. She relentlessly shares her story to provide inspiration, safety, and hope to anyone hiding in a closet. Apryl currently lives in Michigan with her wife and two dogs. Find out more about her at www.aprylpooley.com

CPSIA information can be obtained
at www.ICGtesting.com
Printed in the USA
LVHW051242071121
702657LV00005B/857

9 780692 730027